**Performing English with a postcolonial accent:
Ethnographic narratives from Mexico**

the Tufnell Press,
London,
United Kingdom

www.tufnellpress.co.uk

email contact@tufnellpress.co.uk

British Library Cataloguing-in-Publication Data
A catalogue record for this book is
available from the British Library

paperback ISBN   *1872767 877*
ISBN-13   *978-1-872767-87-1*

Copyright © 2008 Angeles Clemente and Michael J. Higgins
The moral rights of the authors have been asserted.
Database right the Tufnell Press (maker).

All rights reserved. No part of this publication may be reproduced, stored in a retrieval system, or transmitted in any form or by any means, electronic, mechanical, photocopying, recording or otherwise, without the prior permission of the publisher, or expressly by law, or under terms agreed with the appropriate reprographic rights organisation.

Printed in England and U.S.A. by Lightning Source

Performing English
with a postcolonial accent:
Ethnographic narratives from Mexico

Angeles Clemente and Michael J. Higgins

ETHNOGRAPHY AND EDUCATION

The *Ethnography and Education* book series aims to publish a range of authored and edited collections including both substantive research projects and methodological texts and in particular we hope to include recent PhDs. Our priority is for ethnographies that prioritise the experiences and perspectives of those involved and that also reflect a sociological perspective with international significance. We are particularly interested in those ethnographies that explicate and challenge the effects of educational policies and practices and interrogate and develop theories about educational structures, policies and experiences. We value ethnographic methodology that involves long-term engagement with those studied in order to understand their cultures, that use multiple methods of generating data and that recognise the centrality of the researcher in the research process.

www.ethnographyandeducation.org

The editors welcome substantive proposals that seek to:
- explicate and challenge the effects of educational policies and practices and
- interrogate and develop theories about educational structures, policies and experiences,
- highlight the agency of educational actors,
- provide accounts of how the everyday practices of those engaged in education are instrumental in social reproduction.

The editors are
- Professor Dennis Beach, University College of Borås, Sweden,
- Bob Jeffrey, (Commissioning Editor), The Open University,
- Professor Geoff Troman, Roehampton University, London and
- Professor Geoffrey Walford, University of Oxford.

Titles in the series include,
- Creative learning: European experiences,
  edited by Bob Jeffrey;
- Researching education policy: Ethnographic experiences,
  Geoff Troman, Bob Jeffrey and Dennis Beach;
- The commodification of teaching and learning,
  Dennis Beach and Marianne Dovemark;
- How to do educational ethnography;
  Edited by Geoffrey Walford (2008);
- The school and the animal other,
  Helena Pedersen (2008).

Contents

Acknowledgements	vii
Foreword	viii
by Suresh Canagarajah	
Prologue	1

Part 1

Chapter 1   7
   The premise: Performing English with a postcolonial accent
Chapter 2   30
   'I'm very proud I didn't have to pay to get into the Centro': The social and economic context for performing English with a postcolonial accent in Oaxaca

Part II

Chapter 3   60
   'They think that because you speak another language you have changed!': Ethnographic portraits of how students perform at the Centro de Idiomas
Chapter 4   118
   Exorcising the ghost of the native speaker in the contact zone: The use of safe houses in the construction of learning cultures
Chapter 5   147
   'It is not about the accent, it is about having the confidence to say what you want': Moving between language learning and language use

Part III

Chapter Six   197
   Towards a politics of language affinity

Appendix	209
References	215

Dedicated to:

Rebeca, Erika and Jessica
Alianna and Arwyn

All the students that made this book possible:

Adriana Cruz Domínguez, Angélica Morales Santiago, Araceli Valenzuela Ricárdez, Berenice Cisneros Villalba, César Francisco Yescas, Cinthia Paola López Díaz, Claribel Guzmán Guzmán, Claudet Ortiz Ramírez, Damian Villavicencio Valdez, Efraín Calvo Gómez, Efrain Pinacho Juárez, Elvia Jerónimo García, Ervin Méndez Ortiz, Fatima Karime Aragón Aquino, Facundo Santiago Canseco, Gabriela Merlín Osorio, Hassina Hernández Pineda, Heydi León García, Itayetzi Carapia Pedro, Itzel Mendoza Cruz, Itzel Pacheco Maldonado, Jimmy Dei-ly Abad Hernández, Jorge Luis Martínez Antonio, José Manuel Alvárez Nava, Judith Reyes Hernández, Karla Paola Ricárdez Calvo, López Cázares Dalila, Miriam Castro Hernández, Odelma López Arreola, Rebeca Lavariega Bautista, Rhomani López Herrera, Roxana Castro Hernández, Sarahi Cruz Dionisio, Tomás Toral Hernández, Viviana Escamirosa Ortiz, Yadira Castañeda Antonio, Yolanda Merino López, Research Methodology Class, Speaking Skills Evaluation Class, and all the many students who participated in this project but, for reasons of space were not include in the final version of this book.

Acknowledgements

The journey taken to write this book has been a long and fruitful voyage. A great diversity of people, in different ways and styles, have helped us along on this adventure. First and foremost, there have been all the students and faculty at the *Centro de Idiomas*. As we said in the dedication, we would like to acknowledge all of the students and teachers who we were not able to be included in the book. It seemed that each of them had a profound and engaging story to tell. We simply lacked the time and space to present all the stories of how these students performed their English with a postcolonial accent. Of the faculty at the *Centro* we would like to particularly thank Vilma Huerta, Mario López, Donald Kissinger, Sam Johnson, Peter Sayer, and William Sugrhua. We also want to acknowledge the human and financial support of the current administration of the *Universidad Autónoma Benito Juárez de Oaxaca*.

We offer a very special thanks to Adam Sederlin, for his thoughtful and critical editing suggestions for this work; and to Alba Vasquez Miranda, for her suggestions on our argument. With both of them, the discussions around our work were certainly delightful and productive. And special thanks to Erika Santiago Clemente for her work on the graphics and cover of the book.

From the area of applied linguistics we have received a wealth of useful and critical advice. We offer a special thanks to Suresh Canagarajah for his guidance and contributions towards the development of this research; to Alastair Pennycook, Bonny Norton and Vaidehi Ramanathan for the time and concern they showed in offering ideas on how to strengthen our performances; to Adrian Holliday for his support, encouragement and problematising questions; to Chris Candlin for his generous reading and editing of earlier drafts of chapters; to B. Kumaravadivelu for his encouragement to fully explore our ideas, and to John and Jane Kullman for their help and support while we worked on parts of the book in Canterbury, England.

In the area of anthropology, we would like to thank Matt Gutmann for his ironic support and criticism; Enrique Hamel for his critical questioning of our premises and methods; Marco Jacquemet for his transidiomatic suggestions; Roger Lancaster for his useful editing suggestions, Margarita Dalton for her invitation to the seminar on *Gender and Identity*, where we were able to present aspects of this work; and Bob Jeffrey for his encouragement to submit this work to their education and ethnography series published by the Tufnell Press.

Further, we would like to thank the graduate students from China, Mexico, Brazil and Venezuela that were in Adrian Holliday's seminar on language studies at Christ Church University in Canterbury, England, where we presented earlier versions of several of the chapters in this book. Also we will like to thank all of the various people who attended the numerous presentations we made about this work at conferences in England, Mexico, Turkey and the United States. Further, we would like to acknowledge all the friends and colleagues in Oaxaca, like Julia Barco, Vilma Barahona, George Colman, Michelle Gibbs, Vilma Huerta, Lupe Ramirez and many others, that have kindly listened to our comments and worries over the last four years on this journey.

Foreword

Suresh Canagarajah

In the context of globalisation, where linguistic and cultural borders are porous, English enjoys a vibrant presence in almost every community. As we see in the narratives and scenarios in this book, even communities not formerly colonised by Britain find English a significant medium of communication, calling into question the traditional distinction between ESL (English as a second language) and EFL (English as a foreign language) countries. As members of diverse communities actively use English in their everyday life, it is understandable that English would display a different trajectory of development, acquiring codes and conventions different from the traditional norms. In Oaxaca (when teachers and students get together informally) and outside (when the authors present their work at conferences), I have heard these dynamics discussed with great enthusiasm.

Granting these developments, the question for many would be: Does English enjoy enough currency and history in Mexico to develop a structure of its own? Is there a Mexican English? When does one recognise certain variations from the norm as constituting an independent language variety? How much variation does a language need in order to be classified as a new system of communication?

However, such questions are becoming irrelevant. These concerns show a structuralist bias toward languages. The underlying assumption here is that languages are separate from each other, each with its own closed system of stable grammar, which serves as the primary source of communication. These notions are being revised in the light of recent social and philosophical changes. Among other things, we now agree on the following assumptions:

+ grammar is always emergent, not predefined; as language finds its place in social practice, its form changes according to the uses to which it is put;
+ form doesn't govern the speakers of a language, speakers negotiate with form to use it for their interests;
+ competence in a language doesn't mean that one has mastered the whole grammar system; it is the ability to strategically choose certain features as needed and integrate them into other codes and symbol systems in diverse modalities and media of communication;
+ the notion of discrete bounded languages is questionable; languages are always mixed and hybrid in communication.

The terms invoked in the title of the book, *performance* and *accent*, denote the new way of looking at language. The notion of performing in English marks a big departure from traditional notions of competence and performance. Competence gives primacy to the mental and cognitive representations of the form of a language. In the context of this dualism, though performance places more emphasis on the realisations of a language in a social context, it still assumes that usage depends on the underlying core grammar stored cognitively. However, when performance is linked to Austin senses of performativity, it moves away from these assumptions. It gives primacy to acts of creative and strategic communication motivated by the enigmatic purposes of complex individuals. It draws attention to playfulness, fabrication, strategic negotiation, situationally motivated shifts, multiple identities, hybridity, repertoire, irony, and paradox! It resists essentialising language or culture or grounding them in a specific identity, and defies traditional distinctions such as inner/outer; real/illusory, and deep/surface.

So what exactly does performance in English mean? It means doing things with words, not just expressing ideas or displaying one's grammatical proficiency. Even with ungrammaticality one can accomplish one's interests effectively and project desired identities. Sometimes, the desired identity and purpose are precisely those that require resisting conventions and norms associated with a language. Similarly, one might have to draw from multiple languages to achieve one's interests in some specific contexts. Code mixing and code switching are some ways in which one can perform in English. Ben Rampton coins a new label for such usage: *crossing*. A mere display of a token from another language (even without full proficiency in that language) is enough to project certain identities and achieve one's interests.

Performance in English means constructing new, even imagined, identities for oneself. Just as we remove language from its mooring in one common core or base system, we now remove identity from unitary and bounded notions. We perform shifting, contextually relevant, strategic identities to accomplish our interests. Multiple languages, even alien and imposing ones like English, are rich resources for constructing desired identities.

Performance in English means that *you* speak the language and not let the language speak you. This means that you exercise your agency to populate the language with your values, meanings, and intentions. Performance therefore means gaining voice in a language by appropriating its forms and conventions for your purposes. To gain voice is to stamp the language with your identity. It often means that you must go against the grains of the language to reshape it to your expectations. Paradoxically, then, to gain voice in a language is to resist the language.

All this would mean that English takes on a different identity and structure when local people in their everyday life use it in Oaxaca for meaningful communication. English would become *accented*. It would become accented not just in the phonological sense. Accent also refers to the emphasis one gives a language, the twists and shifts one gives the structure to represent oneself. Accent is therefore ethos—one's own voice, one's identity. For that matter, we can't think of any situation where speaking English meaningfully in everyday contexts is not accented in some form.

From this perspective, the debate whether there is a Mexican English or not is moot. There are Mexican ways of using English. Wouldn't such accented-ness constitute an English specific to Oaxaca? Whether it is a recognisable system that can be named is not purely a linguistic or historical issue. It's not only a structure that can be described or a lengthy tradition of using the language locally that determines the outcome of this debate. There are also social considerations. Much depends on whether Oaxacans themselves perceive the reality of a language that is their own. The narratives in this book show that there is a consciousness of a unique or personal way of using English. The very publication of this book will help develop this consciousness both in that community and beyond—i.e., among linguists and practitioners elsewhere.

That a radical social and linguistic consciousness is evolving in Oaxaca has become clear to me from my visits there at different times in the past twenty years. I first went to Oaxaca in December 1987 when I was a graduate student at the University of Texas at Austin. With the university closed for the Christmas holidays, I did the next best when I realised that I didn't have the money to buy a plane ticket to visit Sri Lanka. I jumped into a Greyhound bus, crossed the Mexican border, and then used the local bus system to travel slowly all the way south to Merida. My stop at Oaxaca one lazy Sunday morning was memorable. I went to a Methodist church and tried to mingle with the local people. I thought that at least the Christians would know some English to communicate with me. I was an immediate curiosity when I told them that I was from South Asia. People gathered around me and wanted to see if there was a cobra under my turban! They were disappointed to see that I had neither. Because no one knew English, we had to resort to communicating in sign language and code mixing (me using much of the Spanish I was picking up during the trip). In the nights, I slept in the Zócalo on a bench, with my backpack for a pillow. In the mornings, I took the local buses to visit the other historic indigenous villages (Mitla, Zaachila) outside the town centre. Life was pleasantly rural when I sat one afternoon in Mitla, with cocks crowing belatedly to welcome the morning and goats walking calmly all around me. I saw men hailing each other by whistles and clicks as I would have done in Jaffna. The peacefulness and familiarity lulled me into thinking I was back home in my village in Sri Lanka.

When I went to Oaxaca next in January 2004, it had changed a lot. No more sleeping in the Zócalo, as *Centro de Idiomas* put me up in a comfortable hotel. Nearby, old women were still going to the Catholic Church every evening for mass. But the Methodist church was gone. The building was now used by a broadcasting station. Urbanisation and commercialisation were taking over. There were advertisements everywhere asking students to 'learn Oxford English!' Even the Zócalo had changed its character—as I saw sipping beer in the evenings with Michael Higgins. Mariachi singers and vendors created a raucous late into the night. I wasn't sure the Zócalo still had the quietness that would have let me sleep there as I did before. Just a few blocks away, transvestites were gathering for their midnight rendezvous. In fact, they could speak the language that the Methodists couldn't speak during my previous visit. More importantly, I could talk to local students and teachers in English and skirt dangerous knowledge relating to linguistic resistance.

Despite the inroads of globalisation, the rich linguistic and ethnic diversity of Oaxaca wasn't lost. In fact, people were more conscious and expressive of their identities now. Gays and transvestites did not inhabit the secluded areas of the downtown any more. And I didn't have to go to Mitla to see indigenous people. People were bolder in sharing their unconventional and richly hybrid identities. More remarkable was the collaboration among diverse sections of the community in struggling for issues that mattered to them. In fact, my next visit planned for summer 2006 was postponed as Oaxaca captured the world's attention with the mass mobilisation of students and workers against the Governor, Ulises Ruiz Ortiz. And English was playing a role in this struggle as international news agencies descended on Oaxaca. Local people were using English to communicate their aspirations to the world. The bilingual placard displayed in front of the sit in at the Zócalo has become history, '*SORRY for the annoyances. What happens is that we are busy making our HISTORY. As soon as Ulises gets out of here, we will welcome you again with open arms. Attentively, the citizens of Oaxaca*'.

This book takes me once again to those times when I reached across cultural boundaries to establish community with people with another history—in the English language! In addition to being a window into globalisation and English in the global periphery, this book invites us to do more networking among diverse communities. The narratives remind us of the struggles all of us wage to shape English to express our interests and aspirations. The book makes us think about the commonalties beyond our diverse histories in English, our ability to share our stories in the once-foreign language and, even better, our need to collaborate in developing radical knowledge that would transform teaching and talking in ways that are relevant to our people.

Suresh Canagarajah
Kirby Professor in Language Learning
Penn State University,
USA.

Prologue

The phenomenon to be discussed is very widespread and obvious, and it cannot fail to have been already noticed, at least here and there, by others. Yet I have not found attention paid to it specifically.

(Austin, 1962:1)

Often our English teachers give us a story to read, and then they will ask us to report on what we think the reading was about. However, for us, using a language is not only about interpreting other peoples' ideas, but also about producing our own ideas! When learning and using English, we want to leave behind that level of interpreting the ideas of others or reporting what other people said. That level is only practice. We need to go beyond the idea of only practising and acquiring skills. We need to start expressing what we think and what we feel in English.

What we need exactly is to be ourselves in this other language!

(*Braulio and Freda, offering their views on the use of English*)

To establish one's identity in respect to the language one speaks is important. However, at the moment, I do not know what type of English I speak. I have never been in England or in the United States or any other English speaking country. So I do not have any reason to say that I speak a specific type of English. Sometimes I think that I have created my own style, with my own peculiar errors. So far, these mistakes have been tolerated, but I know that it will not be like that all the time. I am also aware that I have not adopted a native speaker accent. To sum up, I have a Mexican accent. English is mine from the very moment I put it into practice and I am able to establish communication. But when I say that the English language is mine, I do not mean to say that I want to take the culture that comes with it.

(*Raimunda's views on speaking English with an accent*)

We talk in English a lot and ... when we don't have anything better to do, you know ... just hanging around, just talking. In the middle of a conversation, then we realise that we need a word in English. Sometimes we look it up in the dictionary; we were really surprised that we found *cabeza de chorlito* in English. It is 'scatterbrain'. We use it a lot now ... Well, with 'donkey' it was different, we used it so much in Spanish, and of course we didn't need to use the dictionary. It is perfect for *burro*. When somebody does not understand something in the class, that's a donkey. Or when someone is slow, that's also a donkey. It is a joke. It is just between us. It started one day when we did not have anything better to do ... and now it is so common among us.

(*Freda, talking about the way she and her clique use some English words*)

The above are some observations that students at the *Centro de Idiomas* (Language Centre) at the state university in Oaxaca have made about their pursuit of learning, using and teaching English as an additional language. How can we understand the concerns of these students? What do Braulio and Freda mean by wishing 'to be ourselves in this other language?' What is the range of social and cultural issues that would support Raimunda's desire not to give up her Mexican identity as she pursues the learning of English? What is the importance of Freda's desire to play with this other language?

Their questions and observations provide ethnographic texture to the concerns of applied linguistics and cultural anthropology concerning the relations between language, agency, identity, culture and social context. Folded into their comments are questions about the discursive properties of Standard English and English language instruction. These students want to know who controls how they perform languages; when they can play with them, especially if these are languages that are not theirs *per se*; and how, as young Oaxacans, can they locate themselves in these social and cultural dynamics and issues. These are not questions solely concerning the language learning realities of Oaxacan students. With the dominant role that English plays in the contemporary globalised political economy of the existing postcolonial world, students and educators from Sri Lanka (Canagarajah, 2006a) to East Los Angeles are confronting the same questions (Pennycook, 2007).

In dealing with these issues, the students in Oaxaca are composing forms of linguistic activities that we refer to as *performing English with a postcolonial accent*. For us, the postcolonial condition represents the political, social and cultural realities of what constitutes the everyday lives of the actors entangled in the 'whirlwind of globalisation' (Castells, 2000a). How these students learn, appropriate, modify, and redefine their use of English as a series of multilingual social and cultural performances is what we mean by a *postcolonial accent*.

We argue that the *Centro* represents a contact zone in which the students confront the demands of Standard English through various forms of language play in both Spanish and English (Canagarajah, 2004; Pratt, 1991). They use their cliques as safe houses where they can play with both languages. Within these safe houses, these students are constructing various language learning cultures as they play with their own styles of language creativity. For us, learning cultures involves two coexisting domains: the social and cognitive dynamics of language learning, and the overall social and cultural context of that learning. Through an ethnographic analysis of the linguistic, social and cultural activities of these students at the *Centro*, we can illustrate how their performances provide them with the means to explore various identity locations that give them space to move beyond the hegemony of native-speakerism (Holliday, 2005).

How do we plan to address the questions and issues we have raised above? First, we will provide a brief description of the setting of this research and our methods.

The Ethnography of the *Centro de Idiomas*

The *Centro de Idiomas* is the language teacher training centre for the *Universidad Autónoma Benito Juárez de Oaxaca* (UABJO), the state university of Oaxaca. The state of Oaxaca is located in the Southwest region of Mexico and has a population of over 3.2 million people. The state of Oaxaca is noted for its ethnic diversity, stunning ecological variety and extreme poverty in the countryside. The university is located in the city of Oaxaca which has a population of close to half a million, and is the political, commercial and communication centre of the state. The city is noted for its colonial architecture, ethnic and social diversity and culinary excellence. Oaxaca is also a city that has many of the problems associated with urbanisation in Mexico: shortage of housing, limited employment possibilities for those in the popular classes, traffic congestion, and almost daily political protests. In terms of European colonialism, the peoples of the Americas could be said to be the first postcolonial societies. Mexico's history of dependency on the United States, and Oaxaca's history of internal colonialism, can be seen as social formations in which the social actors continue to navigate the hegemonic terrains of postcolonialism (Gutmann, 2002).

We have been working over the last four years on an ethnographic representation of the cultural and language activities of students and teachers at the *Centro de Idiomas*. We have collected various life histories of students and professors and conducted a census survey of over four hundred students and faculty. We have also carried out numerous interviews with the students on a wide range of issues dealing with language learning and use and the various investments that students have made in pursuing their goals. We have had lengthy conversations with students on how they have formed their own learning cultures and how these learning cultures provide them with safe houses for their pursuit of English. We also have collected observational data on student social life and their styles of participation in their classrooms. We have presented these ethnographic data bases in their various narrative styles throughout the text. We contend that the strongest method for knowledge formation is through the narrativisation of the actions and behaviours of the social actors being represented (Bial, 2004). We are not doing an ethnography of speech, communication or language *per se*. We are doing an ethnography of the social and cultural context of the performances of these students' language practices. Our data, therefore, gathered in the form of interviews, observation notes, speech transcripts, protocols, etc., is woven together in a narrative form with the purpose to illustrate and interpret the context within which these actions take place. This mode of presentation also allows us to show how these students perceive and interpret that context and their location within it. See the appendix for an expanded explanation of our methods.

To illustrate and represent these performances we have divided the book into three main parts. Part I (Chapter One and Two) sets the framework and context in which we are basing our analysis and reflections. Part II contains the ethnographic narratives which are clustered into three themes. Chapter Three and Four focus on students, either individually or within their social groups, and Chapter Five presents these students trying out new roles as language users. Part III concludes by putting together the contents of the two previous parts. What follows is a brief description of each chapter.

The first chapter, titled *The Premise: Performing English with a postcolonial accent* tells the story of the intellectual journey we took in order to understand how these young Oaxacan students were performing English with a postcolonial accent. In this journey we moved from the local perspective of the *Centro de Idiomas* to the globalised postcolonial world of multiculturalism and interculturalism. This involved visiting the discursive locations in applied linguistics and cultural anthropology that address the interrelationships between language, culture, identity and agency. These relations include the deconstruction of native-speakerism, understanding the social invention and disinvention of the language regimes, and recognising the performative dynamics of language practices. The resulting challenge of this journey was to use ethnography in order to account for these processes in the everyday language performances of these students.

The second chapter is titled '*I'm very proud I didn't have to pay to get into the Centro*': *The social and economic context for performing English with a postcolonial accent in Oaxaca*. To set the stage for these performances of English with a postcolonial accent, we discuss the overall socio-cultural and economic context that the students at the *Centro* deal with. To do this, we provide the stories of two students: the first one is about how Claribel was able to get into the *Centro* without paying a *mordida* (bribe); the second story is about how Alberto had to use some *palanca* (influence) to pay someone to get into the *Centro*. From these two stories we explore the following questions: what do these two stories tell us about the complex social and economic dynamics of language education in Mexico and Oaxaca? What do these stories tell us about the structure of the university and the *Centro*? And what do these stories tell us about how students perform their social life at the *Centro*? Moreover, in this chapter we decided to include a brief guest essay narrating the social movement that sprouted in 2006 in Oaxaca. In some way or another, some of the students in this study became involved in it.

The third chapter is titled '*They think that because you speak another language you have changed!*' *Ethnographic portraits of how students perform at the Centro de Idiomas English*. In it we are able to show how the students at the *Centro* are being themselves in this 'other' language. We represent a diversity of learning styles and performances that these students have created for dealing with English. To do this we present ethnographic portraits of the everyday lives of the students in order to represent how, in performing English, they are actively pursuing cultural capital, constructing new identity locations and using their own personal agency. In these portraits we introduce six students from the *Centro* and tell their stories: how Nour has navigated the social locations of gender, ethnicity and social class in the process of learning English; how Facundo found the *Centro de Idiomas* a safe house in terms of his sexuality and social class; how Jorge found the *Centro* to be a theatre for the performance of his politics; how Elena is shifting her class position from the *cantina* to the classroom through the pursuit of linguistic capital; how César is redefining his indigenous ethnic identity (Chinanteco) through the way he performs English and how Yolanda is using her indigenous ethnic identity (Trique) to make a claim on English userhood.

In the fourth chapter, *Exorcising the ghost of the native speaker in the contact zone: The use of safe houses in the construction of learning cultures*, we illustrate how many students like Raimunda are redefining their own identities as Mexicans as they construct and participate in their bilingual speech communities. We show how the *Centro de Idiomas* has become a contact zone for learning English, as well as a place where students can construct their learning cultures and find safe houses that shelter their identity constructions. We discuss how students use their network of friends (cliques), social spaces, and interactions both in, as well as out of, the classroom as safe houses for building up their learning cultures. We also explore how these students' performances of English give them access to the user rights of English and establish relationships of affinity, that is, interculturalism, with other non-native speakers of English.

In the fifth chapter titled *'It is not about the accent, it is about having the confidence to say what you want': Moving between language learning and language use*, we explore how the students at the *Centro de Idiomas*, through performing English with a postcolonial accent, are able to move from their learning cultures to cultures of English language use. This involves a discussion of how a particular group of students at the *Centro* wanted to play a role in the decision making process of the curriculum; the story of a group of students and a faculty member at the *Centro* who created their own poems in English and then how those poems were used to teach English; the narrative of a young teacher who has just left the university and is facing the challenge of teaching undergraduate students; and the story of Ervin, who has found that his English can not only give him satisfaction and money but also misfortunes.

The sixth chapter, *Towards a politics of language affinity*, is the conclusion of our study. In this chapter we connect our conceptual view of applied linguistics and cultural anthropology to the journey of the students as they have been performing English with a postcolonial accent in the multicultural and multilingual context of Oaxaca and Mexico. From these connections we develop our model of the politics of language affinity expressed in how these students wanted to be themselves in these language performances; in seeking the validation of their performance in terms of communicative success; and in their search for modes of contact with other users of English in the postcolonial world in which we live. We argue that their quest is based upon their claim of language userhood and their rejection of the assertions of language ownership. As a means to summarise what we present, we offer suggestions on what our findings imply for language learning and teaching.

It is now time to enter the theatre of these student performances.

Part 1
Chapter 1

The premise: Performing English with a postcolonial accent

Introduction

It is a widely held assumption that we are living in a postcolonial world anchored by a globalised political economy (Castells, 2000a). This is a world in which our everyday lives transpire in a multicultural context, that is, the social fields that compose these globalised postcolonial spaces are filled with a diversity of cultural worlds that are mediated by the social dynamics of difference, inequality and disconnection. (García Canclini, 2004)[1] It has also been suggested that there is a world of interculturalism, a quest for forms of equivalent differences and substantive connections (Dietz, 2003).[2] Within these existing forms of cultural diversity (gender, sexuality, ethnicity, social class and ableness) there are numerous practices being composed that encourage various forms of negotiation that seek to go beyond existing forms of power and authority towards a politics of affinity (Haraway, 1991; Mouffe, 2005); that is, more equitable modes of social interaction and communication (García Canclini, 2004). It is within these various social folds where the interplays between language, agency, identity and culture are performed. These performances of communication and interaction are multitextual and multicontextual, ranging from face to face interactions to the clickings of thousands of mice throughout the cyber cafes of the world (Bauman, 2003). It is assumed that the majority of these social and cultural activities, for various historical, economic and political reasons, will occur in English (Brutt-Griffler, 2002; Canagarajah, 2004; 1999; Hamel, 2003; Holborow, 1999; Macedo et al., 2003; McKay, 2002; Pennycook, 1998

---

1 We recognise that each of these terms are quite problematic: 1) difference or differences can be seen as a rich source of diversity and creativity, though often entrapped in various hegemonic forces of authority and domination or they can be the location of new forms of stereotypes through essentialising; 2) forms of material and symbolic inequality can be the sources for new means of struggle and organization or as social folds in the global marketplace; and 3) disconnection can range from social alienation and exclusion to information networks for political struggles against existing tele-technologies (García Canclini, 2004)
2 Interculturalism has nothing to do with the discourse of intercultural communication. More often than not, intercultural communication is a discourse that attempts to essentialize differences and accept the existence of national cultures. Interculturalism is a form of praxis that seeks a Derridian sense of difference, that is, the deferral of social and political judgment and the construction of a context for the ordinariness of diversity..

and 2004; Phillipson, 1992; Seidlhofer, 2001; Widdowson, 2003). English is either being proposed, or proclaimed, as both the formal and informal language of this postcolonial globalisation. However, it is not clear what the standards for English usage within these social fields will be. Moreover, it has been argued that the most appropriate means to represent these linguistic and cultural realities is through localised and situated presentations of people's everyday activities and practices (Ramanathan, 2005).

Assuming the validity of these social, linguistic and cultural dynamics, this situation calls for a merger of the descriptive prowess of applied linguistics and the interpretative flexibility of cultural anthropology. Through this combination of prowess and flexibility we can demonstrate how various social actors navigate the hegemonic terrains of these globalised postcolonial landscapes in their everyday lives. The complementary strengths of applied linguistics and cultural anthropology can offer descriptions of the social fields of difference, inequality and disconnection, while suggesting interpretations for locating the social folds of communicative reciprocity and social equity (Clemente and Higgins, 2005).

Drawing upon the discourse of applied linguistics we can ask such critical descriptive questions as: How has English come to play such a central role in this globalised postcolonial world? How are English and other languages performed in these multicultural contexts? What are the roles of identity and agency in language performances? Who sets the conditions and standards for language access and performance? What is the role of educational actors and institutions in these processes?

Drawing upon the discourses of cultural anthropology, we can ask such critical interpretative questions as: What are the social compositions of these multicultural contexts in which English and other languages are performed? What are the levels of social and cultural diversity in the construction of identity locations? How is agency (both personal and social) used in these language performances? How do social class, gender, ethnicity, age and sexuality mediate who has access to English language learning? How are other languages ranked in relation to English? What are the cultural politics of Standard English in this globalised postcolonial world?

Of equal importance is the fact that since both disciplines encourage the use of case studies or ethnographic accounts, these trans-historical questions of language and culture can be framed in the more immediate context of people's real actions and practices. With such a framework we can explore whether the spread of English works to expand the multicultural world of difference and inequality or if it provides a means for a communicative interculturalism.

What we plan to do in this book is to explore the above questions through the analysis of various localised interplays between language, culture, agency, and identity in the postcolonial context of the city of Oaxaca, Mexico. Specifically, we will be looking at how the above dynamics are played out in social fields in which young Oaxacan university students are pursuing their goals of learning, using and teaching English. Our major premise is that these young students are performing English with a postcolonial accent and that these performances can be read as a counter-hegemonic discourse to Standard English. How these students learn, appropriate, modify, and redefine their use of English as a series of multilingual social and cultural performances is what we mean by a *postcolonial accent*.

Now, let us first explain what we mean by *postcolonial*. For us, a discursive bridge between the disciplines of applied linguistics and cultural anthropology is the area of postcolonial studies (Kumaravadivelu, 2007). Those writing within these discourses have attempted to shift the ways in which the socio-cultural relations are composed in the globalised world. The prevailing argument is that those of the 'third' world are largely in a situation of economic and cultural subordination to Europe and North America. Postcolonial studies seek to change radically the way people think and behave in order to produce a more just and equitable relation between the different peoples of the world (DeHay, 2007; Young, 2003). The postcolonial condition represents the political, economic, social and cultural realities of what constitutes the everyday lives of the actors entangled in the 'whirlwind of globalisation' (Castells, 2000a).

In terms of what we understand postcolonial discourse(s) to be, we suggest (with cautious humility) two broad panoramas of argumentation and interpretation: 1) The domains of critical deconstructionist analysis of the postcolonial condition (see Derrida, 1998; Spivak, 1999; Bhabha, 1994) and 2) The critical focus on historical and socio-cultural dynamics of the postcolonial condition that illuminates the particularities of the systemic and epistemic violence that framed, and continues to frame, the realities of colonialism and how the social actors in those contexts have resisted those forces (see Ashcroft, Griffiths and Tiffin, 1998; Canagarajah, 1999; Mignolo, 2005; Pratt, 1991; Young, 2003). Like any kind of heuristic interpretation, our classification hides the fact that there are more divisions *within* these categories than between them, and that many advocates of the postcolonial discourses work in between these focuses; such is the case with the classic works of Said (1993) and the innovative writings of Kumaravadivelu (2007) or Pennycook (2004).

Though we have been informed by the work on deconstruction, our use of *postcolonial* is more historical and socio-cultural. It can be said that the Americas, particularly Latin America, represent the first postcolonial societies in terms of European imperialism (Galeano, 1985). Furthermore, these postcolonial societies were, from their beginnings, embedded in the hegemonic networks of the United States (González Casanova, 1986). The complex and difficult histories of Mexico and the United States are woven into those networks. In the formation and development of the nation state of Mexico, social and economic dynamics of internal colonialism were established between the metropolitan and provincial zones of the country. It was in these networks that racial, ethnic and class systems of the stratification of Mexico emerged and thrived in Oaxaca and other similar areas with a high percentage of indigenous peoples (Barabas and Bartolomé, 1999; Hernández Díaz, 2000; Nahmad, 2000). It is these historical realities that have made contemporary Oaxaca a postcolonial society.

The socio-cultural postcolonial arguments we make draw upon Mignolo's emphasis on the colonial difference (2002), Pratt's concept of the contact zone (1991), Pratt's (1991) and Canagarajah's (2004) ideas on safe houses, and the issues of languages ideologies within the contact zone (Bourdieu, 1991). *Colonial difference* refers to the geopolitics of the production of knowledge and the question of who has the power to claim the authority of knowledge. It is those in the metropolitan zones who assert this right to produce universal knowledge that dominates the local knowledges of those in the colonies or post colonies (Mignolo, 2005). Mignolo states that globalisation is a continuation of modes of socio/economic authority and power that emerged in the construction of capitalism as a modern/colonial world system. Colonial difference refers to the geopolitics of how knowledge was, and is, produced, accessed and reproduced within that complex historical context (ibid.). In Mignolo's words:

> the difference between centre and periphery, between the Eurocentric critique of Eurocentrism and knowledge production by those who participated in building the modern/colonial world and those who have been left out of the discussion. (ibid., 63)

The idea of *contact zones* refers to the dynamics of transculturation, where reciprocal influences of styles of representation and cultural practices between the colonies and the metropolis, or between the metropolitan centres and the periphery, take place (Ashcroft, Griffiths and Tiffin, 1998: 233). Pratt stresses that contact zones are social spaces where 'disparate cultures meet, clash, and grapple with each other, often in highly asymmetrical relations of dominance and subordination —like colonialism, slavery, and their aftermath as they are lived out many parts of the world today' (Pratt, 1991: 6). She further points out that the imperial metropolis tends to understand itself as determining the periphery, but habitually blinds itself to the ways that the periphery determines the metropolis (ibid.). Pratt's argument about contact zones has focused on the historical dynamics of Western imperialism in the Americas with a particular interest in the contacts between Spaniards and the indigenous peoples of this continent.

We are using the idea of contact zone in a somewhat more localised sense. For us, the *Centro de Idiomas* is a contact zone (which is not constrained by the physical boundaries of the school) where young Oaxacans are entering into the world of learning how to perform English. This arena for learning English certainly contains reciprocal influences of highly asymmetrical cultural practices between the domains of the metropolis and the periphery in terms of the native/non-native dichotomy. There is also a parallel in how the gatekeepers of Standard English clearly assume that they are in charge of the kind of English that should be taught, with little concern with how the Englishes of the periphery will alter the standard.

For students at the *Centro* this contact zone is the stage where they played out the social dynamics involving the colonial difference (Mignolo, 2002). In the dynamics of the geopolitical knowledge production, those in the interior of the system have the authority to define its reality; those in the exterior to the system (the colonised) are silenced (ibid., 63). For us, these dynamics of the colonial difference are played in the *Centro* in terms of whose voice has the authority to set the standards for English and Spanish performances: the hegemonic voices of the language regimes of standardised English and authentic Spanish or the voices of the language performers themselves?[3]

Pratt suggests that actors in contact zones construct *safe houses*. She refers to safe houses as 'social and intellectual spaces where groups can constitute

---

3   It seems to be ironical the way the position of internality and externality (Mignolo, 2002) has reversed as the discursive regimes of Spanish and English confront each other in this contact zone. As the students enter the *Centro*, its interior is dominated by the realities of the Spanish speaking world of Oaxaca and Mexico. English is exterior to these dynamics, though offering the hope of the accumulation of linguistics and cultural capital that can be converted into economic gain. As these students begin the process of
cont/

themselves as horizontal, homogeneous, sovereign communities with high degrees of trust, shared understandings, temporary protection form legacies of oppression' (1991: 18-19). Going further than Pratt, Canagarajah's ideas on safe houses stress that they are sites where students develop modes of accommodation and resistance towards language learning (2004: 120-123). Canagarajah argues that the activities in these safe houses are subversive; they nurture the 'dream of alternative possibilities in educational and social life' (ibid., 134). He contends that language learning students (like most students) are involved in the construction of various identities to deal with the power-laden reality of the classroom. In the school setting, safe houses are sites that are 'relatively free from surveillance, especially by authority figures, perhaps because they are considered unofficial, off task, or extra pedagogical' (ibid., 121). These sites can be almost any space or time frame in which students are free from being watched or controlled. He assumes that students construct safe houses to develop their own group culture and alternative identities as a means to mediate their overall educational context. These spaces give the students the means to learn ways to negotiate how to express their learning desires within the classroom, how to practice suppressed discourses, and how to use their various identity locations in the learning process (ibid., 2004).

In terms of *language ideologies*, this assertion involves issues of language usages and the question of which language in the contact zone will be the voice of authority (Derrida, 1998). The ethnographic texture of these social dynamics

> learning and using English these locations are reversed. Now, English, particularly Standard English, dominates the interior of learning spaces within this zone and the students own desires and hopes about what they want to do with English, are removed to the exterior of the learning process. Thus, only those methods of learning and evaluation that maintain the interior authority of Standard English are seen as valid. All forms of curriculum change, whether they are seen as traditional methods or those that are novel or student-centred, still required that some model of English (a standard) be coded as the goal or direction for instruction and learning. The students' desires and hopes for their own language use rights to the performance of English are maintained to the exterior of this contact zone of learning. In the dynamics of this geopolitics of knowledge, the maintenance of the separation between native and non-native speakers of English masks the continuance of the colonial difference in this process of language learning.
>
> A further ironic twist is that in the desire to be themselves in this other language, these students, through their postcolonial accent, are challenging these geopolitics of knowledge production by repositioning themselves in terms of the internality and externality of the use rights of language performance. As young language actors situated within the multicultural and multilingual dynamics of working and middle class realities of Oaxaca, they are aware of their agency and how to use it to envision their hopes and desires (Ortner, 2006). They bring such feelings and sentiments within them while constructing their various learning cultures and safe houses in this contact zone. Through various explicit and implicit usages of their own local forms of knowledge they have begun to deconstruct these colonial differences through what we have referred as exorcising the ghost of the native speaker or what Pennycook has referred to as disinventing English.

will be developed in more detail throughout our argument. We concur with the postcolonial sentiment that stresses: 'Every colonial encounter or contact zone is different and each 'postcolonial' occasion needs, against these general background principles, to be precisely located and analysed for its specific interplay' (Ashcroft, Griffiths and Tiffin, 1998: 190).

How did we arrive to this position? In other words, how are we proposing this idea of performing English with a postcolonial accent? The answer to this question entails a long story about how we have been searching for ways to locate the realities of university students of Oaxaca within the social dynamics described above. This story begins by reading their language performances as part of a counter-hegemonic discourse to Standard English. Let us start this narrative with some episodes from Angeles' notes when we started this project:

> During a discussion session I asked my students about the English they wanted to learn and teach in the future, when one of them asked me, 'And what English do you speak?' I realised that I didn't have a clear answer. After the usual type of English instruction in secondary and preparatory public schools in Mexico City, I started 'my formal exposure to English': a B.A. in English Literature at the National University of Mexico (UNAM), where most of the input was in British English. When I graduated, the only job possibility for me was as an English teacher. I taught English in a state public high school in Mexico City, where the approach was to teach ESP (academic purposes) in Spanish. This was a period of total absence of oral practice. Four years later, I moved to Oaxaca, where I found a very rich environment in which to develop my linguistic skills. Many of my friends in Oaxaca were from the USA and other parts of the world and they used English as their lingua franca. Another important influence upon my English was my graduate school training: an M.A., a PhD and an Academic Fellowship at the University of London, which entailed three years of living in England. To all this I should add that in the last couple of years, another strong source of English interaction has been with my partner, who is American.
>
> I was astonished that it was so difficult for me to answer that question. However, during a recent academic visit to England I got an answer from a well known scholar who has known me for several years, 'You speak Standard English with a Mexican accent'. My reaction was very strong: I did not like it. I have always had problems with the idea that somebody

else sets the standards for everybody to meet. Although I knew that she was praising my English as academically competent, the qualifier 'with a Mexican accent' sounded to me like 'second rate', not good enough because it is not native. However, if she had said British or American, I would not have been happy either, because I know that my English does not have the distinctive features of those varieties—nor do I identify with them any more.

As can be noted by the above comments, this has been both a personal and professional journey for both of us. Therefore, instead of the more traditional presentation of our conceptual or theoretical framework for this study, we will present a travelogue of our journey through the discursive fields of applied linguistics and cultural anthropology that brought us to these locations where the young students of Oaxaca were performing English with a postcolonial accent. To orient the readers to how this journey developed, we first need to locate ourselves in these processes:

> I, Angeles, have been a professor of applied linguistics at the *Centro de Idiomas* for more than 20 years; have lived in the city of Oaxaca for more or less the same amount of time. I was born in Mexico City, and I am more or less a balanced bilingual in terms of Spanish and English. Within these social folds I am sort of an insider. However, in terms of the social diversity of the identity locations of the students, I am an outsider. And, like them, I am an outsider to the discourse of Standard English and its hegemonic authority.

> I, Michael, as an anthropologist, have been doing ethnographic research in the city of Oaxaca for more than 35 years. Though by no means an insider, I have been ethnographically moving into and out of the various fields of social diversity found in Oaxaca. And being from the United States and an uneven bilingual at best in English and Spanish, I have a somewhat of an insider view on the hegemonic authority of Standard English.

Our journey through applied linguistics began with a desire to understand what the boundaries were between cognitive language learning strategies for acquiring English and the socio-cultural context for those language activities (Clemente, 1998). Interplay between these dynamics transpired throughout a diversity of social spaces that earlier we had referred to as learning cultures. This is where the journey through cultural anthropology began, a search for what we meant by both *culture* and *learning*.

Searching for culture and learning

From this journey, we learned that *culture* is not *per se* about traditions, customs or rituals of particular peoples. It is more about how people can construct new ways of seeing and acting upon the world in which they live (Kramsch, 1993). It is often stated that culture represents learnt behaviour and not genetically determined modes of activity. That being the case, we arrived to the conclusion that styles of learning are central to the dynamics of cultural systems. Bauman (1973) argues that culture is a mode of human praxis in which knowledge and interest are one. Culture is about the possible, the potential, and the desirable (ibid.). Thus, we defined culture as a system for representing the symbolic, intuitive, and behavioural worlds that people construct, live in and act upon. People mediate these systems through cultural tools of interpretation, through the construction of meaning and through the development of strategies for problem solving. The specificity of particular cultures is formed by historical processes within a material and social context. The reproduction of specific cultural systems involves the intergenerational interactions of its members in mapping previous depositions—or what Bourdieu (1977) calls *habitus*—onto the social context of everyday life. It is in the social spaces of everyday life where the cultural realities are composed, performed and affirmed (Clemente and Higgins, 2003).

This is why *learning* is central to the process of cultural behaviour. Accepting that the actual dynamics of learning are both cognitive and social (Wertsch, 1991), we argue that learning is about moving away from the actual and reaching the possible. Learning challenges existing realities through the search for deeper meanings of concepts and actions. Learning is how one can construct a critique of the existing personal and social realities. To paraphrase Bauman's idea, we suggest that culture as learning or learning as culture are forms of praxis (Clemente and Higgins, 2003).

From this critical perspective, Braulio and Freda's quest to be themselves in this other language, Raimunda's demand to keep her Mexican identity while using English, and Freda's desire to play with English are all part of how they are creating the possibility of being creative and capable language users in their own bilingual *learning cultures*. These students are constructing these diverse language learning cultures as a means to invest in their quest for attaining and using English. We started considering language learning cultures as forms of creative interactions between both individuals and these individuals with the institutional context of their learning. We concluded that learning cultures provide space for social actors to negotiate their own learning activities and to locate each other within their respective histories of social and cultural diversity (Clemente, 2003).

To understand the construction of language learning cultures it is necessary to represent the two coexisting domains of socio-cultural-activities and practices: first, the socio-cognitive domain of language learning, that is, the actual activities and practices of language learning; second, the overall cultural contexts of gender, sexuality, ethnicity, social class, age, and nationality. These two domains engender each other to produce and reproduce the particularities of learning cultures. These students compose their cultural activities in Bauman's sense of culture as praxis (1973), that is, they are not protecting their past languages activities, but seeking new possibilities of language usages. It is within these social fields that the students are relocating themselves outside the dichotomy of the native/non-native speakers as they perform their English with a postcolonial accent (Clemente and Higgins, 2006).[4]

Leaving these discursive fields of culture and learning, our journey then proceeded toward those discourses that have used a socio-cultural approach to second or additional language learning.

Moving on to areas of socio-cultural analysis

Over the last several decades, the idea of a *socio-cultural focus* within the discourses of applied linguistics and second language acquisition (SLA) has become quite salient (Candlin, 2001). This focus has come from scholars in applied linguistics and SLA who have been advocating the need for a more socially-oriented and interdisciplinary approach (Lantolf and Thorne, 2006). Block argues for an applied linguistics that will look at the real world problems of language learners (Block, 2003: 2). Along the same line, Rampton has argued that in applied linguistics and SLA, the starting point for understanding real-world problems should be the study of culture and social organisation. According to him, this could be developed through the use of various interdisciplinary sites of research with a strong focus on ethnographic representation and analysis

(Rampton, 1997). Cook argues for a model of multilingual competence that recognises most speaking contexts as highly diversified in which speakers are able to negotiate numerous linguistic domains (Cook, 1996). Rampton has reinforced these ideas with the suggestion that instead of stressing the 'second' in second language acquisition (which in most cases is English), we should see these learning activities as the process of attaining an additional language in already complex linguistic contexts (Rampton, 1997). Block emphasises the need to pay more attention to questions of culture and identity and supports Breen's contention that applied linguistics needs 'to try to relate a theory of culture to the focus of its investigation' (Breen, 2001: 178). Block sees culture as a social process which allows actors to engage in acts of symbolic representation that stands at the cross roads of structure and agency. He declares that the use of the concept of culture in applied linguistics would have to deal with the relation between structure and agency as cultural activities (Block, 2003: 128).

This area seemed to offer very strong support for what we were attempting to represent with our argument of language learning cultures. We were looking for ways to compose more critical interpretations of the realities of these young students in Oaxaca: What were the dynamics of multicultural worlds of difference, inequality and disconnection in learning English in Oaxaca? Was there evidence of communicative interculturalism within the learning cultures of these young students? How did the youthfulness of these students factor into the dynamics between these complex social and cultural forces?

Moving further on to forms of critical interpretations

This required a visit to the discursive spaces within applied linguistics that are closely linked to the discourses of *critical interpretation* in social anthropology (Gutmann, 2002; Hymes, 1971; Geertz, 1973; Stephen, 2005). We were aware that there are several ways that critical interpretation has been expressed in applied linguistics. The works of Candlin (1990), Halliday (1978), Holliday (2005), Kramsch (2002), Pennycook (1998), and Widdowson (2003) offered broad and critical readings about what directions and opportunities applied linguistics could take from a sustained critical position. Many others—such as Pavlenko (2002), Pennycook (2001), and Rampton (1997)—suggested that such a critical focus must have the means to provide a look at what the role of power and authority in language learning was. Others, like Canagarajah (1999) and Norton (2000), worked with a bottom-up approach using ethnography to understand and interpret the everyday activities of language learners and users. It was then that we realised that our approach attempted to link this research to issues of social justice and language use through what is referred to as ethnographic praxis: connecting one's research objectives to the desires and concerns of those with whom one is working (Higgins and Coen, 2000). Furthermore, ethnographic praxis provides a means to link the particular expression of human agency to structural features of a cultural system.

Our journey had taken us into the conceptual spaces where we could support our model of language learning cultures with a strong definition of what we mean by culture and learning (Bauman, 1973); how those ideas were part of the discussions within applied linguistics on social and cultural factors in language activities; and how that could be represented critically through a form of ethnographic praxis (Clemente and Higgins, 2005). Now we were ready to move on to the questions about English and its performances.

Locating the hovering ghost of the native speaker

As we travelled towards the social fields of learning and using English as an additional language, we encountered the hovering ghost of the *native speaker* of English. No matter how often one attempts to deconstruct the assumptions about who or what native speakers of English are and no matter how frequently one notes the importance of pedagogical and methodological constructions made by non-native speakers of English, the ghost is ever present. For Holliday (2005) this ghost is a discourse or ideology that he refers to as native-speakerism. This is the belief that the native speaker teacher of English represents a Western culture from which the ideals of both English language and English language teaching methodology spring (ibid., 5). Native-speakerism is based on the assumption that the 'native speakers' of English have a special claim to the language itself, that it is essentially their property. Holliday rightfully contends that much of the teaching world of Teaching English to Speakers of Other Languages (TESOL) is dominated by native-speakerism and that this domination encourages the use of 'dualist' assumptions about the value of the language speakers. The native speaker is framed as *us* and the non-native speaker as *them*. The native speaker is located in a superior position to that of the non-native. The difference between the two is seen as one of culture: the native speaker of English not only claims ownership of the language but to the culture associated with that language as

---

4 It is clear that there are several features that are similar between Lave and Wenger's concept of community of practices (1991) and our idea of learning cultures. Both are focused on localized forms of social activities that provide a context for the performance of identity expressions. For us, the model of learning cultures seeks to represent both the cognitive and social dynamics of these students' performances and to emphasize Bauman's argument that culture is about the construction of the possibilities of new realities (1973).

well, thus further distancing the non-native speakers of English from any equity in these discursive spaces. For the non-native speaker, English will always be a foreign language and the native speaker will always represent the norm of how the language is to be performed. The non-native speaker's different use of English is marked negatively. It is the role of the native speaker to bring the language to the exotic non-native speaker. For Holliday, these social oppositions are engendered through the process of essentialising culture and difference, and as such, are an expression of the colonialist legacy of English (ibid., 11-12).

Holliday's framework made us reflect on the fact that within some discourses of second or additional language acquisition, the opposition between the native and the non-native as language users is ironic. There is an inversion of the discursive positions of the 'native' and 'non-native'. As a noun in the colonial context, the *native* is a powerless and voiceless person, whereas it is the *non-native* who has the power, the authority and the voice. In the colonial context the symbol of native was changed from a representation of someone who was born to the land into a pejorative term where the native was categorised as one who was regarded to be inferior to the colonial settlers or administrators. *Native* became a symbol to indicate the savage, the uncivilised or child-like person. The colonial discourse was anchored on the assumption that it was the colonisers who were to bring modernity or civilisation to the natives (Ashcroft, Griffiths and Tiffin, 1998: 158-159).

Within the context of teaching English as a second language, this relation between the native and non-native as language speakers has been subverted. The terms in this context, used as adjectives qualifying the noun *speaker*, have been inverted: in the colonial context the native is a sedentary social actor, whereas in the English language learning context, the native becomes a mobile actor travelling with his or her voice. The native speaker of English has the voice of authority and with that voice, the power to impose what the standards of English usage are to be. Conversely, the non-native speaker of English is voiceless. There are suggestions of primitivism in terms of concerns about fossilisation of errors and not moving beyond the stage of interlanguage. Furthermore, the non-native speaker is powerless against the regulations of Standard English imposed by the language gatekeepers. A perfect example of this double use of the term is represented by the good old days of the British Council whose representatives while working in remote places within the dichotomy of *us/them* would use *native* in both senses: *they*, the *natives* and *we* the *native speakers*.

The hegemonic terrains of language and power

From this location of native-speakerism, we moved on to confront Bourdieu's work on language and power and how we could relate it to the issues of the use of English (Bourdieu, 1991). Bourdieu stressed that linguistic exchanges are about relations of symbolic power between speakers in their respective speech communities. For him, these power exchanges take place in particular linguistic fields, in which different styles or modes of expressions are accorded different value forms. The more highly-valued language forms become the legitimate and standard forms of public expression. Those who can attain skills at expressing themselves within these standard forms hope to accumulate cultural capital. And conversely, those who cannot compose verbal or written expressions within these standards are seen as deficient users, generally connected with their complex location within the different social fields of class, gender, sexuality, ethnicity and nationality.

For Bourdieu, language interactions are about power relations between speakers in terms of who has control over the language fields (ibid., 39). Bourdieu defines the official language as that language produced by authors who have the authority to fix and codify the appropriate means of verbal and written expressions (ibid., 45). In order for one mode of expression to be imposed as the *only legitimate one*, the linguistic field has to be unified and different dialects have to be measured against the legitimate language and its usage. The legitimacy of the official language has nothing to do with norms or standards but rather with the sanctions imposed and adjusted to maintain the advantages of those regulating the input and output of these linguistic spaces. The formulations of these language gatekeepers are stated to be authoritative and with the power to regulate ordinary uses of the language. For Bourdieu, we cannot account for the power of the legitimate language or its standards without also taking into account the dynamics of the actors and linguistic fields that have produced these requirements (ibid., 45-55).

It seemed to us that one could use Bourdieu's comments on legitimate language to rethink how we could understand the linguistic activities taking place at the *Centro de Idiomas*. At the *Centro de Idiomas*, young working-class and middle-class Oaxacan students learning English, and how to teach it, were pursuing various forms of linguistic capital. They were aware that learning English was valuable and that it could place them in a different social context in which they would enjoy access to different forms of social rewards and status.

Their access, however, was covered by a glass ceiling: the evaluation of their language skills revealed a separation between native and non-native speakers. There would be limits to the amount of linguistic capital they could accumulate because they can never become native speakers. The gatekeepers of these fields use the symbol of the standard native speaker to allocate differential rewards.

Travelling beyond Mexican English

At this point of our journey, we thought we could get beyond this division of power and authority between the native and non-native speakers of English by proposing that what these students were doing was constructing their own style of *Mexican English* (Clemente and Higgins, 2003; Sayer et al., 2004; Sayer et al., 2005; Kissinger, 2006). The question of the emergence of Mexican English was not about how good the English of these students was, but about the social dynamics involved in the way they were learning and using *their* English. Instead of striving for some native speaker-like competence, we felt that these students were using their agency to move into locations where their language performances were framed between a continuum of novices and experts. That is, in the context of their learning cultures, novice students were learning from their teacher, from other students and from the media with differing levels of expertise (Clemente, 2003). It was within these social locations where speaking and writing styles, reflective of the cultural and historical contexts of the speakers themselves, could emerge. The uses of these styles and practices would not be an attempt to move towards the standard. They would be examples of the diversity of appropriate styles of English (Canagarajah, 2004). Thus, instead of regarding the English styles and practices of these students as deficient, it was better to see their activities as examples of how speakers had constructed multi-competence models within their own social contexts (Block, 2003; Cook 1996). From this view, these student-teachers in Oaxaca were not attempting to break through this glass ceiling. Instead, they were attempting to accumulate new forms of cultural capital, which would allow them simply to sidestep this obstruction.

Furthermore, we thought these students were expressing their language agency or praxis by constructing Mexican English. For us, Mexican English was not about interlanguage. In other words, we were not thinking of Mexican English as a stage in attaining a more standard form of English. Nor were we interested in placing Mexican English within some kind of hierarchy of World Englishes or suggesting that Mexican English should be included in one of the circles of English proposed by Kachru (1986). We argued that these students were constructing a counter hegemonic discourse to the idea of Standard English.

Though we travelled a great distance with this argument, it was something of a conflictive journey. First, no matter how often we stated the disclaimers summarised above, many read our argument as an attempt to declare a new language form or linguistic entity. Or to the contrary, we were criticised because we did not make a stronger case why Mexican English should be either an example of World English (a form of lingua franca) or where Mexican English would fit in the circles of World Englishes. It was interesting to us that when we stopped to present this argument to primarily English speaking audiences we encountered various forms of scepticism (Clemente and Higgins, 2005), whereas when we were in front of bilingual audiences we encountered more support for the assumptions we were presenting (Clemente and Higgins, 2004). Also, we had our own self doubts about relativists' suggestions within our argument. That is, by calling the English of these young Oaxacans *Mexican English*, we seemed to be implying something about all Mexicans attempting to perform English. This could encourage labelling any group that was learning English with a geographical modifier. In one sense this would be fine, if we had been interested in mapping out the 'spread' of English throughout the world. Our interest, however, was to show how these young Oaxacan students were using their quest for, or their investment in, English as a means for entering and leaving various identity locations (age, gender, sexuality, ethnicity, and social class) as they sought diverse cultural and linguistic capitals. And so we felt the need to travel outside of the discursive boundaries of what constituted language, and particularly, English and its standards. We needed to represent how these students were performing English as a means of identity construction. But where would that take us?

A journey beyond language

Fortuitously, this journey brought us to an encounter with Makoni and Pennycook (2006) as they were mounting their discursive challenge to many of the central assumptions of applied linguistics and TESOL. These scholars reject the claim that languages existed as *discrete describable units*. Their position is that languages and the way in which we explain languages are social inventions that have emerged in the discursive spaces of colonial and postcolonial times (ibid., 1-5). For them, languages, conceptions of languages, and metadiscourses about language, are all forms of inventions (ibid., 2). They contend that applied linguistics and TESOL need to understand the social and historical import of the metadiscursive regimes that engender these discourses on language use and what the historical and material affects of these social actions have been (ibid., 3). They want to disinvent these metadiscursive assumptions so that we see reconstituting languages as:

> a process that may involve both becoming aware of the history of the constructions of languages, and rethinking the ways we look at languages and their relation to identity and geographical location, so that we move beyond the notions of linguistic territorialisation in which language is linked to geographical spaces. (ibid., 4)

Their central premise is that we need to seek an understanding of the social and historical interrelations among metadiscursive regimes and language inventions and 'strategies of disinvention and reconstitution' of those connections (ibid., 5). For Makoni and Pennycook, unless we actively engage with the history of the inventions of languages and understand the need to disinvent the 'metadiscursive regimes' that maintain these 'languages' through forms of 'epistemic violence', we will do 'damage to speech communities and deny those people educational opportunities' (ibid., 32). This engagement also calls into question many of the 'icons' of critical applied linguistics (Pennycook, 2001). If languages are inventions, so are such related concepts as multiculturalism, additive bilingualism, or code-switching (ibid., 44). For Makoni and Pennycook, without strategies of disinvention, many of these notions, though assumed to be critical, may actually aid in the reproduction of mainstream linguistics. That is 'multilingualism, may, therefore, become a pluralisation of monolingualism' (ibid., 35).

In terms of our concerns, Makoni and Pennycook challenge the existence of second language acquisition or English as a second language (ibid., 56). They do not see the value in separating and counting languages. They ask 'what would language education look like if we no longer posited the existence of separate languages?' (ibid., 56). They suggest that language education should lie in understanding language in terms of what they refer to as 'majority world local knowledge' and relocate language learning from 'additional to transidiomatic practice' (ibid., 56).

It should be clear that Makoni and Pennycook are not arguing that people do not have languages and that people do not communicate through language codes or practices, but that these languages' practices have real histories and material consequences. Furthermore, they are not attempting to return to a Saussurean separation of language and speech or to a Chomskian division of competence and performance. These are the types of dualism that they attempt to disinvent in order to move beyond to conceptual frameworks that can represent how language is used in the existing conditions of our everyday lives. We think their ideas are on the same line of Derrida's claim 'I have only one language —yet that language is not mine' (1998: 1-6).

From here, we moved on to how Pennycook (2006) applies these ideas about disinvention to a set of questions about the existence of English. For him, all the common sense assumptions, empirical claims and rational deductions about the existence of English are illustrations of a metalanguage or metadiscursive regime, which, in turn, are the base for the invention of English. Such are the claims for a Standard English. He states that 'the standardisation of English produced not so much standard English but rather discourses about standard' (ibid.,153). The construction of Standard English was a project that produced a set of ideas about what English was supposed to be, 'but not a 'real thing' called standard English' (ibid., 154). For Pennycook, the idea of the invention of languages 'suggests that languages may exist but they only do so as a product of human interests' (ibid., 155).

Moreover, it is not just that different languages have been invented, but that the discourses about them are also inventions. Thus, in addressing the question about the existence of English, it should not be about the worldwide spread of English nor the importance of its varieties, but 'rather about English as the currently most significant invention amid all the other invented languages of our times and the acknowledgement that the 'effects of its repeated construction and reconstruction are very real.' (ibid., 155). He states that we have to understand how 'English is involved in global flows of culture and knowledge, how English is used and appropriated by users of English around the world, how English colludes with multiple domains of globalisation, from popular culture to unpopular politics, from international capital to local transaction, from ostensible diplomacy to purported peace-keeping, from religious proselytising to secular resistance' (ibid., 156). Pennycook claims that through a more 'contextual and contingent understanding of language use' the claims about World English or World Englishes become mythical. For him these are historical and material affects of 'a particular set of claims about language and English' (ibid., 162). Drawing from the work of Kandiah, Pennycook points out that most approaches to the new Englishes miss the crucial point that these Englishes 'fundamentally involve a radical act of semiotic reconstruction and reconstitution which of itself confers *native userhood* on the subjects involved in the act' (Kandiah, 1998: 100).

This leads Pennycook to see English as a 'social, ideological, historical and discursive construction, the product of ritualised social performatives that become sedimented into temporary subsystems' (ibid., 169). These 'social performatives are acts of identity, investment and semiotic (re)construction ... and are used to perform, invent and (re)fashion identities across innumerable domains' (ibid., 169). Pennycook states that we need to understand what the 'multiple investments people bring to their acts, desires and performances in 'English' are' (ibid., 169).

These wanderings through Makoni and Pennycook's suggestions on the invention and disinvention of languages have led us to rethink our idea about Mexican English. Were we falling into the trap of the myths of English or World Englishes? We wanted our argument to be about agency, identity, and culture, but it was assumed that we were treating English as a *discrete unit that was describable* (with a grammar or describable dialect). Although we wanted to express the diversity of how these students were using English in a bilingual context to move beyond native-speakerism, we may have been adding to the 'pluralisation of monolingualism' (Makoni and Pennycook, 2006: 35). Though we thought the idea of Mexican English was a way to move beyond the dichotomy of native-speakerism, we were struck by Pennycook's use of Kandiah's idea of how the construction of a language performance 'confers native userhood' (1998: 100) upon the speakers involved in the act. We realised that perhaps the students were already disinventing the opposition between the native and non-native speakers in their performance of English. We felt that we could, through our ethnographic narratives, show how these young students in Oaxaca were involved in the 'global flows of culture and knowledge' as they performed their English, how they asserted their 'native userhood' in these performances, and that these performances were anchored in their 'multiple investments' to bring their hopes, desires and identities into these activities. We felt we could provide a more 'contextualised' narrative on how these students were mobilising their language efforts through the use of their agency in the construction of learning cultures. Such narratives could illustrate how these students were locating themselves in these complex language chains and identity locations. Most importantly, we could capture how through performing English with a postcolonial accent these students were producing a counter-hegemonic discourse to Standard English.

What is performing English with a postcolonial accent?

To define what we mean by performing English with a postcolonial accent we will start with Austin's idea that a performative speech act is one 'in which to say something is to do something; or which by saying or in saying something we are doing something' (Austin, 1962: 12). Hedges reads this kernel idea of Austin as a semiotic gesture about being as well as doing, that is, it is a doing that constitutes a being, 'an activity that creates what it describes' (Hedges, 2006). This kernel notion of *an activity that creates what it describes* has engendered a great deal of interest in the domains of postcolonial discourse, and for Pennycook, it suggests ways to bring back issues of performance in applied linguistics that can deal with the process of linguistic actions, identity locations and agency (Pennycook, 2004: 7). Drawing upon Butler's work (1999) on identity and gender, Pennycook states that performativity can be seen as a way in which we compose identities as a series of social and cultural performances rather than as an expression of pre-existing identities (2004: 8). The contexts for such performances are local contingencies that frame these identity activities as they are 'purported to be'. That is, these are the social fields of the production and reproduction of various identity expressions and locations.

For Pennycook, this perspective allows for a way to think about the 'productive force of language in constituting identity rather than identity being a pregiven in construct that is reflective in language use' (ibid., 13). In terms of our argument, the question should not be whether native and non-native speakers of English speak differently, imposing upon them pre-existing identities, but rather how they *do* their nativism or non-nativism with words (Cameron, 1997). It is in the performance of those identities where the differences between them are constructed and where the actors come to believe in their reality (Butler, 1999). To paraphrase Butler's comments on gender construction, in the tacit collective agreement to perform, produce and sustain the opposition between native and non-native speakers of English, a cultural fiction is 'obscured by the credibility of it own production' (ibid.). These performances conceal the genesis of the constructed opposition and offer compelling reasons to believe in the necessity of the dichotomy. Thus, understanding performativity allows one to show how the production of identity is in the *doing* not in the *being* (Pennycook, 2004: 14). In other words, it opens a way to envision the transformation of this dichotomy.

The separation between the native and the non-native speakers is maintained through constant repeating of the performances, the *doing*. 'In the breaking or subversive' of those performances, new identity possibilities can be presented (ibid., 161). The reality of native-speakerism is performative, thus, it is real 'only to the extent that it is performed' (ibid.).

This privileging of *doing* over *being* allows us to use performing in other ways. We are aware that performance theory is a complex discourse ranging from issues of comparative drama (Schechner, 2003), the theatre of ritual (Turner, 1974) and the presentation of self in everyday life (Goffman, 1959). It has become a discourse that attempts to portray forms of transgressive actions of resistance to existing expressions of hegemonic forces (McKenzie, 2004). The emphasis on performance allows one to avoid validating standard bodies of knowledge and encourages the narrativising of emerging knowledge formations (Bial, 2004: 1-5). Further, in terms of the discursive realities of language activities, a stress on performance subverts the assumptions that there is a link between language and one's nature or that there is some kind of essential quality to language use. A focus on language performance illustrates how actors are quite fluid, inconsistent, and creative in how they use language (Canagarajah, 2006a).

For us, it is in the context of performing where we can provide ethnographic texture to the interplay between language, agency, identity and culture. As we stated earlier, how these students learn, appropriate, modify, and redefine their use of English as a series of multilingual social and cultural performances is what we mean by a *postcolonial accent*. These performances are presentations of the use of English in the multicultural context of postcolonial Oaxaca. These students, by locating themselves in opposition to the standardisation of language regimes of both Spanish and English, are able to open discursive spaces that allow them to play in between the norms and expectations of these languages' regimes. By being themselves in both languages, these students are opposing the spectre of the ghost of the native speaker of English and rejecting the suggestion that they are somehow losing their authenticity as Mexicans or as Spanish speakers by their use of English. *Being themselves* involves a quest to use successful communicative interaction as the means for validating language performances regardless of assumptions about standards and authenticity. Furthermore, in being themselves they recognise that the social folds of the multilingual context of Oaxaca involve more than just the opposition between Spanish and English. Surrounding these language activities are the linguistic locations of the indigenous peoples of Oaxaca, the presence of various European and Asian language actors and the transmission of a variety of multi-media channels of communication (such as radio, television, movies, internet, etc.). Thus, these students are using their linguistic and cultural agency to resist the language demands of standards and authenticity and to seek a language project that allows them to understand their everyday lives in this globalised postcolonial world in which they are a part. Their project also involves using their English to enhance forms of intercultural communication among themselves and other language actors in these globalised social spaces. That is, a composition of a linguistic praxis based upon the politics of affiliation is constructed. It is through such a politics of affinity that the hegemonic force of the 'colonial difference' can be subverted.

This being the case, we are using the word *accent* polysemically, admitting both the definition of accent as an indicator of phonetic difference as well as the action of placing emphasis. The emphasis in this study will be *to accent* how these students use their voices, identities and agencies as they appropriate and perform English. Moreover, it is clear that these young language actors perform their English with a particular phonetic accent. We are suggesting that this accent is a positive marker of their various identity locations, especially that of being Oaxacan. This is also true of their Spanish which also locates them as speakers from Oaxaca. Performing with a postcolonial accent does not hide one's location but privileges it as a factor of being oneself in language activities. This accent emphasises the being of oneself in language performance instead of indicating some kind of language deficiency.

It is on this multicultural stage where these students offer a counter-hegemonic discourse to Standard English by performing their English with a postcolonial accent. These young university students are using the *Centro de Idiomas* as a social arena to break, or subvert, native-speakerism through their performances of English. Along with performing their gender, sexuality, ethnicity, youth and social class, they are composing their identities as particular types of learners and users of English. In this context, English is not a 'pre-given entity' but a context for a diversity of contested performances of what English is purported to be. In the instructional and institutional performances, the script revolves around how and what kinds of English are to be taught and used by the students. This script implies a belief in Standard English and the pre-existence of native and non-native speakers of English in order to justify its curriculum, style of instruction and production learning materials. If this script is left uncontested and there is no search for ways to 'disinvent' such performances, the identities of native and non-native speakers will remain fixed. These students' desires and hopes to be themselves in these languages performances suggest a diversity of possible new scripts. Ironically, to be themselves in this context, they must be able to *do* the language (be successful in communicative interaction) and *not to be* the assumed identity of the non-native speaker. That is, instead of *being* second language acquisition students (non-native speakers) they are *doing* their own performance of English with a postcolonial accent.

The postcolonial globalised world

We accept that the postcolonial globalised world is mediated by the social dynamics of multiculturalism and interculturalism. The social folds of multiculturalism, as suggested by García Canclini (2004), encompass how various social actors contest the locations of difference (whether differences are expressed as hierarchical or complementary), inequality (its acceptance or resistance) and disconnection (alienation or re-connection). Further, it is through the collective activities of interculturalism that social actors attempt to move beyond these contradictions through the construction of affective and equitable linguistic and social formations. Further, because of the political and economic patterns of power and authority, English (in Pennycook's sense) is woven through all these social fields. Because of these political and historical factors, English as standard has been, and is being, located within those social folds where difference is hierarchy, inequality is the given and disconnection is the norm. These realities present themselves as the 'hovering ghost' of the native speaker of English. It will be through all of us, who are seeking to find our own postcolonial accent with which to perform English, that the quest towards a multicultural world mediated by interculturalism can be envisioned. However, as has been suggested, it is at the local level of social and cultural practices these dynamics can be understood and represented. If we can understand this at the local level, such as in the performances of English by the young students at the *Centro de Idiomas*, then perhaps we might learn what the general features of such performances are. That is, since these young social actors have already located themselves in this globalised postcolonial world, perhaps they can be our guides for developing our own postcolonial accents.

Chapter 2

'I'm very proud I didn't have to pay to get into the Centro': The social and economic context for performing English with a postcolonial accent in Oaxaca

Introduction

My name is Claribel. I am nineteen and came from a village outside the city of Oaxaca called Totontepec Villa de Morelos. My father and mother work as peasants to support me and my younger siblings; we are five in total. Since my parents had to work on a farm that was away from the village, I stayed with my grandmother so that I could go to school. I do not remember much about my school years, except that it was nice to get good grades and live with my grandmother. When I was eight, the whole family began living together, which was hard for me to get use to. I was twelve when I entered secondary school, this was a hard time for us because of family problems, but with the strength of my mother, we were all able to stay together. When I finished secondary school, because we were quite poor, my father did not want me to continue to study. Since I was the oldest, he wanted me to work and help out with the family. Quite fortunately for me, one of my aunts, who was working in the United States, offered to pay for my high school fees. Like many young people, high school was a very important time for me. I went through several stages. In the first year I became rather a rebel. Actually, this rebel time was for me a way to learn how to socialise, something that I had not experienced before. However, I only focused on running around with a group of students, getting into trouble and not going to school. Fortunately, I got through that stage, got back to studying and getting good grades. Through the help of friends and teachers, I was able to finish high school with good grades and with the confidence to go on to the university.

However, I still had to figure out how to be able to make my wish to go to the university come true. For me, the way to do that was to start working to support myself, move to another place and get into a university. My father was very opposed to that. He could not understand why I wanted to go to university so much. Actually the first year I started without his permission. Fôrtunately, my mother convinced him that this is what I wanted for my future.

To get into the *Centro de Idiomas*, I had to sleep outside the school and wait in a long line with many others in order get a *ficha*, an entrance form to apply for the school. After a very long wait I got the *ficha*. With that *ficha* I was able to take the entrance exam and I passed. I was very happy that I entered into the school this way. However, later I learned that about half of the students in my class had gotten into through some form of *palanca*, or what we call *recomendados*. Those are folks who had to pay someone to get into the school, but for me I am proud that I entered school the correct way. (Claribel)

My name is Alberto. I was born in 1978. My parents were from a rural background that has a very conflictive history. However, our immediate family has been quite stable. My parents have been married for twenty-seven years and they still get along very well. I have two brothers, one older and one younger, I am the middle one, which has been okay.

In my educational history, I have not always been a very good student. In primary school, I did not do well; in fact I spent three years not going to primary school. Because my grades were not very good in secondary [school] I had to repeat my third year. For that reason I had to go to a high school outside of the city, in Zimatlan. My cousin lived out there and he was friends with the principal of the local high school. He had to use his *palanca* to get me in the school. However, I did very well there and learned to be very good on computers. After high school, I went to the Technological University in Oaxaca to study computer sciences. However, my brother was already there studying in that area, so I chose to go into electrical engineer instead. It was a bad choice; again I did not do well in school. I left that school after only one year. For the following year I did not go to school. Instead I was doing odd jobs and thinking about going back to school. I saw a poster from the *Centro de Idiomas* about becoming an English teacher. Even though I had never been a good student, I thought that being a teacher might be good career. However because of the academic area from high school, I did not have all the requirements for getting into the *Centro*. So we had to look for some *palanca* again. My father had a friend who was part of the faculty at the university, and with a letter of recommendation from him, I was able to get into the *Centro* and now I am about ready to graduate. I have done okay. I was better in the first years, but towards the end my motivation was lower and I did not always work as hard as my teachers wished. But I did okay. Now my love is not English or teaching, but music.

(Alberto)

Political economy of English language education in Mexico and Oaxaca

These brief portraits of Claribel and Alberto illustrate two different kinds of paths that students pursue to get into university and the *Centro de Idiomas* to study English. Some like Claribel, who come from rural backgrounds and with limited economics means, must hope that the system will work the way it claims to operate, with rules and procedures, so that they can gain access to their educational goals. For others, having some kind *palanca*, that is a connection to someone with influence within the university, is how they gain access.[5] As in the case of Alberto, who is by no means coming from an economic background much better than Claribel's, he has had to use his or his family's *palanca* quite often in his educational history. As Claribel found out, over half of her student mates had entered the school through the use of some kind of *palanca*.

There are many social and economic reasons in contemporary Mexico for people wanting to have some level of performance skills in, or command over, English. The reality of globalisation, in particular in terms of the geographical proximity to the United States, causes these young Oaxacans to understand the social and economic importance of English. Their employment chances in government, education or commerce are believed to be much better if they have studied English. Further, how well they can perform English provides them with

---

5   *Palanca* involves using a person that you know within the system who can influence someone within to your favour. Within the university, as in many other institutions, a palanca is not necessarily a person with a high position. A secretary or a janitor may work equally or better than any other. The key is to be positioned well. Usually janitors or receptionists are the ones that hand out the fichas to get the exam or the ones who turn in the documents. They may also have a good relationship with other key people, like coordinators or heads of schools. Given the few possibilities that the state offers in general, this resource is very common in Mexico. One is not ashamed to say that s/he approached her/his sister, uncle, neighbour or godfather (actually to have a handy palanca to assure the future of one's child is a good reason to ask somebody to become a godparent) for help.

   The person with the palanca does not expect any kind of direct payment, but depending on the importance (getting a job) or the difficulty (getting into a highly demanded school) of the favour, they may get a present or an invitation to eat at home.

the means to accumulate various forms of linguistic and cultural capital that they hope can be converted into economic capital.

These two stories can be read as metaphors for the complexities of postcolonial social and economic dynamics in Mexico and Oaxaca. Oaxaca is located in the south-western region of the country. It is a small state in terms of territorial size and population. The current population is estimated to be moving towards four million. The overall political economy of Oaxaca is a regional variation of national patterns of neo-liberal policies of development (Higgins, 1997). Economically and socially the state can be divided into five regions: (1) the city and valley of Oaxaca, (2) the central sierra regions of the indigenous communities of the *Zapotecos*, *Mixes* and *Chinantecos*, (3) the northern sierra regions of the indigenous communities of the *Mixtecos*, *Triques* and *Chontales*, (4) the Pacific coastal areas, and (5) the eastern lowlands that border the state of Veracruz. Spread throughout these regions are other small indigenous and mestizo communities (people with an ethnic mixture of European and Indigenous backgrounds). The economy of the city is centred on mercantile enterprises, tourism, and small scale 'artisan' production. The class structure of both the city and the state includes a very small upper-class elite, a large and diverse middle class and the popular classes. The social and political realities of this social division of labour can be understood in terms of the dynamics of the formal and informal sectors of the economy (Higgins and Coen, 2000).

Both Claribel and Alberto move back and forth between the formal and informal sectors of Mexico's social and economic spaces as they pursue their educational goals. The formal sectors of these social and economic spaces are organised around a set of assumed rational rules and regulations that are supposed to be applied equally to everyone. These are the social fields of Mexico's larger industries, the country's vast networks of commercial and financial institutions and national, state and local governmental agencies. This is the world of profits, formal wages, taxes and bureaucratic procedures and processes. The informal sector involves those social spaces where small or larger businesses operate outside the legal requirements of wages, health insurance and job protection. It is where one can get services or products without paying taxes or import duties, or where one, in their dealings with government institutions at any level, can find a way to get something done beyond the actual rules and procedures.

The need to move in between these two sectors is a reality for all social classes of contemporary Mexico and Oaxaca, where one's class position and location affects how effective one's movements can be. This division of formal and informal sectors is expressed differently in rural and urban settings of Oaxaca. The rural areas of Oaxaca are composed of either indigenous or mestizo villages anchored in extreme poverty. Interwoven into this rural social structure, there is a middle income sector that is composed of merchants, small land holders, teachers and government officials. The urban areas of Oaxaca are composed of urban popular classes (ranging from the urban poor to the working class), a diverse middle class of small business owners and professionals, and an elite level divided between the old money of Oaxaca and new money of politics and international commerce.

These rural and urban social fields do not represent a separation of this political economy but rather the mapping out of the globalisation of these social and economic sectors in Oaxaca. How one is located or can be located within these social fields expresses the social diversity of actions and practices of the social actors involved. How well the different social actors navigate and perform within these social fields affects their skills at composing strategies for accessing the various forms of social and cultural capital. Actors can be in equivalent social and economic fields, but still have different strategies on how to use and access these forms of capital or resources. Thus, because of Claribel and Alberto's different locations within the popular class structure, mediated by their rural and urban living styles, they've had to find different routes to the same destination, the *Centro de Idiomas* (Higgins, 1997; Murphy et al., 2002).

Finally, these different routes that Claribel and Alberto took towards their goals of learning and use English illustrate the complex dialectic between performance and context. We do not assume this to be an either/or question, but rather an illustration of how each dynamic is part of the other. The way one performs affects the contours of the context, while at the same time the context sets the parameters of the stage where the performance takes place. Paraphrasing Marx and Engels' claim (1974), we produce the conditions of our existence while, at the same time, being a product of those conditions. This general theme underlines our overall analysis throughout this study.

Educational structures and activities in Oaxaca

Claribel and Alberto's educational journeys that lead them to *Centro de Idiomas* went through the complex context of Mexican public education at the primary and secondary levels. Public education in Mexico is a mixture of national and regional programmes and policies.[6] In Mexico, to gain entrance into universities (both private and public) students need twelve years of previous schooling: six years in elementary school, three in secondary school and three in high school. In general, students enter primary school at age six and leave close to age twelve. The educational objectives of the primary schools are to develop literacy (reading and writing), numeric skills and general information subjects such as national history and geography and both natural and social sciences. The level of classroom enrolments in primary schools varies in terms of the age and social composition of the students. Also there is great deal of diversity in the actual quality of the schools. The more prestigious public schools in the urban areas tend to have larger class sizes, but they are more homogenous in terms of student age and position in the social class. However, in the rural schools and the urban afternoon special schools, the students tend to be from various age ranges and are often poor or from the working class; ironically, the class size is smaller than the prestigious schools. In the urban areas, generally the classroom size ranges from 25-40 students, with a classroom teacher who is in charge of the class during an academic year (from August to June, two hundred school days). Nowadays, most of the urban primary schools are supposed to have computers and it is up to each school how to organise how they will be utilised. In the rural areas, schools often have multiple grade levels, in which teachers work with a mix of students at different age and skill levels. The luckier schools may have a staff of several teachers, but more often than not there is only one teacher for the whole school.

Access to urban primary schools can also involve the use of *palanca*. In the city of Oaxaca, parents will attempt to place their children in an elementary school that they think is a better school or more convenient for them. This puts some schools in greater demand than others. There are formal rules by which students should get priority for admittance, such as having siblings in the school, but if that is not the case, parents will use what *palanca* they have to get their children into the schools they desire.

Urban primary schools are centred on Spanish, with no officially mandated amount of English instruction. In the rural areas there may be multilingual programmes that include both Spanish and the local indigenous language. In the

---

6   The information presented in this section is a summary of Clemente's more than twenty-five years experience in Mexico's education system, the interviews of students at *Centro* de Idiomas about their educational history, a summary of research done by Weiss, et al., and data from Departamento de Investigaciones Educativas, CINESTAV, México.

urban areas, there are attempts at bilingual education with English instruction in some private schools. English, or any other foreign language, is not an official requirement in the public schools of Mexico at that level. Thus, parents who can afford it often send their children to private language schools for either English or other language instruction. At the *Centro de Idiomas*, students in the English teaching degree programme are encouraged to do their teaching practicum in the public primary schools of the city. This is a popular programme because it means the schools can offer English without having to bear the cost. Students, teachers and parents are very happy to get English instruction from the student-teachers.

In Mexico, three years of secondary school are required and the average age of students ranges from twelve to fifteen years-old.[7] In terms of organisation and focus, secondary schools are more elaborated than primary schools. The educational objectives of secondary school are to continue developing literacy as well as numeric skills; provide a deeper knowledge on subject areas introduced in primary school; and introduce students to new academic areas such as physics, chemistry and English. At the secondary level, English is taught three hours a week for the duration of the school year. The quality and importance of these classes are problematic for many of the students and their parents. For some, this is a good educational option because they are aware of the necessity to have English as a tool. For others, though they are aware of the need for learning some English, they do not feel that the classes are taught well. English classes become a burden because it is a difficult subject and there is a high failure rate. This, in turn, engenders a set of contradictory perceptions: though students want to have access to English, they feel that they do not learn anything in the classes that are offered. They feel that classes are repetitive and not well organised. From their viewpoint, they are not able to develop any practical skills and they are always relearning the same basic content.

In rural Mexico there are not many regular secondary schools and often communities have to share schools which causes problems of transportation and access for the students. An alternative for students are called *telesecundarias*, which are programmes for distance learning in the rural schools. This is a federal programme, whose primary goal is to be able to reach the most isolated rural areas. In Oaxaca, this is the programme currently providing the majority of rural students access to secondary education. A *telesecundaria* school has three grades levels, with a teacher assigned to each level. Often class size is small, with

---

7 Only primary and secondary school in Mexico is compulsory.

an average of ten students. The school is equipped with TV monitors, where students watch the content programmes that cover the different subjects they are studying. Teachers and students watch the programme on a certain subject (i.e. mathematics) and then, after the viewing, they have time to work on the corresponding printed material of the subject matter. They have to finish these assignments within a strict time frame in order to be ready for the next class broadcast (i.e. history). Since these classes are nationally broadcast, students and teachers have to be ready at the time the lessons are presented. There is no system for making up missed classes, neither for those who are absent for some reason, nor when there are technical problems and the broadcast is not received. Furthermore, they cannot work on the printed material nor do the assignments without having seen the programmes. In the regular secondary schools, teachers are trained in the areas that they teach, but in *telesecundarias*, teachers have to cover all the subject materials presented. For these teachers, the most difficult subject to teach is English. Most teachers feel unable to explain or clarify the content of the English programme and are insecure about how to pronounce the new words to the students. Therefore, students who graduate from these *telesecundarias* are academically disadvantaged compared to students from regular secondary schools, particularly in the areas of English language studies (Martínez Vázquez, 2004a).

For those students who can finish secondary school, they have to decide if they wish to continue studying or attempt to enter the labour market. In Mexico one is not legally allowed to work until the age of eighteen. This is rarely if ever enforced. If you wish to go beyond the secondary school level there are basically two public school options: a technical or trade high school or the academically-oriented high school that prepares students to enter a university. Each type of high school is for three years, and the technical schools are supposed to provide various skills for attaining a job in one area of study. Of those students going to high school, more than seventy per cent choose to attend the academic schools (Weiss et al., 2006).

For the first two years in the academic high schools, students usually study the basic areas introduced at the former levels. For the third term, the students need to decide on an academic area (such as basic sciences, social sciences, biology and humanities) on which to focus. In theory, this involves a career decision for the students. However, it only works that way for some of them. For the rest, the decision is based on more general criteria, for example whether they like or dislike a subject (such as avoiding mathematics or not), or if they wish to stay with their same group of friends. But even for the students that are sure of the area they want to follow, the system may not work because of the limited spaces available in the universities.

Access to high school is not automatic; in fact it can be quite limited. It often requires students or their parents to queue for long hours (which often involves sleeping over in the street) to have an opportunity to apply for a place in the school of their choice. For various economic and social reasons, described above, there is a high attrition rate in the public high schools in Oaxaca and throughout Mexico. Those who do graduate and find a way into a state university have an advantage because these universities have very low tuition rates (Martínez Vázquez, 2004a.)

Also, the students who do graduate from high school want to get into the university immediately after graduation, since neither they nor their parents wish to 'waste' a year. The hope is to finish university studies as soon as possible and get a good job corresponding to the degree studied. Their perception is that once they get their degree, jobs and opportunities will be available. As in many other countries, this educational myth does not often match the everyday realities of contemporary Oaxaca or any other state in Mexico. Many cannot enter the university as early as they like, and, often, they cannot study the programme they desire for lack of space. Furthermore, the employment opportunities available at the end of their studies are much more limited than anticipated. One of the attractions of studying English is the hope that the myth of achievement and rewards is more attainable (Clemente, 1998).

For English education, the academic high school does not offer a higher level instruction than the secondary level, neither in its approach nor in its content. Students still complain that it is useless (since the outcome is almost nothing), boring and difficult. From their point of view, the only positive points about high school English classes are that they don't last long. In high school, English education is either for two years or three terms, depending on the type of high school. They may receive additional English if the area they choose is connected to tourism.

The cultural and political context of the state university of Oaxaca

Claribel and Alberto's successful journeys through the public education system brought them to the educational spaces of university education in Oaxaca. There are numerous private and public universities in the state of Oaxaca. *Universidad Autónoma Benito Juárez de Oaxaca* is the largest and oldest public university in the state. The current enrolment for the university is around 22,000 students. Some schools and programmes have long traditions and are very popular, for example, medicine and law. Others, such as, accounting and business management are fairly new, but there is also a strong demand for them. The university governance system is that of rectorship. The rector is the highest university official and is elected by universal vote of all the members of the university community: faculty, administrators, workers and students. These elections are usually contested and often involve the use of armed gangs of students called *porros*.[8] The directors of the schools in the university are also elected and depending upon the school, there can also be conflicts and actions of *porros* (Martínez Vázquez, 2004b).

The requirements to get into state universities are few. The students need to have a graduation certificate from their high school along with other locally required documents (such as birth certificate, photos, etc.). They also need to take a national entrance exam offered by the Mexican National Council for Evaluation or the UNAM. General tuition fees are low and some programmes, such as nursing, may have extra fees for laboratory use. Most students qualify

---

[8] This election process is quite political and volatile. Different factions in the university mount vigorous campaigns for candidates, and use armed students, *porros*, to create disruptions or to pressure people to vote for their candidate. The current rector is taking measures to get rid of these pernicious forces; however, it will take more than one administration of four years to clean the university of them. *Porrismo* is carried out by *porros* who present themselves as discontent students fighting against the injustices of the university. However, they have established connections inside or outside the educational system. Within the university, they may work with teachers or administrators, representing a strong force which can oblige the authorities to make a decision. Outside the university, they have connections with political parties or individuals who call on their services when they need a show of force or mobilisation. They usually work in groups and sometimes can act rather violently. The diverse interests and busy lives of *porros* force them to regularly miss classes and fail courses. They cannot hold full-time jobs, so they need a source of income to support themselves. One of the sources of their income has been to act as middlemen to help people to get into the universities. Their fees vary according to the school they are applying for, but they range from ten to fifty times the regular fees. Usually people without access to someone with *palanca*, or whose connection did not have enough *palanca*, make use of *porros'* services. It is generally the poorer students that find themselves using *porros*, and such students are from the rural areas of the state. To pay a *porro* five to twenty thousand pesos means that a poor rural family needs to sell what property it might have or go into debt. And there is always the risk of losing the money. The *porros* do not hand out receipts or have a permanent (nor temporary) office to receive complaints or give refunds. There are many stories of people that ingenuously come to attend classes in the belief that they have been properly registered and accepted. Unlike when one uses *palanca*, one does not openly say that s/he had to pay extra-officially to get into the university. Some of the more naïve students and parents may have been taken in by the belief of a *porros'* official role.

Porro groups are created at university high schools, and recruit students from there. There are also groups in undergraduate schools. The most well known are in accounting and law, although other schools have been somewhat infected. At the *Centro de Idiomas* we do not suffer from this problem. Here, some *porros* have enrolled in the programme but left it in the first semesters because of a lack of support and obligatory attendance to classes. All the *porros* that make deals with people queuing for *fichas* are outsiders from the *Centro de Idiomas*.

for entrance; the problem, however, is the availability of openings in particular programmes. Each school or programme is only allowed to accept certain number of students each year, and each year there are always more students than spaces allocated. This is a problem experienced throughout all the public universities in Mexico and it is particularly the case in Oaxaca. For example, close to a thousand of students take the exam for entrance into the *Centro*, but less than a hundred can be officially accepted. Thus, many students are not formally accepted into the university. Claribel is actually one of the few students who was accepted into the university through its formal requirements. The other students use strategies like those of Alberto; they enter through the use of some kind of *palanca*. Ironically, one can also use contacts within some groups of *porros* to gain acceptance. For money, *porros* will attain *fichas* that will get students into the schools. What the *porros* do is either occupy the school, thus shutting it down, or threaten to do so, in order to attain *fichas* which then will be sold or offered to their sponsors.

The *Centro de Idiomas* was founded thirty years ago as a language centre, with the main focus on English. During this time it has grown into an important academic programme for the university. Its main academic focus is the training of undergraduate students in the area of teaching English as a foreign language (TEFL). It also offers a master's degree in Applied Linguistics, courses in various languages, and Spanish and other subjects for foreign students (Clemente and Kissinger, 1994).

The current undergraduate students (numbering around six hundred) come mainly from the city and region of the valley of Oaxaca. They are mostly from middle and working class backgrounds, often being the first in their family to study at the university level. The majority of the students are female. Most of the students at the *Centro* are from a mestizo background. Very few of the students come from the indigenous communities of Oaxaca, though many of their parents or grandparents have come from these communities. The majority of the students enter the university with plans to study other programmes but for various reasons gravitate towards the *Centro*, thinking that they are going to be studying a variety of languages. Many are surprised to find that the degree offered at the *Centro* is in *teaching* English.

The faculty at the *Centro* is also a diverse group. There are only five full-time faculty positions and a large number of part-time teachers. The part-time faculty is divided among those who are more or less permanent part-timers and have worked there for many years without formally getting a full-time position and the short-term part-timers who are generally hired to teach English or one of the other languages offered at the *Centro*. Of the full-time faculty, there are only two Mexicans, with the rest being from the United States. Of the somewhat permanent part-time teachers, most are Mexican, while the more casual part-time teachers are international.

Locations and identities of the students at the *Centro de Idiomas*

Now that Claribel and Alberto have been accepted into the study programme of the *Centro*, they have had to learn what the social lives of the students' at the *Centro* were like, what their attitudes and beliefs were, what kind of political views they hold, what they thought about their quality of their education. To give an idea of the social context that they had to deal with, we will provide summaries of various student comments about the *Centro*'s students personal lives in terms of identity, social class, gender, sexuality and the quality of education as well as the social ambiance at the *Centro*. These comments were gathered from a series of public debates that students organised on the above themes. Thus we will be alternating the voices of the students in the debates with the ones of the organisers that summarised their classmates' points and added their own view about their statements. The views expressed are very general and often the students offered comments that were more about how things should be than detailed comments on their everyday activities. Although 'thicker' comments on the lived experiences of students will be presented in the following chapters, what we want to present here is a glimpse of how the students perceive their social world at the *Centro de Idiomas*.

Issues of identity and learning English

In reviewing the comments made by both the participants and the organisers on the issue of identity, we found a tone that suggested that learning English could add to, or enrich, their existing identities as young Mexicans. For these students, English did not indicate a loss or denial of their Mexican identity. There was, however, an element of seeing themselves as different from those others who did not have some command over English. They tended to see themselves as being somewhat more open to other cultures or being more cosmopolitan because of their English language skills.

> When you are learning English, the cultural factor is very strong, but it depends on you, on what you take and what you leave behind. You do not have to adopt the culture, it's up to you. (Pedro)

> Well, we live in a state that makes its living off tourism. So it is logical that we want to learn English here, and that we have a lot of contact with foreign cultures, but I haven't changed because of that. (Ana)

> I haven't changed because I am learning English. I am still Mexican, and for me being Mexican means to value your own culture, your roots, like the Zapotec or the Mixtec, but sometimes we do not appreciate that enough. (Luis)

Nevertheless, the students felt that their families thought differently about their social and personal identities as well as the social rewards they were attaining by learning English. This is how they summarised it:

> Students think that their parents are happy about their choice of learning English. This is seen as attaining some kind of new status or a form of social progress. Many students commented that their families would ask them to speak English to others, 'Show them what you can do. Tell them something in English'. However, at the same time, parents were worried that as English speakers their children would change their identities and become more like *gringos* (foreigners, particularly North American). They said that their parents complained about their musical choices and their international companions. They worried that their children would pick up bad values from these kinds of contacts ... Also some students reported that their parents valued more that they were studying at the university than that they were studying English. That is, for them, a university degree in any area would be good for their children's future.
> (Mayra, Luisa and Diego)

Most of the students rejected the idea that learning and using English would change their identity. In this context, their concept of identity was deeply connected to nationality. They wanted to be sure that people knew that they did not want to 'become American'. They were very happy and proud of being from Mexico. It is also connected to the criticism that they get from the community.

They are seen as *malinchistas*, someone who wants to be like the *gringos*. Because they talk to foreigners, they listen to foreign music and they are interested in the language, they are supposed to be *gringo*-oriented. It is these kinds of presuppositions that they feel are unfair. As stated by a student:

> I already have my identity and I won't change because I am learning English. *Chicanos* change their culture because they live there, but living here you do not have to change. Besides, it is a personal decision to change your identity. Learning the language won't change our identity.
> (Martina)

It is within the context of these contested identity locations over language and culture that many of these students find the idea of performing English with their own accent a compelling idea. This can be felt in the following comments:

> There are a lot of Englishes, so there could be a Mexican English! Why not? When we say we speak English with a Mexican context, we are saying that although we speak this language we are at the same time rejecting the culture of the United States. Mexican English is as valid as USA English. Mexican English conveys everything that means being Mexican but in the other language. (Martha)

Social class and language learning

Whereas the students are quite clear in their perceptions of English language learning and their identities as Mexicans, their views on social class are a little fuzzier. Even though the academic world of Oaxaca is highly stratified between private and public universities and many students at the *Centro* come from working class backgrounds, they wish to contend that their differences in social class are not important:

> Most students think that there are not many social differences among them. They also seemed to agree that when student cliques are formed it is on the basis of personalities, interests, ways of thinking and chemistry, but not social class. We also feel that social class differences should not be important in the school. And we are very happy that most of the times students do not take them into account. (Flora, Naty and Elva)

It is true that there is not a wide range of social class differences among the students at the *Centro*. Given that the university in Oaxaca is public and in one of the poorest states in the country, the *Centro* student community is formed mainly by working and low middle class youth. Many students from the middle and upper classes either go to private universities in the city or go out of state. For the many working class and urban poor youth, going to any university is a limited option (Higgins, 1997). The social histories of many of the *Centro* students involve stories of them coming from first generation middle class families whose backgrounds are framed in terms of either urban working class or marginally 'well-off', so to speak, rural households. There are scatterings of students from urban and rural poverty. However, students do not seem to take into account these aspects of their socioeconomic backgrounds. They see themselves as basically all from the middle class with differences concerning personalities, interests and ways of thinking. This can be noted in their various comments:

> There are not social differences here in the school because most of us are middle class. Although some have more money and some have less.
> (Luis)

> It is not so much about social classes, it is about stereotypes. And if someone comes very well dressed there are many that want to follow them and start dressing like them. (Anabel)

However, they do express an awareness of class difference among themselves, but devalue its importance:

> Yeah, It is because some come in car and the *'chavas vienen muy fashion'* [girls dress according to the fashion], with boots and the latest fashions. For me that's not important. I come here to study. The clothes are not important. (Fernando)

> Yeah, some students come in 'nice' clothes but most of us come in *garras* [rags]. We do not care what we wear. We gather together according to the way we are, the quiet with the quiets, the rebels with the rebels. That's the way it is in the school. (Juan)

One of the ironies of these social perceptions is that within the university student world, the students at the *Centro* are seen as *fresas*, which tends to mean middle class preppie students who think that they are somewhat better than others, more often associated with students in private universities:

> Yeah, I have heard that we are called *fresas*. Outside the main campus people think that we are different here, that we are *fresas*. (Carlos)

Gender and sexuality at the *Centro*

On the surface, the students seem to convey a sense of consensus on the issues of language, identity and social classes. When addressing the issues of gender and sexuality, however, their views became more challenging, more so in the area of gender than sexuality:

> Some of the students' comments coincide; there was, however, a diversity of opinions. At times our views seemed contradictory. When some said that women were more responsible than men, numerous men agreed, while at the same time, some women declared that quite often young women were irresponsible. This was interesting because it showed diversity among the women over what they thought about their own gender roles. In contrast, it seemed that men were more interested in defending themselves as individuals than defending their own gender. A lot of them saw that their gender roles were framed in terms of the social and cultural contexts of Mexico and Oaxaca (Cris, Marlen and Yury)

On the issues of whether women or men were more responsible, their views were mixed:

> I don't think that women are more intelligent than men, it is just that we are more patient than men, and so we can be better teachers. (Guadalupe)

> That's right. There aren't so many patient male teachers. In fact, I do not think that any of my male classmates want to be teachers. (Carmen)

> I think that most women come here because they have that maternal instinct; they love children. (Lalo)

On the question of how well they relate to either female or male teachers they responded in the following manner:

> I have always got along better with male teachers, more hanging around, less formality. I have tried to do the same with female teachers, but they are not like that, they like to use more words to say things, they are more formal than men. And I am not talking about the academic quality. I am talking about interpersonal relationships. (Flor)

> Talking about quality of teachers, for me it is the same, men or women can be as good, well prepared, and knowledgeable. And about hanging around with teachers, it is because of the personality not because of the gender. (Mario)

> I think that now the school prefers to have women teachers, because they are more responsible than men and I do not know if it is true, but scientifically they say that women are a little more capable that men, they have a little bit more of intelligence. (Mercedes)

> I think that it is not right when scientists say that one is more capable that other. The difference is how we are able to develop ourselves. (Itzel)

> I still think that women are more responsible than men, talking about education, but they are not in other aspects of their lives. Women say that they think about what they do and then they get pregnant! (Saul)

The students' comments reflect their relatively young age and the degree to which they reflect or question conventional assumptions about their own gender roles.

This last comment moved the students quickly into the area of gender politics and sexual diversity. What interested the students was the reality of the uneven gender balance at the *Centro* where there are more female than male students. Perceptions went along gender lines:

> I think that there are fewer guys here because guys think that the school here is too quiet. If guys want to be shit disturbers they go to other schools in the university. And here at the *Centro* the boys who come are more study-oriented. (Marino)

> I think there are more women here at the *Centro* because we talk about sexual issues among ourselves and there is more freedom here. In other schools it does not seem to be like that. (Cinthia)

> I don't know why they say that there are no men here. There are men, like me. I don't know why they make those kinds of generalisations. I don't know why this claim is made. Maybe it is because we don't find the girls that we want here. Maybe they also want something different. Maybe that's why, women want us too much! (Carlos)

These comments moved the discussion into the area of the role of fidelity and virginity. What follows again is a mixed set of feelings and sentiments. In terms of fidelity, these young women had the following outlook:

> I have known some folks that have tried to have two partners at the same time, but usually works out that only the *novio* [boyfriend] is free to do that. (Marcela)

> That's because our society still accepts that men can have many partners but if a woman has two *novios* she is a *cualquiera* [goes with anyone], but we as women contribute to that kind of thinking. We criticise women who run around by saying that they are *cualquieras* but if it is a man we say that he is so attractive that he has all of them. It is our fault. (Janet)

Though the males were quiet about this issue, they were more open about the question of virginity.

It depends on your background. I have some friends that won't accept a woman who is not a virgin. It depends on their family, your parents saying that you should want a well-behaved girl, not a *loca*. 'Watch out with whom you go out'. Personally, I don't care. (Alberto)

That's right, they demand female virginity. A girl has to marry as a virgin *a huevo*. Not long ago, in the Isthmus, if a woman was not virgin they hanged a *totopo* [a kind of *tortilla*] on the front door of her house, meaning that she had slept with numerous men. I always tell my mother 'Finally, who's going to sleep with her, you or me?' And she replies that I have to prove to people that she was virgin and I respond 'OK, if they want to come, tell them to come tonight'. *Me encabrona esa mentalidad* [I get so pissed off with that kind of thinking]. And it is not that I am studying another language and that's why I am more open. It is simply my way of thinking. (Ignacio)

Some of the young female students were equally open on this question:

This question is so unjust. They only talk about female virginity. It is not fair that men demand virginity from us and they can go to bed with whomever and it does not matter. As a woman you will accept a man that is not virgin, no problem but when they know that you are not, they say '*Pinto mi raya*' [I leave immediately]. It is unjust that men can and we can't, isn't it? (Clara)

My parents are young and they do not care about my virginity. They have never told me 'You have to remain a virgin'. Instead they have said, 'The day that you think you are prepared, then, that's it. You do not have to be virgin'. They are not afraid of me changing my values because I am studying English and meeting people from different cultures. Sex has never been a taboo at home. They say things like, 'Think about what you want' or 'You may not be ready for that yet' or 'Be careful and take precautions'. I have aunts that think differently, but my parents are educated, that's the difference. (Patricia)

There were also more conventional comments. Below are the views of an older female student:

> For me it is important that kids are virgin when they marry. I did it that way and I have four female teenagers and I want them to do the same. We are Christians and we believe in that. Our daughters have understood this and agree with us. I have talked to them about sex, about menstruation, that's very important. When I had my first period I got so scared. My mother never told me about that. Now I have told my daughters, told them that it is natural. I am close to them and they are happy and agree with me. (Soledad)

Though there are ranges of difference in terms of gender politics among the students, there is a general agreement on the need to respect sexual diversity. These views were summarised in the following comments:

> Most of our classmates think that it is not good to stereotype people because of their sexual orientation. However, there are some who think that it is good to follow the gender and sexual patterns imposed by society. We agree with the majority, people's value depends on them as human beings and on their knowledge and ideas. (Cris, Marlen and Yuri)

These views are expressed in the following comments by a female student:

> As teachers we need to share our views on these subjects with our students. We should teach them that people are not more or less because of their sexual preferences or because they are a virgin or not. The other day my niece told me that there was this boy in her class that everybody was calling *puñal* [slang word for gay]. And I told her that classmates should be more sensitive and not to call him names. I have said the same thing to my mother. She says that if my brother was gay she would throw him out of the house. I joked with her, telling her not to worry and that there is nothing wrong if he were gay. I think we have a responsibility to teach children tolerance about all this. (Flora)

Student politics at the *Centro*

As was explained earlier in this chapter, the university in Oaxaca is a politically contested institution. This affects the everyday realities of the students at the *Centro*. For the majority of students their most pressing political issues are focused on who will control the rectorship, the different ways students can enter the *Centro* and the role of *porrismo*.

The following expresses some of their concerns:

> Our university here in Oaxaca has such a bad reputation, even students in other state universities say that this is a bad school. But we are not the ones to blame. For me, what they are referring to are the political activities of the administrations and the unions. (Fausto)

> There are some *porros* among us, but they are few and they can't do anything. *Porros* are people that are looking for advantages for themselves. They want to form groups, alliances, and move people according to certain ideologies. Someone told me that they do not come here because there is nothing to gain here. They do not find that kind of people that want to get things by means of violence, taking schools or closing streets. (Francisco)

> We see *porros* from other schools when people are lining up to get a place in the school. They are so noticeable, sitting by the fountain in the patio. It is not a stereotype but it is so easy to identify them. They come always together in groups trying to look tough. The folders they carry contain the documents of the people who pay them to get a place in the school. But the leader is not actually the one that moves them from here to there. The leader is someone above. It is all so corrupt. They get money from what they do and the ones above also get something, money and control. (Alfredo)

Unlike other schools in the university that have large blocks of radical students, the *Centro* has fewer students directly involved in such activities. There have been small groups of leftist/Marxist students at the *Centro* that have attempted to maintain a voice in the social and cultural activities of the students. Often these students put up bulletin boards that attempt to link the learning of English to more global political and economic issues. Currently, because of the turbulent political movement for social justice taking place in Oaxaca, many of the students became involved through translating the demands of this struggle into English. (see chapter three)

The educational context of the *Centro*

An interesting part of this ethnography is the general feeling the students have about the quality of their language education at the *Centro* and what they feel about the ambiance there. As we stated earlier, and will elaborate upon more in Chapter Four, the *Centro* is a contact zone where English and Spanish confront each other in terms of use and understanding. Within that zone, students use their learning cultures as safe houses to perform English with a postcolonial accent.

The students in these debates expressed a variety of views about the quality of education at the *Centro*, Here are some of their views on teachers and their teaching styles:

> We have a variety of teachers here, all with different styles of teaching. But it depends on the students, if they like them or not. Personally, I like all my teachers. I have always got something from them. (Flor)

> For me the important things about the teachers are their personalities and how they integrate the learning materials in the classroom and keep a good dynamics going. (Karen)

> I think that teachers are well prepared here. They try to teach us to be fluent speakers of English and to use English grammar. (Paula)

The students were interested in expressing what they thought to be the importance of having teachers who are native speakers and on how thoroughly they should be using English at the *Centro*.

> I think sometimes we prefer native speaking teachers over non-native speakers. But we have learned that the non-native speaking teachers can also be very good. It depends on their personalities. (Lorena)

> Sometimes the non-native speaker can be a better teacher, because he or she can understand what we are going through in the classroom. And honestly some of the native speaking teachers are not very good teachers, what they can bring to the classroom is an understanding of the cultures where English is spoken. (Luz)

Concerns range on how English should be used at the *Centro*, from demands for English-only-context to contexts that encourage playing with a mixture of Spanish and English.

For example, one student says:

> I speak Zapotec and I learned Spanish because teachers in the primary school prohibited me to speak in Zapotec. That's what we should do here. (Pepe)

Along the same line of thought, another student suggests:

> I think a good solution would be to put signs up that say *'It is banned to speak in Spanish'*. You know, the same way they put things up that say like 'It is banned to do graffiti', we could do the same for using Spanish!. (Roberto)

Others assume a more relaxed approach, such as the following comments:

> I think that 'to prohibit' is a very strong word. And even if we did that here, we will always find the ways to speak Spanish. (Itzel)

> We are Mexicans here and all that stuff about practising our English is good, but, come on, when I want to tell a joke, I want to do it in Spanish. In English I have to think for too long and then the joke is not funny any more! (Marian)

> I think that the issue about not speaking Spanish and practising your English has to be more than just posting a sign that will be gone in a couple of days. I think that improving your English is not enough. The school has to give us more tools and to have better teachers who can teach how to use them. (Saul)

Student social networks at the *Centro*

For many students the ambiance of the *Centro* is also an important factor in how well they can perform English:

The ambiance at the university is so different from high school, especially for those that are not from the city. People's way of thinking here is more open. And for the students from out of town it is difficult to start making friends because they are shy. On the contrary, people that are from the city already have networks with their friends from high school.
(Xochitl)

Here students think a lot about your look or your style. I do not have a great style and I've never had it. Here you start noticing that people criticise everything, your shoes, your clothes, even your hairstyle. It is on the basis of these prejudices that cliques build up, and then you have the *maditos* (hard workers), the 'irresponsible ones', and so on. (Mayra)

When you start here it is very difficult to make friends, it is so difficult. So many things come into play, if she sits next to you, if she works in a similar way, For instance, in my own case, I am not a *maditita* but I take into account the way the other person works in her studies. And you only get to know some of them, never the whole class. You only know them superficially, their style, their physical traits, maybe their names. After three years of being together, at least we have learned everybody's names! (Amanda).

Summary

In this chapter we have tried to show how Claribel and Alberto's vignettes about how they entered the *Centro de Idiomas* offer a general overview of the social and economic context of the city and region of Oaxaca, the political economy of language education in that context, and how various students at the *Centro* are attempting to understand and act within these conditions. This represents the stage from which they will begin to perform their English with a postcolonial accent. Here we can note the multicultural drama of contemporary Oaxaca and the possibility of composing a means for intercultural communication through how these students explore the themes of their identities, social class position, gender, sexuality and the quality of language education. In the next chapter, we will present detailed ethnographic portraits of how six students at the *Centro* are finding ways to be themselves in this other language. This *being themselves in*

English entails how they are locating themselves through their various identity locations to appropriate this other language for their own uses and desires.

Postscript

The people of Oaxaca have a long and complex history of social movements and struggles in their quest for social justice (Martínez Vázquez, 2007). Over the years, various alliances of indigenous peoples, students, workers, university members and artists have attempted to change the political and economic map of the state. Two central groups in these struggles have been the public school teachers and some organised indigenous communities. Towards the latter part of our research, Oaxaca erupted with a state-wide social movement that emerged from the annual teachers' strike. Many of the students of the *Centro* were actively involved in these events that were reported around the world. We felt it would add to the 'thickness' of our ethnography to offer some information on these events. Peter Sayers, one of the professors at the *Centro*, graciously offered to give us his account and impression of these events.

The social and political situation in Oaxaca

Peter Sayer

Background on the social and political situation in Oaxaca during 2006-2007

This essay describes the dramatic social and political events in Oaxaca during 2006-2007, called 'the APPO movement'. What started as an annual occurrence—the public school teachers' yearly contract negotiation and work stoppage—grew into a perfect storm of social dissent that left a score dead, hundreds injured and hundreds more jailed or missing. It was an attempt to redraw the political map of a state that, along with the southern, indigenous states of Chiapas and Guerrero, counts among the poorest and most marginalised in the country in all social indexes: income, health, and education. It was an attempt to break the power of the *Partido Revolucionario Institucional* (PRI) which, although it lost the presidency in 2000 after more than seventy years of 'democratic' rule, still maintained a deeply corrupt and nepotistic control of governorship of Oaxaca.

The Magisterial Movement and the plantón

For more than fifteen years, the public school teachers migrated to the city of Oaxaca to commence their *plantón*. Strictly speaking, the *plantón* was not a strike (*huelga*), but an annual late spring work stoppage aimed at pressuring the government by leaning on the capital city's business interests. A forty-block area around *zócalo* became an encampment to accommodate the 70,000 teachers who belong to the union.

The teachers' demands were essentially the same each year: better pay, expanded benefits, an increased education budget to improve material conditions in the schools, and programmes for schools in marginalised areas, including school breakfasts. The *plantón* and the *movimiento magisterial* (teachers' movement) disrupted the daily life of Oaxacans in the city: traffic became even worse, the historic downtown became a tangle of plastic sheeting and twine, the streets collected garbage and smell of urine, and the people stopped going downtown to spend money. Each encampment had a sign announcing its school and region. The teachers took turns manning their encampment, so each person was responsible to spend two or three days and nights at the camp each week. Oaxacans were divided between those who thought the teachers were lazy and the union was corrupt, and those who thought the government leaders were lazy and corrupt; many more agreed with both sides but sympathised with neither.

Recuerdos del 14 de Junio

In 2004 a new governor was appointed in Oaxaca. Ulises Ruíz Ortíz (URO) was from the long-ruling PRI party, and he had promised the business leaders who supported his narrow victory over the leftist candidate that he was going to use *mano dura* (iron fist) on the teachers. In addition to their usual demands, the *magisterio* had added two more to the list. First was a demand for 'rezonification,' that pegs the teachers' wages and retirement benefits to the economic zones within the state; many teachers attempted to get transferred to coastal resort towns during their last year to receive the increased benefits. The second was a call to resist the national *Reforma Integral de la Educacion Secundaria* (RIES), a country-wide reform of the national curriculum by the Ministry of Education. The *magisterio* saw this reform, which emphasised technology and science-related subjects at the expense of subjects like Mexican history, as yet another step towards the privatisation of public education.

The *plantón* stretched into June. The kids had been out of classes for a month, and the government was threatening that all students would lose their academic year. On June 14, just before dawn, around one thousand state police moved in to force the *desalojo*, or break up, of the teachers' camps. They came with police batons, riot shields, torches and tear gas. Plastic sheeting and nylon tents were slashed, aluminium poles and metal cook-stoves smashed, banners torn down, and huge piles of plastic were set ablaze. At 5.30 a.m. groups of teachers rushed panicked through the streets, seeking shelter from the tear gas. They found refuge in the churches, parks, the Law School of the university. A police helicopter swooped low, firing tear gas canisters at the fleeing teachers off the Alameda plaza. The police advanced behind their Plexiglas shields, lobbing gas to push the teachers back, and levelling the camps as they pass.

At 8 o'clock bands of teachers regrouped. Teachers who were not sleeping at the *plantón* were roused by Radio Plantón's urgent call to arms, and were arriving by the thousands to reinforce the teachers who were on the streets. People were calling on their cell phones, figuring out where the police were, where to meet. As the police continued advancing, they were met by a group of teachers who did not flee. Instead, the teachers stood their ground, picking up the gas canisters and throwing them back; they threw bricks and chunks of concrete. News of the clash was spreading. At 9 a.m. bricks were flying at the police who had run out of tear gas canisters. They fell back towards the *zócalo*, past the cathedral and into the Alameda. In front of the post office there was more space, too much space, and the police were not able to hold their line. Metal pipes cracked and splintered the plastic shields, and the police were routed. They dropped their shields and clubs, and ran in groups of twos and threes back towards the *periferico* at the edge of downtown.

Hundreds and hundreds of people milled about, and in front of the Cathedral they hung a burning effigy of Ulises Ruíz over a traffic light as the TV crews arrived and the crowd chanted what was to become the movement's main rallying cry, '¡Ya cayó! ¡Ya cayó! ¡Ulises ya cayó!' (Ulises has fallen!) A spontaneous procession of university students carrying a large banner reading NO A LA VIOLENCIA marched from the campus to the *zócalo*, also chanting denunciations of the governor. As they passed, the teachers encouraged them on, shouting '¡Ese apoyo sí se ve!' (This is support that we can see!).

The APPO movement

The Peoples' Popular Assembly of Oaxaca was formed on June 17, 2006, only a few days after the *desalojo*. In those days, the state police as well as the municipal law officers had withdrawn, leaving the city centre under the control of the teachers and the surrounding neighbourhoods under martial law. Fearing that the police would return in force to try another *desalojo*, the *magisterio* reinforced their *plantones* with barricades constructed out of logs, barrels, barbed wire and scrap metal. Meanwhile, there was an outpouring of support for the teachers,

as well as a rejuvenation of many dissident groups that had been around for years, but that had been less active. Here, they saw, was an illegitimate governor from a corrupt party using force to disperse workers who were well within their constitutional right to install a *plantón*. In public spaces throughout the city, groups met and discussed, and quickly a broad coalition emerged that included some 365 groups:
- Militant teachers' union,
- Left-wing political party members (PRD, Workers' Party, Communists),
- University students, intellectuals, bohemians, anarchists,
- Indigenous peasant and guerrilla groups (EPR, FARP),
- Many small NGOs: women's rights, street kids group, AIDS coalition, etc.,
- Unemployed and disenfranchised.

The APPO controlled the Oaxacan capital from June until November of 2006. During that time, the temporary barricades that had been set up by the teachers became permanent fixtures built from sandbags, captured buses, sheet metal, and barbed wire. The coalition group was organised around town-hall style meetings held in the various plazas around the city. Graffiti proliferated to the point where, with no exaggeration, there was not a single building in the downtown area, including private homes and churches that were not painted with multiple APPO slogans.

The APPO set up a parallel fleet of taxis as an alternative to the PRI-controlled city taxis. In some villages, alternative markets were installed. The APPO controlled all the radio stations in the city, and shut down the local government TV station. Meetings, marches, and rallies were daily events, especially formal assemblies and roundtable meetings with officials. There was a great diversity of activity from 'The Peoples' Guelaguetza' (mid-July) dance and cultural festival, to 'Day of Protest against McDonald's' (October 16) set to initiate a boycott organised by a group called *Resistencia Narcopunk*. There was a 'Popular Open-Air Film Festival' (28 September-1 October) organised by the *Okupación Intercultural en Resistencia*, and a rally by the Communist Party of Mexico (October 4) in the *zócalo* in which large posters of Marx, Lenin, and—with no apparent ironic intent—Josef Stalin were the backdrop for calls to end oppression. With so many groups involved, there was a diverse and at times incoherent set of goals. APPO supported the teachers' demands, but had many other demands as well, ranging from the end of a housing development project in the town of Zaachila, to the end of the privatisation of education by the federal ministry, and the end to US imperialism across the globe. However, the single issue that all groups did share, and even many citizens who did not side with the APPO, was the call for the resignation of the governor.

During the summer, the APPO movement and the teachers' *plantón* continued to gain momentum, with the protesters and the pro-government sides each claiming to represent 'authentic Oaxacans,' and accusing the other of stalling and not wanting a real dialogue. Several successful 'mega-marchas' (demonstrations) mobilised tens of thousands of people. The 4th Mega-marcha on June 28 brought out 500-800 thousand people, over 10% of the entire population of the state, into the city's streets. In September, several thousand people marched for 13 days from Oaxaca to Mexico City to demand that the federal authorities do away with the governor. Meanwhile, some barricades were becoming notorious as sites for drug-dealing and centres of criminal activity, and in others, teachers and protesters were shot at and killed by pro-government paramilitaries. During the first three months, several APPOs were killed in separate night-time drive-by-shootings, and half a dozen more in other shootings as violence occasionally flared during demonstrations or at checkpoints.

The conflict had devastated the economy, and many people—hotel and service industry workers, artisans and market vendors—who might otherwise have supported the movement more, were suddenly facing destitution. Most foreign embassies had issued advisories against travelling to Oaxaca, and the number of tourists arriving plummeted to almost zero. By late summer, things looked grim for governor Ulises Ruíz Ortíz (URO). The body count was mounting, and the congress had sent a special committee of senators to analyse the 'state of governability' in Oaxaca which would have been the first step to declaring the 'dissolution of powers.' Most felt that URO, who had only entered office the previous year after a dubious election, would soon be forced from office by his own party. In October, faced with the split with the teachers' syndicate and a vote on whether to maintain the *plantón* or head back to classes, the radical elements of the APPO stepped up the campaign. The hijacking of city buses—especially targeted at the *Sertexa* line and others said to be owned by PRI members—escalated, and a string of bombings hit the PRI headquarters, Scotia Bank, and Burger King. At the end of October, a few days before the Day of the Dead celebrations, the violence flared, leaving several APPOs and a US American IndyNews reporter dead; outgoing President Vicente Fox ordered the federal police (PFP) into the state to restore the rule of law. The arrival of thousands of PFPs clad in black body armour lead to several massive confrontations as the police cleared the barricades and drove the APPO out of the downtown. On November 2, there was a huge clash at the main gates of the university when armoured tanks attempted to smash down the last of the barricades. For more than six hours, the APPOs hurled rocks, bricks, Molotov cocktails, and fired home-made rockets at the swarming police and helicopters that bombarded them with tear gas and chemical sprays. Although the police eventually had to retreat, the APPO victory proved to be their last. URO was still in power, and the thousands of PFPs were encamped throughout the city.

A tense stand-off continued for several weeks. On November 26, less than a week before Felipe Calderón took office, the APPO held the 7th Mega-marcha. As the march arrived at the PFP encampment, people started pushing and shoving, and the tear gas started to fly. The PFP moved swiftly, and in the next few days made hundreds of arrests. Those arrested were swiftly transferred to federal jails in Nayarit and to the far-off northern states. Ulises Ruíz emerged to give a press conference on 27 November, and declared that the movement was over. By the week after the new president was sworn in, almost all of the APPO leaders had been arrested. By Christmas, the conflict had been 'resolved,' the PFP withdrew, and the outward signs of the struggle, the graffiti, broken windows, and burned vehicles, had been cleansed.

Part II
Chapter 3

'They think that because you speak another language you have changed!': Ethnographic portraits of how students perform at the *Centro de Idiomas*

Introduction

In this chapter we will show that as students at the *Centro* are pursuing their goals of learning English, they are also involved in a set of complex performances that accent their various identity locations (Baron and Kotthoff, 2001). At their age, they are naturally dealing with who they are, or who they could be in terms of gender, sexuality, ethnicity, social class, and both social and personal responsibility. We contend that these are the general social dynamics for how young people construct their selfhoods whether they are studying English or chemistry and whether they are in Mexico or anywhere else (Blackman, 2004; Holland, et al., 2004). However, where they are located, and who shares those locations with them, influences what can or cannot be envisioned or performed. Thus, for students at this point in their journey towards adulthood, learning English is part of the context for how they understand and act upon their identity possibilities. How they perform their gender, sexuality, ethnicity, social class and selfhood is interwoven with how they are seeking to use English. These social activities are folded into who they think they are and how others think of them. They enter into these social fields with varying levels of social, linguistic and cultural capital. Through their personal agency they may be able to combine these funds into forms of symbolic capital that can help them along their journeys. With the use of ethnographic narratives, we will illustrate these dynamics in the lives of six students from the *Centro de Idiomas*. Also, by reading between the lines of their narratives, we will focus on elements that show how these students deal with the colonial difference (Mignolo, 2002) and what we refer to as the politics of affinity (Haraway, 1991; Laclau and Mouffe, 1985).[9]

---

[9] Throughout our analysis we will refer to these narratives as ethnographic portraits. This involves the blending of the descriptive prowess of applied linguistics and the interpretative flexibility of cultural anthropology. To compose these portraits into ethnographic narratives we have integrated information from our observations of the everyday behaviour of these students (particularly within the classroom and the social context of the school), sections from interviews with them, written and spoken material of the students themselves, analysis of their language games and performances and our interpretive reflections about their performances.

Ethnographic portraits of how students perform at the Centro de Idiomas   61

In these portraits we will tell the stories of the journey of Nour, who had to navigate the social locations of gender, ethnicity and social class in the process of learning English; Facundo, who found the *Centro de Idiomas* to be a safe house in terms of his sexuality and social class; Jorge, who has used the *Centro* as a theatre for the performance of his politics; Elena, who was shifting her class position from the *cantina* to the classroom through the pursuit of linguistic capital; César, who was re-defining his indigenous ethnic identity (Chinanteco) through how he performed English and; Yolanda, who was using her indigenous ethnic identity (Trique) to make a claim on English userhood. These portraits are somewhat chronologically ordered, the first one being the portrait of a student we worked with in the early stages of the investigation, and the last being of a student we met more recently. Furthermore, as is the case with ethnographic interviewing, these young language actors used different conversational and narrative strategies, and this is reflected in both the narrative style and in the length of their portraits.

Nour's social capitals and identities

Nour is an attractive and intelligent young woman studying at the *Centro de Idiomas*. She is twenty-three years-old and comes from a middle class family; her father, whose background is Lebanese, is a physician and her mother is a housewife of Spanish heritage.

> My background is Lebanese and Spanish, because of my grandparents. I do not mention this to show off, but for people to understand some experiences that I have had in my life. My mother's mother is from Barcelona, and she had to run away from Spain with her father and brother because of the Civil War. They arrived at Mexico and settled in Miahuatlan. On my father's side, his mother was the daughter of a Lebanese father and a Greek mother. My great grandfather left Lebanon because of the bellicose situation in his country and came to Oaxaca. For different reasons, my great grandmother left Greece for problems in her first marriage. Both met in Mexico. Somehow, I can say that I had three great people as my ancestors that left part of their lives in their home country to look for new opportunities. Each of these stories has determined my own decisions in different ways, particularly because I want to leave my country in search for new and better opportunities for my own life.

Nour has a younger brother. The two children together with their parents form a very solid and cohesive familiar unit. Their financial stability and personal qualities have allowed them to enjoy their family.

> I have good memories when I was a kid. The four of us used to make a 2500-piece zigzag puzzle every summer. It was a kind of therapy for the whole family. Also we used to take short trips to little towns in Oaxaca. Once we went to Italy. Now every weekend we sit in the living room smoking *nargileh* [water pipe] and talking for hours. I have grown up in a great family, a family that is neither religious nor conservative (Great!), a family that has given me the freedom to look for what I want in life. My father has a strong character, he is also intelligent, responsible, with a good sense of humour, and always reading (I've got this habit from him). My mother is the perfect woman: intelligent, strong, patient, sociable, happy, with a smile for everybody. I would like to be like her! My brother is my best friend; we have shared so many things in life!

Nour's previous schools were mainly private institutions. However, she thinks that being in a private school also has its shortcomings:

> I studied in private schools for my elementary and high school years. I don't think that it was better or worse than the public schools. My parents decided to send us to private schools in order to give us the best opportunities. After finishing secondary school, I moved to a different school, because the previous one was too religious and elitist, full of '*hijos de papi*' [children of important and affluent parents], who seemed to be untouchable, superficial and egocentric. The school was managed by Catholic priests. Somehow or another, I have always put limits to religious beliefs. I believe in God in my own way. I do not like to say that I am Catholic, Christian, Buddhist or Muslim because I do not want to be labelled. My parents and my relatives are Catholic.

In her school years before entering the university, she proved to be a hard-working and academically oriented student. She had also developed music and dancing skills and studied French, Italian and Japanese. Before getting into the *Centro de Idiomas*, Nour spent some time in Italy to make up her mind about her future.

I was eighteen when I travelled by myself. I had a lot of concerns and fears about doing things by myself. Before I had always lived with my family and my parents had been always there to solve my problems. When I got there I was surprised that I could do things by myself, going from here to there and making decisions on my own. In Oaxaca I had never even taken a bus because my father had the idea that it was very dangerous for a girl to do that. I understand my father's reasons, but that made me a very frightened person. In Italy, while studying Italian, I met people from all over the world and I decided that I wanted to study something related to languages.

In her quest to find herself in this journey to Europe, she decided to go to Lebanon and meet her relatives:

My grandfather had never come back to his country, so we lost contact with them for one hundred years. In 1997, my father got an email address of one of his cousins and we started the contact again. They and we were very euphoric and nostalgic about all this. And now I had the possibility to go and meet them. I was aware of the war problems with Israel, but I didn't care. After overcoming all the problems and paperwork to get a visa to enter Lebanon, finally on the 8th of March 1999, I took a flight from Italy to Lebanon. I met all my grandmother's brothers and cousins, her children and grandchildren. I still cannot explain the way I felt, how lucky I felt to be there, I spent twenty-nine days meeting my family and getting to know every corner of that beautiful country that is Lebanon. For the first time in my life I felt that I was in my place, the place I wanted to be the rest of my life.

Nour returned to Oaxaca having decided that she wanted to study languages. She went to the *Centro de Idiomas* and joined the programme to be an English teacher. We met Nour because she was recommended by one of her professors and she was interested to work with us on the development of this ethnographic research project. Her professor told us that she was incredibly committed and bright. We worked with her for two years and discovered that apart from being responsible and intelligent, she is very compassionate, humble, and witty. Nour is one of the few students that came to this school because she wanted to be an English teacher. But in spite of all her good qualities, she was not very popular among her classmates. Being very committed to her studies and being quite responsible, she felt that she contrasted strongly with most of her classmates whom she considered not to be very academically oriented. This is how she describes her problems with her classmates:

> I started at the University very motivated, but little by little I grew to dislike the atmosphere. The fact is that I clashed with my classmates. I have been part of this class for five years and I think that most of them are a mess. They are not interested in school, they do not seem to be university students, and they do not care about their academic preparation. Sometimes I think that with them, I am going backwards. They do not even seem to have a life plan. They do not seem to like what they are doing or what they are studying; they are not motivated. They are the ones that cause the university to have a very low academic level, and because I say what I think, they do not accept me.

She is not only critical of her classmates but also of her teachers; 'As a student, I have a feeling of frustration because of the poor teaching of some of the members of the faculty. There are some courses I still wonder why I was there, really poor teaching'. These feelings almost made her leave her studies some years ago, 'In the fifth semester I wanted to quit. I was so frustrated, not getting what I wanted, but I didn't want my parents to spend money to send me away. So I had to stay here.'

Another cause of dispute between Nour and her classmates was political. She supported an academic candidate for the leadership of the school, while most of her classmates were against him, 'I supported a candidate they did not like, and I put forward my reasons but, of course, academic reasons would not convince them.' Nour thinks that most of her classmates do not have the capacity to be critical. 'They do not read. They only sit in front of the TV and accept everything they hear.' This lack of reflection and critical attitude led to the most difficult situation for Nour in her school life:

> A crucial moment for my separation from the rest of the group was about 9/11 [2001]. The media were accusing the Arabs, calling them 'extremist, fundamentalist, Muslim terrorists'. What a title! My classmates knew that my background was Arab, and they were just accepting what they were listening in the news and I wanted to demonstrate that they were

wrong. It was very difficult for me. They were literally attacking me. And I was defending myself and thinking about my relatives that live there. That was when I separated from my classmates. Before that, I had not noticed that kind of racism, and I was not going to stay quiet. And I felt so impotent, so helpless. I had to speak up, but they believed only what the media said. Some of them may have been only joking, but they hurt me so much.

From that moment on, she defended herself by showing an attitude of indifference about the affairs that concerned the class whose members, whether consciously or unconsciously, kept telling her that she was different:

I did not want to be in the generation group photograph because I did not feel part of the group and also because I did not agree with their decisions. Did you see that they decided to wear cap and gown for the photo? Come on, we do not use that here, that's a *gringo* costume, and you know me, I reject everything that is *gringo*.

Even her attitude towards English changed radically:

Because of all this, my attitude towards English has not been very positive. I hardly feel now a motivation to be 'the great English teacher'. With all the imperialist *gringo* politics, and the manipulation of ideas against anybody born in the Middle East, or with an Arab last name, or even with Arab appearance, I have built a barrier against anything that is *gringo* or English ... That's why I still do not know if I will teach English, I am very angry about this and makes me want to reject English.

It is not, however, just her ethnic background and academic skill that cause this clash with her class. According to one of her male classmates, Alberto, there are other reasons that Nour is not as popular as other girls:

Well, I do not know her very well, but we are not blind; she is very attractive ... there is no doubt that she is attractive. We think she is distant, she does not allow the boys to get very close to her. Her appearance is very striking; a lot of guys think that she is so beautiful and so intelligent ... but they also think that they are not good enough for her. Some of them must think that 'I am so poor and look so Oaxacan, you know, with brown skin and she is so white and beautiful'.

However, according to Nour, there are some who do not think the same way:

> They have told me that the boys are afraid of me. But there are also some that have insisted, and gosh, they have been so insistent that I had to ask a friend to come to the school and pretend that he was my boyfriend. I just wanted to get rid of them.

And this situation has also happened with her few male friends:

> Some of my male friends think that because I am their friend I want to have a relationship, so they start insisting. That has happened even with my best friends. And they do not understand that I love them as friends, but they always want more.

Her best friends ended up being her teachers. She became especially good friends with a literature and Spanish professor, who was very supportive of her.

> What helped me to stand up this awful attitude of my classmates was my friendship with some of my professors, in particular my Spanish professor, in spite of the fact that they would say that she was lesbian and that we were a couple. But in this school you can expect any of this kind of gossip. I did not care if she was lesbian or not, I respected her ideas and her decisions about how to live her life. I learned a lot from her. But in spite of her, I still wanted to drop out of the programme. My mother was very important in my decision to finish it.

Fortunately, her project with our research group gave her a new motivation to stay in the school:

> There have been moments when being by myself in the school, with its very active social life, has been very difficult for me, that is, not belonging to a social group. I have come to recognise that I have to adapt myself,

to learn to live with different people. When I started the project with Angeles and Michael, I felt that I was learning a lot. I felt for the first time that I was in a university. That's why I decided to write my thesis on finding out why the students at the *Centro* want to get a degree in English teaching. My investigation has allowed me to understand other people and to understand myself. What am I doing here? What are they doing here? I know that there are prejudices here. At the national level, I have suffered prejudices because I am from Oaxaca and because I studied at UABJO, you know, one of the poorest public universities in the country and with a lot of political crises, but with my study I became aware that since I was neither working class or indigenous, I have had more opportunities. Some of my informants (some of whom were also my classmates) told me that they or their parents had to spend the whole night here to get a *ficha*. Before carrying out my research, I did not know that ... Taking part in the ethnographic project at the *Centro* has helped me to know why we are here, to find answers to understand the way I feel and to understand my classmates, to know about my context, my school and the way we are.

To celebrate her B.A., her family organised a party. They invited many people close to Nour: aunts, uncles, cousins and friends from her previous schools, her former teachers and her university professors. The food and drinks were Lebanese style and the main attraction was the *nargilehs* that most of the guests enjoyed. Now that she has finished her B.A., Nour summarises her hopes for her future as follows:

> I have grown up in the poorest state of Mexico, where there are not many opportunities, where education is suffering one of its worst crises, where the government seems to be the most corrupt and inept. This has motivated me to want do more, even if it has to be outside Oaxaca. Because I have realised that things do not work well here and I have felt the frustration and the injustice to people like me that want to make a difference. But wherever I go I will always stand for my origin: Oaxacan, Spanish, Lebanese and Greek, because nobody has the right to judge me by whom I am or the place I come from.

After the university, Nour applied for a place in an assistantship programme for high schools in United Kingdom. She spent a year there as a Spanish teacher's assistant and decided that most teenagers there were not interested in learning Spanish. Before coming back to Mexico, she decided to visit her relatives in Lebanon. While she was there, the horrific violence of the Israeli army was directed at Lebanon for supposedly not controlling the rebel forces in the southern part of the country. She, along with dozens of Mexicans and other internationals, were evacuated from the country. She is currently back in Oaxaca, recuperating from the shock of experiencing first hand a postcolonial war, and of having had to leave her family in the middle of it.

Reflections on Nour's story

Among the six students presented in these ethnographic portraits, Nour clearly entered the *Centro* with more cultural capital than the others (and no doubt more economic capital also). Given her family's class standing, the professional context of her father, and her mother's family background, her everyday life was a context in which she had access to different forms of cultural capital. One clear example of this is that in our sample of students at the *Centro*, she was one of few who were aware of the academic structure of the university, what kind of programs there were at the *Centro*, and what she wanted to study. She had spent time comparing the cost and programs at different universities and found that for various reasons the programme at the *Centro* was best suited to her needs. She came with an identity of herself as a student with serious goals and desires about her studies and what she thought a university setting should be. This required a series of performances that could balance these goals with her desire to be or not to be part of the in-group of her class.

This also involved composing her performances so as not to be hindered by the perceptions and actions of other students concerning her gender, sexuality, and ethnicity. She is an assertive young woman who was not hesitant to express her views, particularly about her fellow students or teachers. She felt that she had an awareness and understanding about what a university education was, and she demanded that students and faculty be able to act accordingly. In terms of her student identity, she chose to maintain these beliefs over winning social approval. Further, she did not use the perception of her attractiveness as a means to gain social approval or to soften her assertiveness.

The way she performed her gender and sexual locations was expressed in how she dealt with others' perceptions of her attractiveness and her personal style. Some read her assertiveness as her way to distance herself from the other students, and others saw her attitude as she thought that she was so attractive that it was not possible for others (especially young men) to approach her. Her understanding of the dynamics of the personal politics of sexuality was expressed in how she knew that some young men were only offering friendship and access to their social networks in anticipation of certain presumed sexual favours from her. To confront this, she used her own agency. Having a male friend to act as her *novio* was her strategy to ward off the attentions of other young men. Furthermore, she was confident enough about her own sexuality so as not to be concerned about how other people at the *Centro* read her friendship with her Spanish professor, who was perceived to be a lesbian. For Nour, her friend's lifestyle was an example of an alternative way to plan one's life, independent of their sexuality.

A dramatic example that illustrates the combination of her cultural capital with her various identity locations and her personal agency is how she dealt with the concerns over her ethnic background. She is quite aware of her Arab heritage through her father's family and her own visits to Lebanon. Moreover, she has had various travel experiences outside of Mexico and was quite aware of the diversity of ethnic and political issues in the contemporary world. She felt that many of her classmates saw the events of the 11th of September, 2001 in terms of stereotypes about radical Arabs. She challenged them to see these complex events more critically. For this, she was chastised and further marginalised by her classmates. Though she was hurt by these actions and felt that it was in fact an expression of racism, she committed herself to doing even better in her educational pursuits. In fact, by participating in this ethnographic project and through her final project, she came to have a reflective understanding of the colonial difference in the context of her social locations and those of her classmates. She became aware of the ways class and ethnic locations affected students in the university context and her own familial and personal relations in and beyond Oaxaca, especially concerning her family relations in Lebanon. These understandings allow her to find a way to reduce her feelings of distance from her classmates. The colonial difference was now, for her, an issue about what the connections between imperialism and English were, exemplified by the political and economic actions of the United States. In her new found feelings one can note a hint of what we are referring to as the politics of affinity.

And so, the way that Nour performed her gender, sexuality and ethnicity was not a hindrance to her pursuit of the linguistic and symbolic capital involved in learning English. In fact, she was able to enhance the attainment of her educational and personal goals through these performances. Moreover, she will be able to convert these capital 'gains' into her own cultural capital and, in doing so, further her skills and desires to learn and use English. Though her positions within the learning cultures of the *Centro* were often distant and conflictive, she was able to navigate around these barriers towards her own social hopes and goals. Like others at the *Centro*, by performing English with postcolonial accent, she was finding out how to be herself in this other language.

Facundo's safe houses

Facundo is a lively, extroverted student at the *Centro*. He is from a rural working class family from a small village near the city of Oaxaca. His mother has had to support him and his older sister with small-scale vending enterprises while coping with the alcoholism and macho attitudes of his father. He and his sister (a preschool teacher) are the first ones in his extended family to go to university to get a degree. He feels a great responsibility to get his degree since he is the first one who speaks English in his family. His family, however, is not very happy with his choice:

> At the beginning they thought that it was a 'double edged sword', because they thought that either I was going to change and become *agringado*, *malinchista*, betraying my own country and culture, or I was not going to make any progress. They used to say, 'As a physician you earn money, but being an English teacher is not profitable'.

As a child, Facundo was weak and somewhat sickly. He often had to stay at home which prevented him from enjoying his childhood as much as he would have liked. He thinks that was the reason he was so timid, introverted and fearful of speaking when he was in kindergarten. He remembers that once he was lost and had trouble asking for help because of his problems with talking. His life did not change very much during the six years of elementary school and the two first years of secondary school. Aside from that, he became overweight, which was the cause of bullying from his classmates. He depicts himself at that time as a shy, quiet *gordito* (fat boy) who was alone most of the time, preferring to stay in the classroom while his classmates enjoyed their break. He says that his reaction to this difficult situation was to become a lonely but irritating adolescent who would refuse to use public buses or attend school. Because of his slow academic progress, he even failed his English courses. His mother decided to send him to a private Catholic school run by nuns. There, he says, the atmosphere was different and he did not feel alone, and in the religion he found the strength and confidence he was lacking before.

At the end of secondary school he started to think about what he wanted to be in life. Although the idea of becoming a priest was attractive to him, it was actually his desire to learn English that made him start high school in a public school in order to be able to enter the *Centro*. His first year at high school was difficult for him. The atmosphere at this new school was too relaxed and disorienting for him. It was evident that he was different from his classmates. He remembers that he used to go to school wearing slacks and a long sleeve shirt with a tie. Sometimes he found the environment so negative that he would carry his Bible with him thinking that everything in this context was sinful. But he also found that there was a lot of diversity among his classmates, who instead of rejecting him, invited him to take part in their *desmadres* (trouble making). Finally, he decided to change. First he changed his appearance (now he wears jeans and t-shirts) and then his point of view and behaviour. He left his Bible behind and started smoking and drinking, though he points out that he never tried the other drugs that his friends used to take.

These changes in his style of performance were related to his emerging sexual identity:

> I am a boy whose social life is very restricted. Actually, it revolves around the *Centro* and my classmates. However, during this past year I have learned to deal with my reality, a reality very difficult to deal with, since I have had to develop two different personalities and lives fighting against what I am. I am referring to my sexual preferences.
>
> This has limited my social life because it was not until this year that I woke up from the lethargy that depressed me so much because I refused to accept my sexual orientation. Now I have learned how to live as a straight man in front of my family and how to express my homosexuality when I am not with them. I feel that the day I tell my family they will be very disappointed, but for me it will be a sort of liberation because I will not be pretending to be what I am not any more.
>
> The *Centro* is the right place for me. It has been very helpful for me to be here because I feel that a high number of students are gay and that

encourages me and makes me feel that I am not alone any more. Now I know that I am not the only one whose sexual preferences are different.

When Facundo talks about his English learning experience he makes the connection with social status:

> People think that because you speak another language you have a better cultural level, that you are 'in'. For instance, one day a student from the States, with whom I practised my English at school, invited me to the cinema; you know the new cinemas they just opened. The place was full of *fresitas* (show offs), rich young boys and girls that look down at others. They looked at me as if saying, 'What are you doing here? You do not belong here! You don't look *fresa*, or nice, or cool.' But, boy, they were shocked when my friend, a tall blond guy, green eyes, arrived and started to talk to me in English and I answered him back and we had a fluid conversation in English. They were astonished, thinking '*Orale!* (Gosh!) How can HE speak English and we, who think so much of ourselves, can't.' Their attitude simply changed. I do not know how to explain it but their attitude changed, I swear. And that gives you a better status, doesn't it?

However, the gained social status does not always work in favour of social smoothness:

> My friends have also reacted to my learning English because, you know, sometimes I forget the words in Spanish and I say them in English and they start calling me *fresa*, and sometimes the situation turns tense. I guess that they are sensitive to that. They feel that they are left aside; they feel diminished and excluded. And you feel uncomfortable as well; you do not want to leave them aside, but at the same time if I come across a *gringo* that I know, I have to talk in English but my intention is not to say anything I do not want them to know about ... They say that I have changed, that now I am *fresa*, that I am *fresa* because I only hang out with *gringos*. They see you differently, but in fact one has only changed a little bit, but one's essence is the same. They do not see that because they are looking at it from the outside. They think that because you speak another language you have changed. They may think that you

are exchanging them for new people and that you are also changing your culture, and of course you are changing your friends.

Certainly Facundo's attitudes and beliefs have undergone a dramatic change. The following are some of Facundo's ideas a year from the first interview with him:

> I have changed my religion. I do not like being a Catholic any more. It was very repressive. I feel I was forced to believe in something I was against. Like most religions, there are too many restrictions and rules. That becomes very constraining when you have different sexual preferences. In many religions you do not have a place; they tell you that for you 'there is no God.' They regard you as if you have killed a human being; they expel you from their group. They tell you that you are going to hell because you are ... gay! I was really worried about that, always thinking that I was not bad, that my feelings were good. When several priests told me that I needed to feel repentant, my reasoning was sort of, 'If I am straight I could kill somebody, and then kill again and again, but then when I am about to die, if I say 'I repent,' will I then go to Heaven?' Some Sundays I still go to church with my parents but with a strong feeling that it is a farce. Recently I found out about Wicca, a religion where there are no taboos and where they tell you that there is not one alternative but many. I have heard that some think that this is witchery, but they say that because they do not know anything about it. Wicca is about understanding your context and finding a balance. It is about a circular world with you in the middle, and you need to know how to get it balanced, and you can achieve that by respecting and loving others and by doing good deeds.

This change also involves some kind of assertiveness about himself:

> I feel relieved now because my family finally knows that I am gay ... it sounds strange, doesn't it? I am not as tense as I used to be. The atmosphere at home has changed; now it is my parents who are very upset. I just told them last week, but they are processing it little by little. They've just got to understand me.
>
> I would like to tell other gay young people to be strong because you need that strength to succeed in life. Sometimes it is difficult, but we

need to keep in mind that our stay in this world is temporary and that we do not have to be what our parents want us to be. They already lived their lives and it is our turn to live ours!

Reflections on Facundo's story

Facundo's portrait is a compelling story of how, through his own agency, this young man was able to compose a series of complex performances, in terms of social class, sexuality and presentation of self, that helped him to navigate his way through various levels of his familial and educational contexts. Given the shifting and conflictive situations he has found himself in, he has been able to maintain a vision of what he wanted from his life. This is expressed quite strongly in his rejection of his family's concerns about his studying English (they felt that he would become a *'gringo'* and would never make money like a medical doctor does), his acceptance of his new-found sexuality and his religious beliefs in opposition to his family's, and how he hopes to continue with both of these identity locations.

Also, the history of his educational adventures is a strong representation of the social activities involved in the construction and performances of his various identities. From his entry into primary school up to his current activities in the *Centro*, he has been constantly constructing and practising various identities to locate or find himself. He has moved from being a very timid child to being a somewhat confused teenager, and now he is entering young adulthood accepting his homosexuality and exploring forms of alternative religious beliefs. It has also been through learning English in the supportive context of the learning cultures at the *Centro* that he has gained the security to continue these pursuits.

Moreover, in this context of the *Centro*, he has been able to encounter a safe house for himself, where he has been able to understand his homosexuality and further his pursuit of the linguistic and symbolic capital associated with English (Canagarajah, 1999). At the *Centro* he has found friends that share his quest for learning English and who accept his sexual orientation without judgment. He has had to relocate himself in terms of older friends who thought that he was attempting to be better than they were through his command of English and the new friendships he has attained. Within this more open context his self-esteem seems to have increased with his willingness to be open about his sexuality and his exploration of new forms of spirituality. He is finding that through the pursuit of various forms of linguistic and symbolic capital in the context of the learning cultures of the *Centro*, he has enriched his cultural capital and he can manoeuvre better in this postcolonial world. Like Nour, his identity performances have helped, not hindered him in learning and using English.

Furthermore, Facundo's performance of English with a postcolonial accent accents what we have stated about the generalities of the maturing process and the specificity of those actions taking place in the context of attaining a command over English. While seeking to learning English, Facundo found ways to redefine his relation with his family, his friends, his personal beliefs, his education and his selfhood. At this point in his quest (as you will also see in the case of Yolanda) English was his safe house in which the question of confronting the authority of the native speaker was yet to come. Within the social folds of English, he could define his sexuality, change his religion, confront the class prejudices of middle class youth and feel free to be himself. He could also use his linguistic capital accumulated by learning English to redefine how he wanted to perform his Oaxacaness or Mexicaness. Perhaps the same social possibilities would be present in other fields of study, but in the multicultural and multilingual context of Oaxaca, English can be a useful tool in building forms of intercultural communication.

Jorge's political weapon

Jorge is quite an interesting young man. When we began working with him, he was in his early twenties and was in his second year at the *Centro*. In this context he is one of the most politically knowledgeable and active students. He sees himself as a Marxist revolutionary and contends that he needs English to be able to connect with various social and political movements throughout the world. Like Nour, he came into the *Centro* with various forms of cultural capital, but his came from an understanding of different political and institutional dynamics more than educational ones. He came to his politics through his father's involvement in the national teachers union, which often used very radical rhetoric in its political positions. Jorge has involved himself with some of the more controversial politics of the university in terms of relations among the university administration, the *Centro*, the unions and the student groups. Currently, his strongest identity location in the context of the *Centro de Idiomas* is focused on his political and ethical performances. For Jorge, the performance of English with a postcolonial accent is a means towards the attainment of more political and symbolic capital.

Jorge's family history is similar to that of many other students at the *Centro*. There is a social pattern in which the students' grandparents' generation come from rural areas with limited economic means, whereas their parents' generation has had access to the various changes in the Mexican political economy from the 1960s through the early 1980s. These changes allowed their parents to enter into more advantageous economic and social fields and allowed Jorge and his generation the 'luxury' of pursuing university education within the state systems (Higgins, 1997).

Jorge's maternal grandmother lived in a village in the costal area of Pluma Hidalgo, Oaxaca. At very early age she worked picking coffee on nearby plantations and was never able to go to school or have decent paying jobs. As a young adult she married and moved with her husband to the town of Miahuatlan (about an hour west of the city of Oaxaca). Soon afterwards, her husband died and she had to maintain the family by running several small scale enterprises like selling *tortillas, atole* (a common hot corn beverage) and beans. As the oldest female in the family, Jorge's mother was his grandmother's main helper. When his mother finished secondary school in Miahuatlan, she left to go to high school in the city of Oaxaca. She did not like the high school programme, so she transferred to the *Normal* school in Oaxaca (the teacher training institution). She spent four years of study there, acquired her teaching degree and was able to get her first teaching job.

During her first year of teaching, Jorge's mother began to date a young man, Jorge Luis, who was to become her husband and Jorge's father. Jorge Luis was born in the city of Oaxaca, where his parents ran small businesses such as stores or small restaurants. Jorge's grandmother encouraged her children to seek a good education or find good jobs. His father became a history teacher and militant union member.

Given Jorge's parents' history as school teachers and their political involvement, Jorge is an articulate young man who has always had a strong desire to study English and to become a teacher.

> I have always thought studying English would be very cool. It has been a real satisfaction trying to learn English, and now I feel that I am really learning it. Knowing English changes how people look and interact with you. You get chosen to do different kinds of things with English and it can isolate those who do not know it. Now, many jobs in Mexico require that you have some level of English, even to be a receptionist. It will be hard in the future not to know English. Here at the *Centro*, for those students that have not had any English, it is harder. In our classes, especially linguistics

classes you have to be able to read materials in English. That's when you realise knowing English makes a difference. The fact that I have taken English courses helps with these classes. Knowing English will make my life less difficult in comparison to someone who does not.

Also, I want to be a teacher. My parents are teachers, but that's not why I want to be one. I just feel like being a teacher. And I say this knowing what it is like in these days to be a teacher, with all the problems. I know that you suffer; you have to be studying all the time and then you have to find a job. But as a teacher you can try to change the things in this world that are wrong. It is exciting to think that you can attempt to change things from your own point of view. I can try to help students to see the world differently, to be aware of relevant events and to change their attitudes towards social issues. I would want to make my classrooms and the way that I teach very egalitarian, not just with empty words that everyone is equal, but with really treating all students in an egalitarian way. Teaching gives you the potential to make important changes, that's why I want to be a teacher.

Jorge also offered us some narratives and statements on how he was able to use his pre-existing cultural (or political) capital to locate himself within the complex university world.

I have always been rebellious; it comes from the politics of my parents. My father was militant in the national teachers union. When he was in the *normal* school he was active in the union and was one of the student leaders. Although my mother agrees with his ideas, she is not as militant and she is still very much into the church. I think I got introduced to socialism through all the protests I went on with my father for the teacher's union. I would go to the sittings, either here in Oaxaca or in Mexico City. In Mexico City it was hard, we would sleep in the streets with cardboard sheets and it was very cold. We would get woken up at three in the morning by anti-union vandals who would attack us. That's where I learned what the struggle was.

There are some in the university who think that the political group that I am involved with is nothing more than just *porros*. But that is not true, we are not. We do sometimes take very spontaneous actions, like anarchists, so maybe it looks like *porrismo*, but it is not. But I have had my own problems with groups of *porros*. They were collecting money from the students to help one of the founders who was in jail and the money was going to buy him drugs. I want no part of that kind of behaviour. Also there have been students in our group who were acting like real *porros*, we had to kick them out. In fact, sometimes it is hard to tell who are and who are not *porros*. *Porros* seem to be driven more for the money they get paid, where the more militant students are driven by their ideologies, but sometimes the actions are the same.

Within the context of *Centro*, Jorge needed to find a mentor in order to feel comfortable with how he wanted to present himself in that context:

When I started here at the *Centro* I did not like it. The *Centro* had a reputation of having students that were very *fresas*. Then I met Ilhui, one of the professors here. She was very good and that helped me to starting to like the place more. And also there were a lot of students that I know here, and that also helped. I have done well and I have got good grades. I am still improving and I would say that I like here for sure. My parents are pleased with my work here, and in fact they are thinking of sending my younger brother here to study English. But I am not here to please my parents. That would be silly. They know who I am and how I was in high school, there I was a real shit disturber. But they know that I want to study and get my degree. My friends that are not here at the school think it is cool I am studying English here. They think that I might be able to help them get into the *Centro* in the future. They also think that it is cool that I am studying with all these *fresas*. I think the academic level at the *Centro* is very good, better than in law or accounting. Here the focus is really on studying and that's good. Even the entrance exams are harder than in the other schools in the university.

Feeling comfortable at the *Centro* has not stopped Jorge from criticising what he does not like:

Among the students at the *Centro*, politics seems more personal, more about envy. If you speak up too much in class they start to dislike you for that. If you have new clothes, they hate you for that. And then if you do not speak, they hate you because you don't speak. Damned if you do damned if you don't. Everything bothers them. There are also a lot of differences in terms of social classes. For example, in one of my classes, when you enter into the room, in the front there are the *fresas* and at the back the *trovadores* [bohemians], those students that think they are more hip and political. In the middle you find the ones who want to be either *trovadores* or *fresas*. The differences are very marked. And there are also some students that think that they can come and shout and give orders to others.

The student council for the *Centro* can be very vicious. They are only concerned with keeping their power and getting themselves re-elected. Excuse me? In my home town that is called a dictatorship! Because of their actions, we (I and other political students) are looking for an alternative political structure for the students. We are all in the second semester here at the *Centro* and we are very close and we try to help each other.[11] We want to go to a student conference on politics and education in Monterrey, in northern Mexico. We are trying to organise events to raise money for the students who do not have enough money. Little by little we will get things done. We are in the same struggle to become teachers of English. We want to be able to teach English without the students having to suffer the way we did. It is difficult but we can do it.

Jorge's passion to find a way to teach English to future students in a way that will be more humane and direct is reflective of his global view of English and politics. As he states:

English has always been a weapon; it has been the spoken weapon for the imperialism of the United States. This imperialism affects everybody and everything here in Mexico. But, English can be our weapon also. English can be a way to communicate and express your views to the rest of the world. Using English in the way we are learning it, we can fight for the rights of the people, and it gives us weapons to fight with, that is, intellectual weapons.

Jorge's vision of being able to use English as an intellectual weapon in the fight for the rights of people moved from being an expression of youthful idealism

---

11 Here at the university, students all enter and graduate at the same time, they form a generation. They count themselves by semesters. So Jorge's generation of students are in the second semester.

to an actual lived experience during the political crisis that was taking place in Oaxaca (see the postscript in chapter two). The following is a summary of Jorge's narration about the 14th of June (2006), the day that the Oaxacan government sent the police to remove the teachers from the *Zócalo*.

> For days before the 14th, we were receiving calls from people telling us that they were concerned because of rumours and threats that the police were going to attack the teachers in the *Zócalo*. They wanted us to say something on *Radio Plantón* [the radio station of the teacher's union]. Later we learned that the government was sending the police. At one o'clock in the morning we knew that the police had left their base in San Bartolo, and had started blocking the exits of the city. By four o'clock in the morning they started throwing tear gas bombs at the people in the streets and some kind of orange gas that made your body feel numb and sleepy. We had some vinegar, but we could not take it to the people at the radio station who were suffering from these attacks. Very few people knew that vinegar was good against those gases. The police had a lot of gas bombs, it seem like they had almost one for each of us. They threw gas at families with children who were in the streets. I found my mates about six in the morning and we were just running from here to there, hearing the bombs falling next to us. There were also people coming from different parts of the city but the helicopters were still throwing gases. Some policemen surrendered because they were unable to beat us back. At about eleven a.m., the police finally ran out of gas bombs. The neighbours in the area around the *Zócalo*, opened their houses to let us in for protection and they also gave us some food and stones to keep fighting with. In a moment I was passing out and they took me to a nursery school were a nurse gave me a shot and told me not to come back, but I had to come back so they gave me a *cubrebocas* [disposable inexpensive surgical mask] soaked in vinegar. The police told us that they did not know what they were there for, that they have been told that it was a supporting act for the PRI [ruling party in Oaxaca]. During the battles, our people had caught some police and took away their helmets and shields. That night, my buddies and I met in a secondary school to make decisions with the teachers of the union. The following day we called for a demonstration with students. A girl form the *Centro* that I did not get along with came with students from the Law school. There

I learned that, in spite of our differences, we were fighting for the same ideal. We marched together with more than seventy students from the *Centro*, with banners in English. Before, nobody at school had shown any interest.

Of course we had some problems with some students that were supporting Calderón for president (Calderón was the conservative candidate in the presidential elections). They had learned from their parents that rich people are the ones that count and that the poor are the ones to blame for being poor. These students were spreading the rumour that we were *porros*.

We also worked as translators of the teachers. People would come from all parts of the world and they wanted to know, so we translated this poster:

> SORRY for the annoyances.
> What happens is that we are
> busy making our HISTORY.
> As soon as Ulises gets out of
> here, we will welcome you
> again with open arms.
> Attentively,
> the citizens of Oaxaca

Fig. 1 APPO poster translated by *Centro de Idiomas* students

We thought that it was great that the teachers were trying to communicate with the people in those terms, 'Sorry for the annoyances ...' That was so cool! So we decided to translate it. We made another good one with Ulises as Mussolini 'Wanted for tyrant'. We also sent emails, made T-shirts, banners and posters, all this in English for the world to know about our struggle.

Reflections on Jorge's story

Jorge, like Nour, came into the *Centro de Idiomas* with forms of cultural capital that were advantageous for his educational goals. For him, however, these were insights into how to perform within the political and institutional structures of the *Centro* and the university. Given his parents' history as school teachers and as activists in the teachers' union he was quite attuned to the possibilities of social action within this context. He saw his actions as a continuation of his 'shit disrupting' style from his high school times, but in the *Centro* he found a safe house for the expression and enactment of his radical political beliefs. Thus, his strongest identity performance was that of a political actor. He recognises the functional benefits of English in the postcolonial world of Mexico, but for him the attainment of such linguistic capital is a means for more symbolic capital that will strengthen his political hopes. He is not looking to convert his social capitals into economic gains, but rather political ones. Performing English, and especially the teaching of English, are for him the venues for the attainment of his social and political goals. He sees teaching as an arena in which one can construct an atmosphere for students to perform in a more equalitarian style of social interaction. For Jorge, performing English with a postcolonial accent is anchored around his quest to be an authentic political actor. He wants to be able to express praxis of English language teaching that removes the separation between the classroom and the social community. Furthermore, he wants to use English not as an identity location that can make him better than others, but rather as a tool towards a struggle for the betterment of all. For Jorge, English can be an intellectual weapon to subvert the authority of the colonial difference. These are very idealistic performance goals (though also part of the journey of youth), but given his parents' political histories and his own, he is both hopeful and critical of possibilities present in the social and political fields of postcolonial Mexico. These are also very concrete goals for him; at the time of this writing, he continues to be actively involved in the state wide political struggle that has been narrated above and he is developing his senior thesis on how to teach English with content, and in this case, political content. For us, this suggests a form of political action that we refer as the politics of affinity; that is, they are using their language activities as a means to enhance forms of intercultural communication, which is a theme of how these students use their English with a postcolonial accent.

Elena's roles in life

Elena is quite an impressive young lady whose life has been framed by hardship and adversity. She comes from a working class background of limited but adequate income, and her parents were a hard working couple attempting to raise a family of eight children. When Elena was in secondary school, her family's lives were tragically altered with the death of her father. The family's primary source of income was a *cantina* that her father had been running at the time. Elena's story moves from the tables of the *cantina* to the pursuit of an English teaching degree as she locates herself as a young woman looking for the means to do what she desires.

Her father, Genaro, was born in the village of Talea de Castro in the Sierra Juarez of Oaxaca. His mother had abandoned the family when he was only three years-old. His father was a strong and difficult man. After his wife left him, he lived with several different women with whom he had several more children. He worked at various jobs in the village area and was known for his heavy drinking and fighting. Genaro began to work at a very early age and received little attention from his father. When he was thirteen, he left his village and family to find better work. At first he could only work as a *campesino* (peasant) but later he found jobs selling different things, such as popsicles or other food products. It was better than being a *campesino* because he worked fewer hours and made a little more money, and most importantly, he was good at it. He was married at the time, but he found that his wife was better at spending rather than making money from their small food vending business, so he left her and went to the city of Oaxaca. He was able to establish himself quickly in Oaxaca, where he met Elena's mother, Teresa. He and Teresa married, and together they operated several small successful food vending businesses, and after a few years were able to build a house.

Elena's parents were married for more than 20 years before Genaro starting following in his father's footsteps of drinking, running around with other women and, in one case, having a child with one of his lady friends. In order to provide for his primary family, he put his funds into to a *cantina* business. However, Elena's father's and grandfather's lives came together in quite a tragic way:

> My grandfather was very strict with his children. In fact if they misbehaved, he would use a belt on them. However, at other times he could be very patient and my father cared for him. He died seven years ago, he was seventy-five. I remember this very well. It was my father's desire to take care of the cost of his father's funeral. But on the last day of *novenario*[12] of the funeral for my grandfather, my father started bleeding

---

12 The custom in Oaxaca is that as part of the funeral there are nine days of prayers. Family and friends meet in the house or at the funeral parlour, where a recognized pray leader presents a sit of nine prayers in three sets.

and had to be sent to the emergency hospital immediately. He died three days later. My mother was left with eight children to take care of.

Elena's mother decided to keep the *cantina* going since it was her only source of income. This also provided her with a new challenge: dealing with men as her customers. Elena's mother was from the same village as her father. Her mother's parents were small farmers in the village, and she was the oldest child of the family. She had seven siblings, but two died very young. While still very young, she took care of her siblings, acting almost as second mother. When she was sixteen, both her mother and grandmother died, and she left the village to find work in the city of Oaxaca. Her dream was to be a school teacher, but that never came to be. In her second year of *normal* school, she met Genaro and they married. They had ten children, though like her mother, two of her children died very young. She was always a hard worker and worked in many different jobs to make money for the family.

> Even with all her children my mother was a hard worker; always trying to find ways to make more money for the family. She worked as a maid, in a factory; she would sell fruit, candies and *tamales* in the street in front of our house. She also worked with my father to physically build the house we now live in. So with the death of my father, she became the owner of the *cantina*. Though most of our neighbours have been helpful to us, some have been very mean and have tried to have the *cantina* shut down. One guy has always been very threatening and even stabbed one my brothers once. But my mother has always had the strength to maintain and to fight for her family's needs.

The following is the way Elena describes her life with her family:

> I am twenty-one now, and like all my siblings, I was born here in the city of Oaxaca. When I was two years-old, we returned to my grandparents' village. We were a family that lived in poverty. I remember in my early years when we lived in the village of my grandparents, we only had beans to eat everyday. For us as children, to have some candy to eat was a very rare event. But I think we (that is my sisters and friends at the time)

were happy. When I was seven, we went back to the city. Everything was different in the city. I became very serious and did not have a lot of friends. Then my father died when I was in secondary school, which was very hard on me. Everything changed in the family. Now we were responsible for ourselves and my mother was the only one making money.

Elena was the fourth of eight children. Her oldest sister studied law at the university, is married and has a baby of six months. She and her husband are now planning to open a small store. The next sister, twenty-five, is a nurse, married and has one child. Her oldest brother is twenty-three, does not currently have a job, tends to drink way too much and has not finished his university studies. Her younger sister, nineteen, is a very good student at the technological university in Oaxaca. Her three younger brothers are thirteen, eleven, and nine years-old. She has always been concerned about them:

> They are growing up without a father. My little sister and I have taken the responsibility to take care of them, take them to school and look after them. This is all apart from my other chores at home. I am the one that has to pay the bills, such as electricity, telephone, water. Also I am the one that does the shopping for the house; I buy clothes and shoes for the younger kids and whatever else they need for the school.

In fact, Elena feels that she has been like a mother for her youngest brothers. She has tried to make sure that they are well educated and responsible. Starting with small chores, she is teaching them how to become independent (washing their own clothes) and how to cooperate for the well being of the family (washing the dishes after a meal). She believes that this is how they will become good men (responsible, hard working, taking care of their families).

Elena is candid about the role of the *cantina* in the family history and her work there. She finds her work there not that unusual nor very hard. The *cantina* provides the money for the whole family to live without financial problems. Her mother is the one who is in charge of the *cantina*. For some time, her eldest brother had that responsibility but apart from not being a good administrator, he was an alcoholic, so the family made the decision to take him out of the business. Currently, they have problems with him because instead of getting a job, he wants to be supported by the family. As both part of the solution as well as an attempt to put some distance between him and her other children, Elena's mother bought a little house for him. Although the situation is better now, he is still drinking and not working.

Elena's account of her job in the *cantina* is far from negative. She does not have to go there everyday, only when her mother does not have other employees. She works as a waitress, taking orders, serving the drinks and getting the bills for the customers. Most of the customers are working men who are their neighbours. They like to go there after they finish their working day. The opening hours for the *cantina* are from seven to eleven in the morning and from eight to eleven in evening. The morning hours are very popular for some of their customers.

> I still work in the *cantina*. It is okay. I have not suffered any kind of hassles from my mother's clients. It is a neighbourhood bar and we know all the people. Sometimes they can get kind of rowdy, especially if some of the ladies of the streets come in. Sometimes some girls will come in, and some of the guys will jest with them. They do not bother either me or my sister, thank god. The customers have always treated me and my sisters with respect. Once, I remember that a guy tried to hug me, but one of the regulars of the *cantina* told him to stop. Of course there are some fights, and I have the obligation to try to stop the guys from getting involved. Once, when I was alone taking care of the *cantina*, some men started fighting and they were using their belts to hit each other. Since I was alone, again some of the regular customers helped me to calm them. However, I still have a scar on my shoulder from a belt stroke that accidentally hit me during the ruckus. But actually, the *cantina* is kind of a quiet place. The customers are all about the same age and all know each other. They even help me out with little chores around the bar, like taking the trash out. Sometimes guys will jokingly ask for our phone numbers (that is, mine or my sisters') but I try not to pay any attention to that. When they bother us, we just ignore them.

Elena started English classes when she was around ten. Her father told her that she needed to learn English to make some progress in life. She remembers the first day of the English course very well. Her father took her to a little private English school downtown Oaxaca. He told her to pay attention to the teacher and to wait for him. However, after the class, she waited for an hour and he never arrived, then she made the decision to go home by herself. When she arrived home he was working at the *cantina* and told her that he had been too busy to be able to pick her up.

After that first encounter with English, Elena found out that she wanted to learn it and so she decided to try to get a place in the *Centro de Idiomas*:

> When I finished high school, I wanted to enter the *Centro de Idiomas*, but there was no space, and I had to wait a whole year to get in. During that year I worked in a café near the centre of the city. Also during this time I was able to take a semester of English and French. When I started here, I did not have enough time to continue with French.
>
> I like to stay very active, but now I may be a little too active. Sometimes I do not have enough time to go home to eat. That why I dropped my French classes. I am occupied all day long. It seems all this year I had not gotten home during the day to help my mother take care of the younger kids. This means that often they are left alone, and nobody is around to prepare their meals. But I have to maintain my energies to keep going to school, though I know that the family is very important.
>
> I like here very much at the university, though I do have a life apart from here. I like to go dancing when I can, though I think I often have two left feet when I dance. I only go maybe once a month, if I have time. I work on Friday and Saturday giving English classes to kids. Also, as I have talked about, I have a lot of responsibilities at home helping my mother. But given all that, I am very lucky to have the family that I have. And my mother is a very special person, I am also lucky to have a mother like her. I am happy with my life and with what I have. I thank god for that.

Her four years in the *Centro* have given her an idea of certain social issues. In terms of social classes she does not see much difference:

> I think economically I am okay now. I have enough to live on without a lot of worries. I don't think that my social class background has affected how I am treated here. I do not think that I have been treated differently by the professors here, nor by the students. Generally, everybody seems to treat everyone the same. I think you get judged here more on your behaviour, how you present yourself, than on your class background. However, there are occasions when racism or classism are expressed here at the *Centro*.

> For example, here we tend to treat foreigners very well if they are *güeritos* or *güeritas* [fair skinned ones]. I have heard comments of students here at the *Centro* expressing dislike for some of the visiting black students, but always favourable comments about *güeritos*, no matter where they are from. They seem to think that *güeritos* are better off.

Outside the school, on a national level, she acknowledges some kind of racism:

> Unfortunately, as I see it, many Mexicans do express some kind of racism. It is the indigenous people of Mexico who suffer the worst racism here. People treat them like they are a different race, that they are uneducated and that it is okay to mistreat them. People will criticise their clothing, the way they speak, and what they eat. Sometimes they are treated like animals. The government does nothing, our laws do not protect them, their rights and integrity are taken away from them through the loss of their lands and homes. That is why the indigenous people of Chiapas are fighting for their land.
> Also the urban poor are treated the same way, mistreated and made fun of because their clothes are dirty and they have no shoes.

A view that she does not share:

> I try not to treat people differently because of their social class position. I try to be respectful to people, whether they are poor or rich. Though, if I know someone is better off economically than me, I can act a little reserved sometimes, until I get to know them better. There are some students in my generation that seem to be very well off, they have cars and nice clothes, and have gone to private schools before. They make me feel a little strange around them. I would not be very talkative or friendly. I would worry that when I had to talk in front of the class they would think that I was not dressed right or think that I was from the wrong social class. But as I got to know some of them, it was all right. I would hang out with them and sometimes we would go dancing or partying. We would not pay attention to differences in our backgrounds, we would just be ourselves with each other.

Once she had an experience that may have been seen by others as racism on her part but she explains how it was more connected with some kind of machismo:

> The interaction I had with a visiting black student here might be seen as racist, but I do not think it was. The student was from Atlanta in the United States, and he was my exchange studentship partner. People noticed that I was avoiding him and would not accept his invitation to go out for a coffee or a drink. It was not that I was being racist. He was always trying to kiss me, and I had told him that I had a boyfriend, but he would not accept that. He would still harass me and try to kiss me. It got to be very annoying, so I got out of being his exchange partner.

Elena says that her mother is very happy because she is the one of her seven siblings that chose to be a teacher. Actually Elena is not particularly enthused about her being able to speak English, a fact that has given her a nickname from her friends.

> My mother always wanted that one of her children would be a teacher, so she is happy with me, but she does not seem to be impressed because I am learning English, nor are my siblings. For them it is the same as if I am studying medicine or English. Sometimes my friends make jokes about me, 'Wow! You have to teach me some English!' Or if they see me with a foreigner, 'Wow! What's going on with that *gringuito*?!!' Everything is 'Wow' for them. Also when we are walking in the street and there is a foreigner around, they push me to start a conversation with him. Yeah, it gives you a little bit of status. They also think that I am *fresa* because I am studying this, and also because, you know, sometimes in Spanish I use one or two words that are not common for them, then they also say that I use *fresa* words. When I use some words in English they think that I am showing off, or they make jokes, telling me that I have so much English that I am forgetting my Spanish. Some of them even used to call me 'Sorry', like a nickname, you know, because I was always using that word so much. So I became *La Sorry*!

Now that Elena has attained her degree in English teaching, she thinks that it is not yet the time to become an English teacher because she envisions her near future in a different way:

> Although I like teaching, I think that it could be very monotonous. So I do not want to do that immediately. I do not want to get myself enclosed in a classroom, doing the same thing every day. Before that, I want to get a scholarship to go abroad, meet people, know places, and when I get back, I will work in a classroom. My mother sometimes makes jokes about me marrying an *extranjerito* (foreigner) and going to live very far from Mexico. But these are only jokes. Actually I think that it would be very difficult to have a relationship with a foreigner, to get to know him, their way of thinking is so different. It would be easier to get used to a Mexican way of being than that of a foreigner.

Reflections on Elena's story

Elena's journey towards performing English with a postcolonial accent has been both dramatic and ordinary. It was dramatic in terms of her family's tragic histories and real in that her triumphs were ordinary in the sense that her life journeys were not that different from many other working class youth in Oaxaca. She has had to travel on many challenging routes in her young life; she has moved with her family from rural poverty to a somewhat adequate urban working class life style in the city of Oaxaca and she has had to learn that hope can be constrained by necessity, as illustrated by the story of having to walk home from her first English class because her father could not leave the *cantina* to pick her up. She has dealt with the tragedy of her father's death, which led to the re-composition of a stronger family unit that survived through the *cantina* business that her father left behind. This social world of the *cantina* became the stage from which she was able to move into the university world, to begin learning English and to envision a future beyond her family.

Besides the stage of the *cantina*, she has had to perform in a variety of different social theatres. Because of the death of her father, she moved from being a young girl enjoying the activities of being in school to having to perform as surrogate parent to her younger brothers, manager of household funds, and the aspirant of the mother's lost dreams of becoming a teacher. She also had to learn how to construct a style of performing in the male world of the *cantina* that would allow her to be treated in a non-ordinary way, that is, not as a sex object. This was made possible by the combination of the neighbourhood status of the *cantina* along with the clever skills of social interaction that she and her sister composed. These skills were part of the cultural capital that she took into the social fields of the *Centro de Idiomas*. In that context, she felt that she could perform in a manner that was dependent on her personality and hard work, not on her social class position. She felt that the *Centro* was a safe house in which she could explore what she wanted to do instead of being what she was assumed to be because of her class position. It was also in the context of *Centro* that she found ways to understand the complexities of the social and political realities of postcolonial Oaxaca and Mexico. She came to understand the interrelationships between social class, race/ethnicity and gender in both global and personal spaces. This was evidenced by her explanation of why she did not want to continue her exchange studentship with the young African-American.

The diversity of her particular funds of social and cultural capital allowed her to see the attainment of the linguistic capital that English offers in pragmatic terms. She is proud of her skills, but knew not to overstate their importance. Because of her desire to be good at her languages skills while not looking pretentious in her performances of those skills, she often softens her presentations with the comment 'I am sorry'. This led to her friends to give her the nickname '*la Sorry*'. She knows that English will give her opportunities, but those opportunities would have to be tempered by her commitments to her family and her own connection to her Oaxacan and Mexican identities. Further, she seems to want to use the social capital she is accumulating not to fix a future but to keep seeking the possible, which are worlds that are beyond the now. For her, performing English with a postcolonial accent is a bridge between her multiple social worlds and the possibilities that lie within other social domains.

César's journeys back and forth to his pueblo

César is quite an assertive and ambitious young man. His ethnographic portrait tells the tale of a young man moving from his rural Chinanteco community[13] to the urban world of the university and the *Centro* and his return trip to his community to seek affirmation of what he saw as his symbolic and cultural

---

13 The Chinatecos are located in the north-eastern part of the state of Oaxaca in an area called the Chinantla. The area is located in the River valley of the Papaloapan River and is surrounded by mountains. As of 1995, the population for the Chinatecos was around 116,271, with over 68% of the population being bilingual in Spanish and Chinateco. Their primary economic activity is fundamentally agriculture; they grow corn, chilli, tobacco, coffee, beans, and rice. Except for the corn and beans, the crops are sold in the local and regional markets (Barabas and Bartolomé (eds.), 1999).

capital achievements. Along this journey, through his own agency, he tries to locate his performance of English with a postcolonial accent beyond the expectations that both his local and university communities hold about what he should be doing with himself. He seeks his own being through the achievements of language and education. He might seem stern and stubborn in these pursuits, but he takes solace in the awareness that he is his own guide in this quest for self-betterment and progress.

César comes from the village of Chiltepec, a Chinanteco speaking community in the north-eastern mountains of the state of Oaxaca. His father drives a taxi and his mother is a nursery school teacher.

> I am wenty-two years-old. My parents have had four children and I am the oldest. I have always been the one in the family that has liked to study and get good grades. My brother Jose is twenty one and he has gone to the States; my other brother Israel, who is seventeen, has already left school, whereas my baby sister, Brenda who is twelve, is still in school. I am very proud of my parents and my family. Until I was a teenager, I lived with my family, but because of my desire to learn English and progress in my life I moved to the city of Oaxaca to attend the university. I am now studying for an undergraduate degree in TEFL.

Though he was engaged by the process of learning English, like many indigenous peoples in the state of Oaxaca, he was not encouraged to learn his own language. César's grandparents spoke both Spanish and Chinanteco, but only his father speaks Chinanteco in the nuclear family. His mother, like him, understands Chinanteco but does not speak it. This linguistic context was the cause of numerous frustrating situations for César when he was a boy, particularly when his grandmother came to his home and she would speak in Chinanteco to his parents:

> I knew she was accusing us kids of doing something wrong. I could recognised the word *chamaco* [boy], I knew that she was telling my parents how bad I had been and I thought that was so unfair. Since I couldn't understand the language, I was not able to defend myself; I could not understand what she was saying about me. It was so frustrating!

Ethnographic portraits of how students perform at the Centro de Idiomas

With the series of narratives below, César explains his community and familiar background, the history of his pursuit of English, the conflicts that he has encountered in his community because of his use of English and how he has located himself as a student within the *Centro de Idiomas*. These narratives are an interesting mixture of oral histories and critical reflections, which in turn, are representations of how he moves from one identity location to another in his various language contexts.

> My parents are very proud of what I am doing. My father is proud that I have been teaching in our community high school during the summer. We live in a very small town and my father hears people saying, 'Hey, do you know who is teaching at La Forestal [name of a local school], César!' My father says that people are surprised that I am teaching at the school because I am so young. But I think that's the way it should be, you should be putting into practice what you have been learning. It makes you feel different and proud to being doing these things for our community.
>
> The teacher that I am working with has been very supportive and has given me a lot of praise for my efforts. He tells me 'I remember you as a young boy in school and now there is a big difference in your behaviour. Now you are not my student and I am not your teacher, we are working together. We are at the same level now. Your English is very good, your knowledge is very high and you know how to run a class. I am proud that you have been my student.' At the end of the school session we had a big lunch, which my parents were able to attend and hear the praises that I received for my teaching.
>
> Often my father will ask me why I want to learn English. I tell him, 'Look! How is that you can ask me that question? Haven't you realised that English is everywhere now?' Sure Spanish is growing in the United States, but it is a two-way street, as Spanish is spreading in the north, English is spreading towards the South—it is a process of mutual influences. That is why I am learning English.
>
> When I enter the English programme here at the *Centro* I was *sacado de onda* [overwhelmed], that is, I was shocked and scared. I quickly learned that I was not the good student I thought I was. Here the teachers gave you thousands of grammar rules to learn. It was overwhelming for me. I saw that most of my classmates were very well prepared and knew much more than me. I could not understand their use of English and I was very

nervous and insecure. There was such a big difference in our backgrounds. How was it that I, who had been such a good student before, now felt so impotent and lacking in confidence? I was working hard and worried that I was going to fail.

My friends at school like me because I am always joking around and making people laugh a lot. People seem to like it. My friends tell me how they never would have thought I had this kind of *onda* [style] from their first impression of me when I arrived at the *Centro*. They say that I looked scared and shy. That was somewhat true; the city made a grand impression upon me and made me feel very submissive. When I left my home my parents were very supportive. They told me, 'You will not have any problems there because it is very easy for you to meet people and make friends'. But it was hard for me because you have to start from scratch to meet people and to get to know them. You have to figure out who you can get along with and who you can work with.

In the above narratives we noted a shift in status from being the local star student who is able to teach English in the local school, to that of being the overwhelmed young university student. In the following narratives César expands on what the move to Oaxaca meant in terms of changes in his life, which involved not only living without his family but also being able to survive in a new schooling environment:

Living here in the city of Oaxaca is very different from where I came from: the food, the streets, the means of transportation, and specially the people! But now I feel like I have family and friends here. In Oaxaca I have found my own way to live. My landlady is a great person. She wants me to call her 'mother' and she wants to refer to me as her son, even though she has two daughters of her own. I get home from school at around three thirty in the afternoon and we have *comida* together. After eating, I will go to my room and watch some TV. I like movies, and stuff like entertainment news and one or two soap operas. In between various show I will do my homework. As I said before, I am a bit of a procrastinator, and I'm really only focused hard on my work when there are deadlines. For example, if I am going to have a quiz on verbs the next day, then I will study very hard the night before. I am lucky that I have a great memory, it is almost photographic. Some students have to spend a lot more time studying than me.

Maybe I am a little egocentric or ambitious, but I am determined to face the challenges of my life. I want to become someone who has respect from others not based upon what I have but based upon what I know. This makes me a little anti-social and different from my classmates. In fact, I do not like most people, I try to, but it is hard for me. In the end I get bored with other people quickly and thus I do not have a lot of friends at school. I prefer to do my school work or to study by myself, behind the closed door of my own room. I love the tranquillity of my own solitude. Though I have to admit that I often put my school work off to the last minute and do everything on the last day.

I think that I am a holistic learner. I do not wait for my teacher to solve my problems but try to solve them on my own. What I really worry about are my grades. I get nervous when I get grades that are only 8s or 9s. My friends laugh at my concerns because they are only getting 5s or 6s (Here the grades go by numbers, with ten being the highest). At night I will study for awhile, then watch some TV and then go back to studying. I try to remember what I have read without going back to the book. Maybe I will make a table or a chart about the problems that I am working on. Then if I want to, I go back to watching some TV. Sometimes I finish my studying on the bus going to school in the morning. I think now I am more relaxed at school. I am more self-assured and confident. I feel more assured of what I want to say in classes. Now, I can even get distracted in class and be able to get back into what the teacher has been talking about.

César, like many young people who have left the provinces in search of new hopes and goals has had to learn—to paraphrase Thomas Wolfe—that you cannot always go home with ease. Below, César provides several accounts of how he learned that his joy for learning English was not shared by others in his community.

Now when I go back home to visit I do not hang out with my old friends any more. The first time I went back there I tried to meet up with some of my old friends to go fishing at the river. But it was not the same; their attitude towards me was very weird. I felt that I could not bring up what

I was learning about English. For me, it seemed natural that we would compare the differences between Spanish and English, just like talking about the difference between living in the *pueblo* (village/town) and the city. But their attitudes were, 'oh there he goes again talking about his stuff ... Yeah, now you want to be a *gringo*, don't you?' to what I answered, 'No, I am only studying English!' I also wanted to show my friends how much I have learned, but they would say:

'You only come back here to show off. We do not know if what you are saying is really English; it could be any old bullshit. You could be trying to fool us, how would we know?'

'No I'm just trying to show you what I am learning and if you want to know a little English I can help. I do not know everything, but we can look things up.'

'Ahh, just shut up, we are fed up with you!'

'Hey I am just trying to practice because I need to practice my English, that's all'

'Yeah, well then go where they speak English, but not here. If all you want to do is practice that shit, then do it somewhere else.'

Sometimes I will defend myself by saying to them, 'So what are you studying? Accounting? There are around thirty people in the *pueblo* studying to be accountants, but there is only one person studying to be an English teacher, and that is me. Further, finding a job as an accountant is going to be very hard'. Because I take this attitude to defend myself people think that I am showing off.

So now I would rather avoid them. I feel that these attitudes will get much stronger over time and I will lose my feelings for my community and the way I used to be. Now the *pueblo* does not seem as important to me. My mother warns me to be careful in the *pueblo*. She says people have told her that I have been saying such and such that made people feel bad. She says, 'You know that I am proud of all the progress you have made in your education, but people here do not see it that way. They are envious of you and they say that you are showing off. They are not interested in what you are learning and they do not want to hear English words!' These really upsets me and I feel like not going back home at all. She says, 'You should not respond that way. This is where you were born; this is where you are from!'

But I tell her, 'But I feel so unappreciated. What is there here for me to come back to?'

This rather odd situation has forced César to look for a new location in his own community:

> Well, anyway, this Easter I did go home. It was nice because I met some international folks who were visiting the area. Since they did not speak Spanish, I started talking to them in English to explain our activities for the holy week. During the procession from the church many people started looking at us and got upset that we were talking in English. Since we were near the river, I suggested to the visitors that we go there for a while. They did not understand the behaviour of the people in the village, so I explained to them that people here were not used to hearing English and they did not like it.
>
> Later that day, when I went back home, my mother and I had the following exchange:
>
> 'Where were you? Why did you leave the procession?'
>
> 'I left because of the way people were acting; it was like they wanted to run us off.'
>
> 'Why?'
>
> 'Because we were talking in English and they thought that we were talking about them!'
>
> 'You should not pay so much attention to them. But you need to change your attitude about the community or you will regret it tomorrow. You do not have to ask why they'll treat you that way, they just will.'
>
> 'Sorry, mum, but this is who I am and I won't change just because they want me to.'
>
> 'But it does not have to end in a bad way. Why don't you take it easy? Ignore them. That would be better.'
>
> 'But why can't they be the ones to ignore me. As soon as I arrive they start to fuck with me. If they want to mess around with me, then they will have to cope with my reactions. If they talk about me then I talk back about them. I can't ignore them and I am not afraid of them. I'll tell them right to their faces what I think. If they want to humiliate me, I will do back to them!'
>
> That is the way my mother and I talk.

As a means to reduce the ambiguity and hostility that César was encountering in his community, he used his visit to his grandmother. With her, he developed an interesting language exchange that moved between Chinanteco and English. Also, he told us that watching films in English provided a safe house to protect his language performances and perhaps his self esteem. In his home he would spend the whole day watching films in English. Through these activities, he could be free of the tensions resulting from his public performances of English in the community. And so, he had two safe houses in which three different languages were being performed.

> They speak Chinanteco here, but I don't. My grandparents speak Chinanteco, but not my parents. Even though I don't speak the language, I can understand some of it. Now, when my grandmother speaks to me in Chinanteco, I answer her back in English. She tells me that it would have been wonderful if I had learned Chinanteco because then I would know three languages. I too think it would have been good for me to have learned some Chinanteco, because it is such a hard language to pronounce. Your tongue gets quite flexible and that would have helped me in my pronunciation of English words. For example, now when I ask my grandmother to repeat words in English it is very easy for her, she does not even have much of an accent. For her it very easy to repeat the English words, hardly with any effort at all. It is that tongue movement of hers from all those years of speaking Chinanteco. I think if she could seriously study English she would be better at it than me. She is always very happy when I come home to visit and is proud that I am learning English and that I will share my English with her. She will ask how to say this or that in English. She tells me I must study and practice.
>
> I have talked to my grandmother about my problems with my old friends in the community. She thinks that the reaction of the others in the *pueblo* is because of envy, they cannot do what I am doing. She says to me, 'It must be difficult what you are learning, no? Do you connect learning English with Spanish?' She is always asking me to say things in English to her and then she compares them to Chinanteco.
>
> I know that this attitude of mine can sound selfish and stubborn. But that's how I feel. I am not planning to go home for Mother's Day, but I know that my grandmother is sick, nothing serious, but I should go and

see her. But why should I go back and get hassled all the time? If people do not want to see me, well then I will please them by not going!

My siblings only speak Spanish and all the movies they like to watch are in Spanish. To tell you the truth, I do not like Mexican movies like *Amores Perros*. I think they are boring. They are about things I already know.

My mother and I had the following exchange about the value of films:

'I think that these new Mexican films are kind of dumb and I do not learn anything from them. What am I supposed learn from *Y tu mamá también*, that two bums can take off and travel around the country? Is that what I am supposed to do?'

She says back to me, 'But what do you get from your American movies?'

I answered, 'Maybe there is not always a message in these films, but at least I can practice my English and check my level of comprehension. Also I can learn some new vocabulary, something that I can use.'

'You know, I write those new words down and then when I am in class I use them and everybody is very impressed with my English. The teacher will ask me where I got those words from and I tell him I heard them in a movie.'

In the following narrative, César reflects further upon the importance of having a command over English in the contemporary world of globalisation, the conflicts this pursuit of linguistic capitals has cost him in terms of his community relations, and his implicit recognition of the colonial difference in terms of the spectre of the hovering ghost of the native speaker. It is interesting that he notes this in terms of relations of authority between Spanish and English and not between Chinanteco and these other language regimes.

Today our society has become very demanding of us. Now, when you go to look for a job, no matter how modest, the main requirement for the job will be knowledge and competence in a specific foreign language: English. No question that this reality has killed the hopes of many people looking for jobs, who more than likely do not even know what a foreign language is. However, this reality has also awakened a desire among many people to seek to learn English as a means to progress in their lives and to improve their lives.

I certainly place myself among these people with the desire to progress. To achieve that progress in my life I applied to this school to get a degree that will certify my quest for an ample knowledge of English. Though this seems like a straight forward goal, I have come to realise that there are many obstacles along this path of progress. This is because there are so many differences between speaking Spanish and English. In starting to learn a second language you have to start so slowly, from scratch basically. It is like we are little children again and we have to be taught all the simple words again, like 'dad', 'mum', 'aunt', 'hello', 'I love you', etc. For me this is very upsetting. I am already a grown up, and I want to be taught more advanced ideas or words. This negative feeling can prevent us from understanding that we have to build a foundation first before we can advance. There can be no progress in life if we do not obey that simple rule.

Besides all these learning pressures, there are what I would call societal pressures. When I go home to my *pueblo* to visit my friends, they are not nice to me any more. They are rejecting me because I am learning English. They think that I am turning my back on my own culture and language. They think that I am only trying to show off when I speak English.

They do not understand how hard it has been for me to learn this new language. I try to tell them that I will never become a native speaker of English, but I am going to work very hard to become competent in this language. Thus, in spite of all these difficulties and all the time it takes to learn English, we have no other alternative but to continue to work hard and do our best. We have to believe that at some time we can speak English with the ease that we can speak Spanish.

Reflections on César's story

Like many of his fellow language learners at the *Centro*, César's performance of English with a postcolonial accent is far from being perfect; not *per se* in terms of his language skills, but in terms of his social struggle in locating himself within the new and old social fields that he is part of. For him this involves issues about his family, his community, the contradictions in his learning community and the global implications of having access to English. His various performances can be read as consequences of his ambition or as the errors of a stubborn young man. However, we feel that a better reading might note the energy and hope that he invests in his endeavours and the courage that he shows in his willingness to be his own guide. To this we need to add his acceptance that his performances often place him in the ambiguous location of being in-between the social folds of his actual and imagined communities (Anderson, 1991; Norton, 2001).

He grew up in a Chinanteco community, one of the poorest regions in the state. His family comes from a somewhat marginal but better off household in the community, thus he is able to pursue his educational desires. He feels a commitment to his community and a hope to fulfil that commitment through teaching and particularly through the teaching of English. He feels that is in contrast to other students of his generation who choose to go into areas that were perhaps more economically rewarding, but not ones that would (for him) directly help the community. However, on many of his trips back to the community, he finds that his attempts to share his English with others are scorned and rejected. He feels great pride in his success at summer teaching in his local school, but anger at his mates in his community who would not affirm his achievements and his willingness to share those with others. He finds that these conflicts put him at odds with his family, like when his mother warned him of the importance of getting along with others in the community. In his youthful stubbornness, he is ready to do battle so that his attempts are seen as a contribution to the community rather than some form of pride and boasting. But concerned by his mother's worries, he avoids these battles by seeking solace in the imaginary world of English speaking films where he could attempt to improve his language skills.

In the social world of the *Centro de Idiomas* he confronts similar tensions in his performances. In his tales, he offers little or no information on his views or concerns about the issues of gender, sexuality or ethnicity. He found his early entrance into this social world challenging; everything was different and more complex than in his home community. He found a safe house in the context of a household where he rented his room and was proud that his landlady wanted him to call her 'mother'. He regards himself as a loner who enjoys his own company while at the same time explains how he is popular with friends and school mates because of his style of humour. He is proud of his struggle to make himself a good student at the *Centro* and of the fact that now he is seen as one of the best students. He is quite aware, however, that some of his study habits, like his habit of procrastinating, are counter-productive and that this can put him in conflictive situations with his professors. He is proud of his 'photographic' memory, but does not want to act like he is better than the other students. He attempts to offer them study guides, but often they feel he is acting like he is better than them.

We could say that he is learning from his social struggle at performing English with a postcolonial accent. One can sense in his actions an embryonic presence of an awareness of the colonial difference in his understanding of the value of languages and an emerging expression of what we refer to as the politics of affinity in his quest to be a good teacher. He moves in-between his various social worlds. He code-switches between the narrative styles of the oral tradition of his Chinanteco community and the styles of critical self-reflection of his university world. He accepts that he loses a little bit of both by being located in-between them. For him, these losses are part of his struggle to better himself through his education and his learning English. He uses his agency to compose his various identities around his goal of progress and to do what he wants to do in his own way. He does not feel that his attainment of English is a denial of his Chinanteco community nor does he feel that in seeking English he is capitulating to forms of linguistic imperialism. Though these feelings may change as his youthful optimism is tempered by time, for now, these are pursuits of his own choosing for his own well-being. This is best evidenced by the language performance between him and his grandmother in which she is teaching him Chinanteco while he is teaching her English.

Yolanda's reaffirmation of her ethnic identity

Yolanda is one of our most recent encounters during this research process. The first time I (Angeles) talked to her, she approached me to ask to get into my course on speaking skills evaluation. She told me she had heard it was a course to improve speaking skills and she wanted to do so. I accepted her in my class and I assigned her to one of the teams already working with a student-tutor. I designed the course in such a way that advanced students would be taught learning strategies for speaking which they, in turn, would teach to novice students. During the course they would report to me about their tutees' progress. According to her tutor, Yolanda was shy and quiet but willing to work. At the end of the course, I decided that I wanted to corroborate the speaking skills of the students, so I was present in their last assignment which was an oral presentation of a topic they had chosen. The range of topics was quite varied and ranged from ghost stories to marriage costumes in the Isthmus. Yolanda chose to talk about the discrimination of indigenous people. When it was her team's turn, she decided to be the last one. She started in a low, paced voice and tried to make her pronunciation clear. However, at a certain moment while she was speaking she started to cry. I asked her if it was all right to go on and she assured me that she wanted to finish. As she was the last one to participate, I sent everybody home and asked her to stay and talk. Then she told me that her speech was not about the discrimination of indigenous people in general but about the discrimination that she and her family had suffered. We talked for some time and she told me that in fact she was very proud of her indigenous heritage. When we finished our conversation, she seemed to be feeling better. The following day, Yolanda came to school wearing, for the first time, her indigenous clothes. This is the way Yolanda tells the story of her family:

> My name is Yolanda. I am a student and twenty-one years-old. I am from San Juan Copala, a small Trique village in the Sierra Mixteca, five hours from the city of Oaxaca.[14] I have two marvellous parents. My father is Mariano, sixty and my mother Catalina, fifty-four. I have six siblings, all older than me. My oldest brother is Fausto; he is thirty-four years-old, is married and has two daughters. My second brother is Sergio; he is thirty years-old and works with my parents. My third, brother is Mariano. He is my mother's headache, but I still love him. He is twenty-seven and studies architecture. Catalina, my sister, is the fourth child of the family. She is twenty-five years-old, has a bachelor's degree in Educational Sciences from the university here in Oaxaca. She is married and has one child. My other sister, Filomena is the fifth child. She is studying to be a nurse, also here at the university. And finally there is me, the youngest and my mother's baby. My parents were each married before, I have two step siblings from my father's first marriage and also two from my mother's other marriage.

14 Triques inhabit the western most part of Oaxaca, inhabiting a territory of approximately 193 square miles, bordering on the Mixteco municipality of Mixtepec, to the north. To the south, it borders on Constancia del Rosario, a Mestizo town. To the east, it is limited by the Mixteco towns of Santo Tomas Ocotepec, and to the west, with the town of Juxtlahuaca, and the Guerrero state line. The Trique area is extremely treacherous, since most of it is located in the Sierra de Chicahuaxtla, which is part of the Southern Sierra Madre. Altitudes vary from 2,625 feet to 10,000 above sea level, allowing for the presence of a variety of ecological resources. Their primary economic activity is fundamentally agriculture; they grow corn, chilli, squash and beans. This agricultural production is mainly for self consumption and for selling in the regional markets. The Trique are also well known for their weaving productions. As of 1995, the population for the Triques was 16, 271, with over 68% of the population being bilingual in Spanish and Trique (Barabas and Bartolomé (eds.), 1999).

My parents are now both Christians. They were Catholic before, but my father told me that, once, when my brother Mariano was a baby, he got very sick and they went to pray to the Catholic Church, but he didn't get better. Then, they went to the Christian Church and the people there got together and prayed with them to get help for my brother. They also helped them economically and the baby got better. He also told me that, on another occasion, he had made a promise to go to a Christian temple, but he didn't go. Instead he chose to go to Monterrey to sell their merchandise in a fair there. He says that God punished him and that's why he was sent to prison there. In jail he got in touch with other Christians and he even got married with my mother while he was in jail. I grew up within that religion. My parents taught us to believe in that, but now I do not feel that religious. I have changed a lot, being here in the school. But I don't want to argue with my parents about it, because my mother has recently been found to be diabetic. We now are controlling her diet. The doctor told us that she could suffer a diabetic comma if we don't take care of her. My father also suffers from high blood pressure. So we are very careful and avoid making them angry. So we go to church with them without complaining.

Yolanda also offered her understanding of the cultural dynamics of her *pueblo* and Trique culture. She provides both praise and criticisms of her background, particularly in the area of gender relations and community violence:

Because of my parents, I speak both Spanish and my indigenous language, Trique. We are noted for the fact that most of the women still wear the traditional red *huipiles* [that are woven on *telar de cintura* (back strip loom)] and an *enahua*, which is a woollen or cotton skirt. Most people in my *pueblo* speak Spanish now. Trique is spoken now mostly by only older people and some women. I lived in my *pueblo* for a very short time, though my father has still a house there. I would like to write my thesis about something connected to my *pueblo*. Nobody in the family wants to stay there, we only go for visits. My half-brother went back and he is an accountant but he is working as a driver because there is no work and his wife is selling meals there for the same reason. It is very pretty there and I think our culture is unique and important. I don't want to say that there are not problems among the Trique, such as machismo and unfortunately, the long histories of feuds between communities which often lead to violence and killings.

In my *pueblo*, people marry very young. A man chooses a girl and he goes to see her parents and they agree on a date for the wedding. She doesn't even know. They pay for the girl. I don't like that. I don't want to get married yet. I have to finish my degree and get a job. I have had the experience of having to take care of children and I don't want that yet. It is a big responsibility and it takes a lot of effort. Men in my *pueblo* are very *machos*. For example, married women are not supposed to look directly at other men. You can still see how they look at the floor instead of looking at people, because their husbands are so jealous. Men do not cook or take care of anything in the house. I do not know if you have noticed that here in the *Zócalo* (central town square), at our market stands, men do not work. While women are selling in the stands they sit in the back and chat with their male friends. They are *mantenidos* [irresponsible and lazy]. In the village they either work the land or go to the States. There are exceptions, like my father. At the beginning he taught us that men do not cook and men do not cry but later on he realised that everybody has to help and that women need to work outside the house as well. My father never made the difference between boys that needed to study and girls that should stay at home. There in the *pueblo*, men have several women living in the same house. My mother was married before and her husband took other two women to live with them and he also beat them. She left him. She said, 'He can stay with the other two. I am leaving'. But women that leave their husbands are *repudiadas* [repudiated], so she left the village.

Maybe I will someday get a *novio* [fiancé], but if I do, he will have to wait till I finished my education. I don't know if I want a Trique *novio*, or somebody from here or a foreigner. Here in the *pueblo*, they think it is bad if couples hold hands and touch. I would like to have a relationship but not in my *pueblo*, it would be impossible to get used to their restrictions. My father doesn't want us to have *novios*. He wants us to finish our studies first. It is taken as a lack of respect to one's parents if you have a *novio* without their permission. When my sister had her boyfriend, my father was very strict with her, very jealous. They thought that she would make a mistake and lose her virginity. They think that a woman that is not virgin is a woman of the street. Virginity is important for them and it is important to me because they taught me that.

The Triques have been part of urban social context of the city of Oaxaca for more than thirty years. They have been primarily street merchants attempting to sell their weaving and other *ropa típica* (typical clothing) within the tourist economy of city. Below Yolanda gives an account of her family's enterprises.

We make *ropa típica* of the Triques: *vestidas, huipile,* [dresses, blouses,] *rebosos* [shawls], and bracelets. My mother weaves different *huipiles* on a *telar de cintura* [back strap loom], my father sews the *manta* [muslin] clothes into garments like blouses or shirts, and the whole family works at selling the clothing, especially when there is a lot of work. In the past, during time of school vacations we went to other states to sell our goods. My parents have a stand in the main market in the city and in the evenings and during the weekends we also sell in the centre of the city. When my parents first arrived to work in the main market it was not very well developed and most the streets were still unpaved. Now it is much better.

We are not involved with middlemen in either the production or selling of our weaving. We make and sell all the weaving ourselves. It is not easy to get permission to sell your goods and it is expensive. I think our prices are just. Clearly the clothing that is embroidered costs more than other items, because these items take a lot of time. In my village, some middlemen go and buy really cheap and they come to the city and sell these things at much higher price. That is not fair. People who make the clothes should be the ones that sell them.

When Yolanda was quite young, her father was incarcerated on very vague charges. Yolanda correctly feels that his time in jail was a reflection of the ways that the indigenous people in Oaxaca (and throughout Mexico) are often exploited because of their lack of Spanish.

Then sorrow came to our home many years ago when my father was put into jail.
My father went to jail because they took him for another person. My father was on a bus going to Monterrey because he was going to a fair to

sell the clothes my mother had made. In the bus he started talking with the man sitting next to him. The police thought this man was involved in illegal activities, he was arrested and they also arrested my father because they thought that they were travelling together. And because my father did not speak Spanish fluently he was not able to defend himself. I think that happens with a lot to indigenous people. And I still do not know if they provide translators for indigenous people when they have to go to court. Besides, it was very difficult for my father to have this trial in Monterrey, where there were no indigenous groups and since it was many years ago, there were not any programmes to help indigenous people caught in the legal system. Later, he was transferred to Miahuatlan, Oaxaca. My mother used to take us to visit him. They actually got formally married while he was in jail. Before they got married, they were only what they called *juntados* [free union]. My father had a twelve year sentence but because of his good behaviour, he got paroled after seven years. As part of his parole, he had to check in each week. After that it was difficult for my father to start his life again. He only wanted to be at home and not go out where people had so many questions for him.

The seven years my father was in jail were a hell for my mother and the rest of us. She didn't want to go out to sell, because she did not speak Spanish at all. But she had to start selling at night, going to restaurants in the *Zócalo* to offer her goods. We also went out to sell. In the morning we sold chewing gum and at night woven bracelets that we made ourselves. There were people that bought from us and people that looked down on us. Once my mother was offering something and this woman called her *pata rajada* [derogative term for poor indigenous people] and my mother started crying and the woman laughed at her. Another problem was the government inspectors. Since we had no money for permits or to offer for bribes, they would confiscate our goods. My father would help from the jail. He wove hammocks and bags and gave them to us to sell.

In chapter two we provided a summary of the political events that surrounded the teachers' strike and the emergence of the popular political movements organised under the structure of people's assemblies called APPO. Like Jorge and Ervin (in chapter five), Yolanda's life and daily activities were framed by these events.

Since the emergence of APPO, there seems to be a feeling of unity among people, we are all united, especially the indigenous peoples. We support each other. Since the folks of APPO had been occupying the *Zócalo*, we watched out for them at night while they slept, and they let us sell our goods in the streets during the day. When the teachers strike began, we were selling our goods at a stand that was in the *Zócalo*. We were not involved with the teachers' strike; we were just there to sell our stuff. However, after the 14th of June, when the governor sent the police to violently remove the teachers, we have gotten involved. The movement had grown from teachers to all other sorts of groups seeking social justice, like us from the Trique communities. This new alliance named itself APPO. If we did not sell anything during the day, the APPO folks would share their food and coffee with us. Thus, for doing the night watching, we would work in two shifts, one from twelve at night to three in the morning, and then a second shift from three in the morning until seven in the morning. I do not know what we thought about the problem of the teachers. But I know for sure that it was very unjust to send the police to attack and evacuate them. I do not know if we were in danger for supporting the APPO. This October, when the federal police had driven the APPO supporters out of the *Zócalo*, all of the stalls of vendors, like ours, were destroyed. Luckily, now that the conflict is over, we haven't been pursued. We do not have to hide ourselves, but the whole thing has affected us. We have not been able to sell a lot because there are no people in Oaxaca. There were more tourists when APPO was in the *Zócalo*, now there are no tourists. The APPO group my father was supporting is now in Juxtlahuaca (a town in the Trique zone). They are not here now, but they are still organised. Many of them came back to a demonstration a few days ago. I do not know if anybody was caught and thank God none of them was sent to jail. The other day we saw a demonstration with the families of the people in jail. They took off their shirts and tied their hands with tape and carried chains in their feet. It was very shocking, very sad.

My father has always liked talking about politics; it is one of his favourite topics. Fortunately, he doesn't get very involved. In our village, people get very political. As I said earlier, they even kill each other over their political views. The major groups in conflict are the MULT (*Movimiento Unificador de la Lucha Triqui*) and MULTI (*Movimiento*

Unificador de la Lucha Triqui Independiente) which are rival groups claiming to speak for the Triques. There is now a new group, called the UBISORT (*Unidad de Bienestar Social de la Región Triqui*). It gets confusing at times. Back in our *pueblo*, my father belongs to a group that supports the old ruling party the PRI, but here in the city he is very supportive of the APPO. I do not understand all of these affairs.

Yolanda pursuit of education is a tale of great persistence and courage. As she states:

> The first time my mother left me without saying anything and I asked my sister Caty what was going on. She told me our mother had to go to work and that I should not cry. I started to cry a lot and she told me:
> 'Don't cry, Mum is coming back'
> 'Why did she go?'
> 'To sell the clothes to pay for the school and the food'
> 'Then I don't want to study. I want to be with her'
> 'No, Yolis [short for Yolanda], Mum wants you to study'
> Caty was the oldest so she was the one to take care of me because my mother told her so. When my parents came back I was very happy. I ran to them and I hugged them and told my mother that she had been very bad because she had left me, and she said:
> 'Do you think I enjoy doing it? I do it because we need the money to pay the school. When I leave my children I suffer a lot, but I love you a lot so I do it.'
> I also remember when I told my father that I didn't want to study. He said:
> 'No, daughter. Study. Study because I don't want you to suffer from sleeping on the floor and to suffer the cold weather or the lack of food. I want you to study and in the future to finish your studies and work in an office. Do you want to keep selling and suffering?'
> 'No'
> 'Daughter, your mother and I have suffered working hard to get money for your school. Don't you see your mother all day weaving, sometimes all night as well. She does it for you. That's why you have to make the effort to go to school'
> 'Yes father. I will do it I will put everything I can to finish my studies'

Then I understood why they worked so hard.

So my siblings and I would go off to school holding hands like our father told us to. We went back from school the same way, walking and holding hands.

When my father was released from jail, I was just finishing elementary school. Then he took me to secondary school and taught me how to go and come back. Later I started high school. I remember once that I went to school wearing my *huipil* [traditional blouse] and the gatekeeper said, 'You are coming to school not to a carnival' and he laughed at me. Then I also started to notice that some guys made fun of my way of speaking, imitating my Spanish and Trique. That made me self-conscious when speaking which I tried to avoid. I was becoming ashamed of my great culture and origins. But I have also noticed that foreign people were enthralled when they saw my mother weaving in her *telar de cintura* and wearing the clothes from my *pueblo*. Many indigenous youngsters suffer maltreatment and bullying because they are not in 'fashion' and that causes them to hide and forget the language that they were taught by their parents. Thank God I have moved from that stage, thanks to my family, and thanks to the people that have told me that it is marvellous to speak two languages.

Now I am studying at the *Centro*. I am in Fourth Semester. My parents do not go to *ferias* [fairs] any more. We, their children, still help them to make and sell the merchandise. Thank God our economic situation is stable, thanks to their efforts and work.

In the following paragraphs we have summarised Yolanda's reasons for entering the B.A. programme and her feelings about her multilingualism.

I've got into this programme because we sell clothes, typical clothes, and it is essential to speak English, because when foreigners come to my stand they do not speak Spanish. Sometimes I speak English with my friends, even with my mother, although she does not understand me. Then she says in Trique '*Ya tú, níca's gringo*' which means 'Stop it, you, gringo's wife'. It is a joke. They also tell me that I will marry a *gringo*, but it is their joke because I speak English. Sometimes with my sister I practice a little. When I am selling, other women get cross with me because I speak English and they don't. It would be good to teach them English. Very often, foreigners really appreciate that we can speak several languages. Once, a woman asked me for the price of one our weavings and I asked my mother in Trique language how much it was. Then this woman told me that it was very good to speak another language and she told me not to lose my language and fight to maintain it. This was very encouraging to me, to meet people who admire that I speak three languages. They even ask us to teach them some Trique. They say, 'What a beautiful language and what beautiful clothes that you sell.'

I do not feel different knowing that I speak three languages. I feel the same. It feels nice to be able to speak English; however it is not that difficult to speak three languages. Maybe I feel that way because I am already used to switching between Trique and Spanish. My father is proud of me. I am the only one in the family that speaks English. I have become friends with many of these internationals, but since they are often only here for a few weeks, there is not much time to build strong friendships. They come and go. I would like to go to the States some day to study for a M. A. or to work as a teacher but not as *mojada* [an illegal immigrant]. In my village a lot of people go to the States. It is almost a ghost town now. But I didn't want to study English just to go away. My need to learn English is to sell in my stand, and also because my father used to tell us that we had to study a degree. I would like to be a teacher in the States.

However, in the classroom, I am afraid to talk, because there are always students that know English better than me and they make fun of you if you get something wrong. Foreigners are more understanding. In the classroom I remain silent. But my grades in English are good. I have never failed any subject. I have a few friends at school, but I get along with everybody. Nayelli is my best friend and sometimes we speak in English in the street for people not to understand us. But I do not speak English with everybody. It doesn't come naturally. It is not spontaneous. And it has to be that way, not be forced. I think my English comes more naturally with a foreigner than with my classmates.

My life has changed with my English because I have met a lot of people at our stand. Before, when they found out that we did not speak English, they would ask us to write the price on a paper and that is not necessary any more and they also tell me that my pronunciation is good. Before, I did not relate with foreigners. Also, before I was the interpreter for my mother because she did not speak Spanish, now I am the interpreter of other Trique vendors, because they do not speak English.

I always wanted to go somewhere else, to another country and meet people. Now I also think that I want to be a teacher and give courses of English in my village or go to the States to teach my Trique language. Now, with what I have learned, there is a lot that I could do for my family or my community.

Reflections on Yolanda's story

Yolanda's story is quite dramatic in its simplicity and a telling tale of the everyday struggles that indigenous peoples of Oaxaca deal with. It is also quite illuminating about how these young language actors move in and out of various identity locations as they are performing their English with a postcolonial accent. Yolanda deals with the colonial difference not only in opposition between English and Spanish, but between these two dominant language regimes in relation to Trique, her indigenous language. English gives her a means by which she can explain and defend her own cultural heritage. With English, she can better explain the important qualities of her culture that are entwined within their weaving and clothing. With English, she can also eliminate the Spanish language as a 'middle person' between her culture and the world outside of the provincial views of Oaxaca. She can use English to counter the lightly veiled racist assumptions offered about the Triques and other indigenous Oaxacan peoples. At this point in her journey, English is serving to reinforce the cultural capital that she has accumulated as a young Trique woman and it has opened new ways for her to understand that background. It may also be the case that, because Spanish is the dominant language in Mexico, English is for Yolanda a neutral language (Kachru, 1986; Kumaravadivelu, personal communication[15]), not loaded with an imperialistic connotation, but a linguistic benefit that locates her in a better position.

As she proclaims the importance of her Trique heritage, she has also become aware of its own internal contradictions, especially in terms of the dynamics of community violence and gender inequality. She moves between questioning

---

15 Kumaravadivelu's insight about a certain neutrality of English in the context of Oaxaca is very useful to our overall understanding of the postcolonial accent. It can be noted through the various performances of these students and those to come in the following chapters. At certain points in the drama entailed in these language activities, they are attracted to and hope to use English as a mode of communication that seems neutral to their national and regional identities and who they want to be. However, that neutrality is constantly challenged by the authority of the colonial difference in the form of native-speakerism.

whether she could live within the restrictive confines of her community's assumptions about gender roles and obligations, while being able to accept the regulation her sexuality to honour her parents' values. She rightfully praises the family solidarity that allowed them to survive the illegal incarceration of her father, while at time recognising where the fissures in the unity were. She is critical of the dubious assumptions about male privilege among urban Trique males and proud that her father was able to move beyond them. She is also aware of the social domain that encompasses the internal dynamics of Oaxaca's postcolonial context, where the Spanish speaking world imposes its domination upon the indigenous world. This awareness is strongly expressed in the way she explains the context of her father's time in jail and her accounts of the racist attitudes that she has encountered in her journey through the educational system.

Clearly César and Yolanda construct their safe houses within their rich ethnic multilingual environments, César in his metalinguistic conversations with his grandmother and Yolanda within her ordinary role as translator between her mother's language and her customers' English. However, they provide an interesting contrast on how one can deal with one's ethnic identity location. César, though equally proud of his cultural heritage, is in conflict with his community for what he felt was its lack of support for the goals that he was attempting to attain and because they did not understand that these goals would in turn, benefit the community. With his youthful idealism, he was going to be their English guide to confront the globalised world. Furthermore, Yolanda seems to want to use her English as means to advocate the importance of being indigenous and to confront issues of social justice. Ironically, like Jorge, Yolanda found herself directly dealing with these concerns within Oaxaca's political turmoil last year.

For Yolanda, the degree in English was not the direct goal of her pursuit of educational capital; her goal was to obtain a university degree. As mentioned in chapter two, her parents held views similar to other parents in that for them it was the university degree that was valued rather than the subject matter *per se*. Again, in wishing to honour her parents' struggles to support her, she too accepts this position. Unlike Facundo, the *Centro* has not been able to represent a safe house, since her ethnic background and her Spanish are at stake there. For her, the safe houses are located in all the encounters that she has when selling her goods to international tourists. It is there where she feels free to perform her English and to present herself as a multilingual young woman, a fact that has been praised several times. It has been in this context in which pursuing

English has been a means to express her identity as a Trique. There, no one told her that she should not wear her *hupuil*. There she found encouragement and support. On the other hand, it was in the context of the *Centro* that she authored (significantly in third person) her declaration of indigenous language rights. It is in the *Centro* where she feels timid about expressing herself in the classroom for fear of criticism from students that she felt were better than her. She found it easier to speak English mainly to internationals, to her friend, and even to her family.

And so, like the other students presented in these portraits, Yolanda's journey to pursue English involves moving through various identity locations—ethnicity, gender, sexuality and social class—while accumulating different forms of linguistic and cultural capital. It is her ethnic identity that currently frames the importance of her other locations, with the ironic twist that English should enhance that concern. These forms of her intercultural interaction are suggestive of what we mean by a politics of affinity.

Conclusion

These ethnographic portraits illustrate how these young social actors are finding ways to perform their various identities within social spaces located in the multicultural and multilingual context of the *Centro*. These performances deal with how they are composing themselves as young adults (Blackman, 2004; Butler, 2004; Holland, et al., 2004; Jacquemet, 2005); how they are using agency to accumulate different forms of linguistic and cultural capital (Ortner, 2006); how they are confronting challenges to the authenticity of their performances (Li, 2007); and how they are encountering the reality of colonial difference in their everyday lives (Mignolo, 2005).

As we have stated, we see the *Centro* as a contact zone where the various language regimens that are situated in this multicultural context confront each other. Though the primary confrontation is between English and Spanish, there is the presence of the indigenous languages of Oaxaca and various uses of European and Asian languages. These young students are playing between these different language regimes as a way to rehearse how to perform the diversity of social elements that they are using to compose their young adultness. This involves their moving in and out of the various identity locations of gender, class, ethnicity, sexuality, and nationality. The particular social dynamics of the *Centro* offers these students access to safe houses where they can hold their rehearsals. The above social practices no doubt can be seen as general to the process of the way young students, whether they be language or geography students or whether they are located in Oaxaca or in Canterbury, compose how they want to perform their young adultness. However, the important social difference is that these performances are taking place in the postcolonial context of Oaxaca and the presence of English in these social folds queers these dynamics, both positively and negatively. Positively in the sense that the addition of English to this multicultural stew offers them new means to the accumulation of linguistic and cultural capital, and negatively because it opens to them questions about their cultural and linguistic authenticity.

The activity of composing a script that can authentically express who one is, or who one wants to be as a young adult is a process that contains numerous challenges, contradictions, confrontations and ambiguities. These young actors are using their agency as a project to compose what they want to be as young adults and to resist what others assumed they should be (Ortner, 2006). For these young adults, with these performances that are taking place in the multicultural and multilingual contact zone of the *Centro*, they find that who they want to be is called into question because of conflicting language ideologies (Gal, 1989; Woolard and Schieffelin, 1994). Nour is never questioned about her attainment of English, for it seems obvious that, with her amount of cultural capital, she would have a command over English. What is questioned is how she wants to express her intelligence and sexuality. Facundo finds acceptance of his sexuality but is challenged by his family for wanting to be something else with his English and was confronted by young middle class Oaxacans who perceived him as someone that should not have English skills. Jorge, like Nour, is not questioned about having English skills also because of his cultural capital, but he has to sort through the contradictions of his politics and the politics of the English speaking world. Elena's skills at social accommodation helps her with both her family and social networks at the *Centro*, but finds that such accommodations produce ambiguous results, that do not *per se* express who she wants to be. César wants his pursuit to be an English teacher to be recognised by his community as a worthy and helpful goal, but finds confrontations and contradictions as he seeks to affirm those goals in his community. Yolanda finds that her quest for English offers hope to her family and community, but opens up for her the contradictions about her community, especially around the issues of gender. The possible value of their symbolic capital becomes a contested site over who has the authority or power to say what can or will count as an authentic expression of selfhood or young adultness.

These conflicts become woven into their language studies in terms of the questions about proper and appropriate means to learn and use language skills, and in the case of English, the presence of the 'hovering ghost of the native speaker.' For us, this is where the stage is set for them to perform English with a postcolonial accent. In this postcolonial context they are confronting the daily reality of colonial difference, that is, the question of the geopolitics of knowledge production: who gets to produce knowledge and whose knowledge has more authority and control (Mignolo, 2002). For Nour, Jorge, Facundo and Elena, their quest for attaining a command over English brings them within the boundaries of these power dynamics, whereas for César and Yolanda their linguistic spaces now deal with ideological claims of both Spanish and English. Thus, for these young students to pursue who they are and who they wanted be as young adults, English can be a 'weapon' or counter-hegemonic stands in confronting colonial difference. In the social spaces of English as a second or additional language, what Holliday (2005) calls *native-speakerism*, is for us an expression of the geopolitics of language learning.

These young students all entered the *Centro* with different types of linguistic and cultural capital and each used their agency to add to or modify their particular funds. Nour and Jorge entered with great amounts of educational or academic capital because of their parents' professional backgrounds. Facundo and Elena entered with a sensitivity to social class dynamics because of their family backgrounds, whereas César and Yolanda came with the cultural capital of their indigenous communities, and Yolanda entered with the undervalued richness of her Trique language. It is clear that Nour and Jorge's forms of capital helped them within their academic pursuits, whereas the others had to modify their existing funds so as to be useful in the context of the *Centro*. How well they moulded, altered and pursued these forms of capital, as they were performing from their various identity locations, would be reflected in the symbolic capital they could accumulate from their activities (Norton, 2000). The diversity of their performances suggests a successful process; but they have all had to deal with questions about the authenticity of who they are (Garcia Canclini, 2004). Thus, for these students to be themselves, and particularly for the way they can be themselves in this other language of English, there is a confrontation of these patterns of power and authority by performing their postcolonial accents. As we suggest throughout our analysis, such performances encourage a form of linguistic praxis that we refer to as a politics of affinity. This is most dramatically seen in Jorge's account of his actions during the last year's political conflicts in

Oaxaca. In the following chapters we will see how this plays out in how these students use their language learning cultures as a means to pursue these goals and how they locate themselves in order to make demands on how they want to learn and use their language skills in both Spanish and English.

Chapter 4

Exorcising the ghost of the native speaker in the contact zone: The use of safe houses in the construction of learning cultures

Introduction

It all started with an assignment in the first year of our studies. We had to work for the whole day at Paulina's house. From that activity, Paulina, Itzela, and Luisa started hanging around together (there were other girls that left the clique because of 'personality differences'). Later Viviana joined it. Although there were some differences we learned how to solve them, making it very tight by the fourth semester. By this time it became evident for our classmates that we were a very close and strong group. The last one to become a member was Itzel, who had been part of other cliques.

We are very well integrated, although our personalities are very different. Maybe the reason for this is that we are always trying to develop a nice ambiance around us. Having been together for three years we are very fond of each other and enjoy our time with each other. Actually our differences have taught us how to get along and know each other better. We think that we complement each other very well. We are also aware that among us we have closer relationships with one or two, but that happens in any social group of more than three people .(*Las Malditas*)

In the last chapter, we provided ethnographic portraits of six different students and their particular journeys towards performing English with a postcolonial accent. We have tried to locate them within the various contexts of their family, community and personal histories. As we pondered the way to illustrate how these young language actors situated themselves in order to exorcise the ghost of the native speaker, it seemed clear that their actions were more collective than singular. In terms of our use of the conceptual frameworks of contact zones and safe houses, we also needed to capture various forms of social interaction as these students constructed their learning cultures. As often is the case, what we were looking for was right in front of us. These students were staging their learning actions from within their own social groups at the *Centro*, that is, it was within their cliques that they formulated, practised and carried out what they wanted to do with English. With the *Centro* being a contact zone between the discursive worlds of Spanish and English, these cliques built their safe houses in which they could construct their learning cultures.[16] In turn, by constructing various language learning cultures, they were able to play with their own styles of language creativity in both Spanish and English. And so, in this chapter we will exemplify and analyse three different aspects of their performances within their safe houses: exorcising the ghost of the native speaker; carrying out transidiomatic practices and; performing as themselves and as the other.

Following Woolard (2005), we argue that within these social fields these students are responding to existing language ideologies about both authenticity (how unpolluted their Spanish remains) and standards (how acceptable their English is). Moreover, they are composing their own alternatives to both language regimes (ibid.). Through an ethnographic analysis of their conceptions of English, their practice routines and their word games, that is, their performances about and with the language, we can illustrate how they are locating themselves beyond the identity locations of native and non-native speakers and how they engage in ludic performances in both languages.

Exorcising the ghost of the native speaker by disinventing English

In order to explore our theme of exorcising the ghost of the native, let us introduce one of the three cliques we have been working with, *Los Gabos*, a name that they chose for themselves. This is a group of three students: Freda, Braulio and Raimunda. All are quite cosmopolitan, have a variety of interests in art, politics and education and see English as a means to give them contacts throughout the world in terms of these interests. Freda is twenty years-old and her family comes from Tehuantepec in the Isthmus of Oaxaca. Her father is seventy two and her mother is fifty nine. She is the youngest of six children, with all of her siblings being currently economically independent from the family. Freda has a very active intellect, which she wants to use to construct a better world. She wants to pass her hopes on through teaching and engaging students

---

16 It seems to us that often in the analysis of language learning and use it is assumed that the activities and outcomes are to be understood in terms of the particular performances of singular actors. However, the following sections will illustrate how learning and knowledge are social constructs (Vygotsky, 1986) and how, referring to the ghost of the native speaker, performances of exorcism are joint adventures involving two or more actors.

in what the world could be. She feels that English is a means to aid her in such quests. Freda and Braulio are *novios* (engaged).

Braulio is also twenty one. Though he was born in Mexico City, he and his family are from the city of Oaxaca. He is the younger of two children. His father has recently passed away, and he helps his mother maintain the household through various part time jobs and projects. He sees himself as an inquisitive person who is searching to know more about the world he lives in. He believes that intellectual and social interaction with others allows one to widen their schemata and knowledge about the world. He strongly believes that through communication one can learn how other people in the world have solved similar problems or share common concerns. He feels that the dialogues can be triggering forces for cultures to understand each other and to be open to reconciliation. He hopes to use English to pursue such goals.

Raimunda is twenty years-old and was born in the city of Oaxaca. She is the oldest of three children. As a child she lived in a town near Oaxaca and went to an elementary school there. It was her desire to go to secondary school in the city of Oaxaca. In high school she studied art and music, but she was interested in studying English, so she entered the *Centro*. However, her interests were in learning the language, and not necessarily in being a teacher. She too sees English as a means to be able to connect with other people throughout the world. After finishing the programme, she is considering either a career in music or studying *lauderia* which is the art of making musical instruments. She feels that English will be useful for her in either area. She is currently enjoying a scholarship that has allowed her to spend a year at Kalamazoo College, in the States.

During our interviews with *Los Gabos* and in different written documents that they produced, we noticed a variety of comments that reflect how they perceive the value of English, their assumptions on how their various identity locations are affected by their pursuit of English, and the way they wish to use English as a strategy to develop various styles of intercultural communication. The following is how Freda describes her quest for English:

> I was eight years-old and in the third year of primary school when my mother told me that I was going to study English. She had always wanted one of her children to study English, and it was to be me. It scared me, but I did not say anything. I like the idea of being able to understand what the *gringos* were saying, but on the other side, the idea of meeting new children was terrifying! The first day of the class is still alive in my

memories. My mother encouraged me with all her heart, 'You can do it! Let's go. You'll see how nice it will be when you speak English' she said. Her words resonated in my head the whole time of that first class. So I decided not to stop. She had faith in me and one day she was going to be proud of my success. I started making friends from other schools and ages. It was fun. In the elementary school I started showing off to other students and started teaching them my English.

I was happy to be learning something that most adults that I knew didn't know. I was also aware that I would have an advantage over other students in secondary and high school. And apart from being easy, fun and useful, it was also a tool to communicate with others. All my teachers were good, and most of them were non-native speakers. It was at high school that I started to think about becoming an English teacher. My introverted side was disappearing and was being replaced by a willingness to be a teacher.

I have never questioned the capability of non-native speaking teachers. For me it was better to have a non-native speaking teacher, because it was easier for her/him to understand my doubts and it was easier for me to approach him/her when I felt confused. I never thought that native speaker teachers were superior to non-native speaking teachers. The former understand and identify the mistakes and obstacles that the learner faces when learning English. For me, I always felt equal to the non-native speaking teachers.

I just see English as an important means of communication. English has become the second language in so many countries. Thus, English is a link to connections to other people and places. It does not matter if I am Mexican and I want to communicate with a Japanese person. With English we have a language in common. It is true that native English has a specific accent difficult to emulate completely. But for me, as long as you pronounce it clearly, your accent does not define your level of knowledge and competence in the language.

I am attracted to learning the structure and complexity of English, but not to the culture that it comes with. When I speak English, I feel that it is mine because it is useful to me; it is a second language that I am acquiring, little by little, it is a tool for communication. It is true that with this language, I have got to know a little bit about the American and British cultures, but I am not attracted to these cultures. I do not identify with them and nor do I pretend to adopt a specific style of life just because I speak English. I like the language, but I already have my own culture, my own context. And that's why I do not find any problem to speak a language of a country like the United States, which I do not identify with at all. I agree that it is impossible to ignore the context and culture of the people that speak a language, but it is up to each of us to take or not the culture that comes with it.

Raimunda also told us about the way she relates to English and she emphasised her rejection for what she calls the 'whole package':

To establish one's identity in respect to the language one speaks is important. However, at the moment, I do not know what type of English I speak. I have never been in England or in the United States or any other English speaking country. So I do not have any reason to say that I speak a specific type of English. Sometimes I think that I have created my own style, with my own peculiar errors. So far, these mistakes have been tolerated, but I know that it will not be like that all the time. I am also aware that I have not adopted a native speaker accent. To sum up, I have a Mexican accent. But I do not feel that I can decide that by myself. Maybe a native speaker has to judge my English and have an opinion about my style and my accent. S/he may say that it is funny, confusing or even near to perfect!!

But whatever s/he decides, I know that the most important thing is to be able to communicate, and to the extent that I can do that, I won't have any problems. I think that people forget one's style and accent, unless one's interlocutor happens to be a purist *gringo* that only accepts people that talk in his same style. But that is impossible. The style cannot be the same, because even in the same country people speak differently.

English is mine from the very moment I put it into practice and I am able to establish communication. I do not completely own it because I am still trying to master it. But when I say that the English language is mine, I do not mean to say that I want to take the culture that comes with it. Culture is something different, it is part of the people that speak the language, but it is not part of me, nor the politics and the way people think and live. I can have information about all this but that's it. In contrast, I can use English to talk about me, about my culture, the politics in my country, and our ways of thinking and living. And I defend all that. English is becoming part of me but I am only taking part of it, not the whole package.

In contrast, when Braulio describes his connection with the language, he stresses the dynamic nature of his learning process:

My first conversation with a North American student was difficult. We both tried to communicate but it was really only very routine types of questions. It was not a pleasant experience for me, I was tense and nervous. At that time, I started to imagine drawings of the things I looked up in my pocket dictionary, and to think about how to do these words through miming. Seeing how to combine all these elements allowed me to discover that it was more important to be understood than to try to speak perfectly all the time. This understanding allowed me to relax when talking and to concentrate on what I wanted to say instead of how I was saying it. This encouraged me to want to learn more about the nuances of English grammar and vocabulary and to take advantage of what it means to speak a second language. My English is mutating, what I know now turns into something to know more about and to understand more. My goal is to learn this all as fast as I can and to be able to have images of how this language works. My brain retains images better than words or phrases learnt by heart.

Reflections

For us, the particular 'language ideologies' of *Los Gabos*, suggest that, as they seek to exorcise the ghost of the native speaker of English, they are engaging in the disinvention of the 'metadiscursive regimes,' (Makoni and Pennycook, 2006) of native-speakerism, (Holliday, 2005) and are challenging the 'epistemic violence' (Bourdieu, 1991) produced by those standards. Their comments also suggest how their performances of English 'are acts of identity, investment and semiotic (re)construction ... and are used to perform, invent and (re)fashion identities across innumerable domains' (Pennycook, 2006: 169). As we stated in the introduction, we feel that as they performed their English, they were asserting their 'userhood' (Kandiah, 1998) in these performances, or as Kandiah states, 'a radical act of semiotic reconstruction and reconstitution which of itself confers *native userhood* on the subjects involved in the act' (ibid., 100).

For Freda, English is hers because it is useful for her desires to communicate and connect with people throughout the world. For Raimunda, English is hers as soon as she puts it into practice. For Braulio, performing English is a creative process of composing images to communicate his wishes and feelings to others. For all three, it is the act of using English that is important to them, not a command over assumed standards or the virtues of native speakers. Their 'radical acts of semiotic reconstruction and reconstitution' (Kandiah, 1998: 100) can be noted in how both Raimunda and Freda make their accents part of who they are as they perform English, or in Braulio's quest to have understandable English rather than to have perfect pronunciation. These acts are also forms of disinventing the standards of English, as neither Freda nor Raimunda grant the native speaker the authority to validate their language performances. They are opposing the 'metadiscursive regimes' (Makoni and Pennycook, 2006) of native-speakerism and proposing a counter-hegemonic claim to have communicative interaction seen as means to validate their language performances in English. Their position implies that they see English as a tool for various forms of multicultural and intercultural interaction. As Freda states, 'English is the link with other people and places. It does not matter if I am Mexican and I want to communicate with a Japanese person. With English we have a language in common.' This quest for communication is seen as a way to vary their own particular identities while at the same time strengthen how they want to express themselves as young Mexicans. In learning English they do not believe that they have to be like '*gringos*' or accept aspects of other cultures that they do not agree with. These actions illustrate the 'multiple investments' (Pennycook, 2006) they have made in order to express their particular hopes and desires in English. These investments aid in their accumulation of cultural and linguistic capital which can be seen in how Freda mentions that by knowing English she will know what the '*gringos*' are talking about (Norton, 2000). But through their imagined communities (Anderson, 1991; Kanno and Norton, 2003, and Norton, 2001), what seems to be most strongly expressed is their advocacy of a politics of linguistic affinity through the use of English. They are claiming that English gives them a means to affiliate with other non-native users of English throughout the postcolonial world.

Transidiomatic practices

Transidiomatic practices are various ways of communication that language users draw upon within the current overall social and cultural contexts of globalisation. Marco Jacquemet has introduced this term in the following way:

> transidiomatic practices are the results of the co-presence of multilingual talk and electronic media, in contexts heavily structured by social indexicalities and semiotic codes. (2005: 8)

We will elaborate on this concept later, but first we want to provide some illustrations of what we mean by transidiomatic practices within the context of the *Centro de Idiomas*. To do this we will introduce the second and third cliques and their performances of transidiomatic practices.

Paulina, Viviana, Luisa, Itzela and Itzel are a group of young women known as *Las Malditas*. They have maintained their clique over the last three years. They, like *Los Gabos*, also come from a more or less middle income social context. Most of them are A+ students, have an above average command over English and are highly committed to their studies. They are also active in the social and educational dynamics of the *Centro*. Three of them recently returned from a semester study programme at UNAM (Universidad Nacional Autónoma de México) in Mexico City. They try to take courses together and while in class they are always making jokes and laughing. They were given the nickname of *Las Malditas* (the Mean Ones) by their classmates because of their strong presence and their sharp sense of humour, which often can be abrasive. They see themselves as a group that is happy, lively, responsible and assertive, though some students would use a more direct description: they are shit-disturbers.

Paulina is a twenty-two year old student with a very extroverted personality and who can at times be quite coquettish. She comes from a middle class Oaxacan family, her father is a lawyer and her mother is an *ama de casa* (housewife). She has one younger brother. She sees herself as a young independent woman who is happy and responsible. She is perceived by her classmates as a talkative and friendly person who is careful with her appearance and who does not have any money problems. Viviana is also twenty-two years-old and comes from a middle class Catholic Oaxacan family. Her father is a civil engineer and her mother is also an *ama de casa*. She attended parochial schools before the university, but did not like them. She came to the *Centro* like many others students thinking it was a foreign language centre, but has come to enjoy her study of English. She sees herself as somewhat of a serious and introverted person who likes to be very well organised in terms of her studies at the *Centro*. She is seen by her classmates as a creative and friendly person who is also a very hard working student. Within the clique, she is by far the quietest and most serious member of the group. Luisa, also twenty-two, comes from a professional middle class family. Her father is a public school teacher and her mother is a speech therapist. She has two older siblings that have already finished their undergraduate education. She has had the opportunity to study English in private schools. She feels she is a strong young woman who has had the advantage of earlier training in English. She is seen by her classmates as a happy and artistic person. In class she is a very attentive student, but outside class she is very talkative and likes to joke and fool around with her friends. Itzela, is twenty-one and was born in Chiapas (the state south of Oaxaca). She was raised by her mother, who is now a retired school teacher. Her father died when she was very young. Like Luisa, she had studied English in private schools before coming to the university. Also, like many of the other students at the *Centro*, she entered thinking that she would be studying various foreign languages, but has come to enjoy her English studies and works part time as English teacher in a private school in Oaxaca. She sees herself as a strong person with an extroverted personality and with strong political commitments concerning gender and racial issues. Other students see her as the leader of her clique and someone who is able to make things happen at the *Centro*. Itzel, the youngest member of the group, twenty, is the only non-Catholic among them. Her family belongs to the Jehovah Witness Church. She was born in Salina Cruz in the Isthmus. Her stepfather is retired from the Navy and her mother is an *ama de casa*. She has two older siblings. She feels her personality is a mixture of being introverted and extroverted; she likes to be with her friends and she enjoys the lively style of her clique. She thinks that her religion makes her find a balance in her life and also feels very committed to her beliefs, something that may not be fully understood by others. Also, she is saddened by her parents' divorce that occurred as she was entering the university. Others see her as happy and, at times, coquettish. She is also perceived to be mature and quite responsible for her age.

In the following comments that these students make about themselves, their cliques and how they play with both Spanish and English, we feel that they are moving in and out of spaces that can be seen as transidiomatic. The first account refers to the *Las Malditas*' practice of code mixing:

When watching TV, we are interested in the vocabulary. We want new words that we have never used before. There are some words that I [Itzela] have seen before but I have not found out how to use them and in what context. In regular courses they teach you correct language, and in the TV it is not correct but appropriate. We want to learn more than just correct language, something more real and not so artificial. We do not want to sound artificial, though when you are learning a second language you sound artificial anyway, so in order not to sound too artificial you need to learn all this vocabulary and pronounce it in a way they understand it. Like when you are playing the piano, or when you are walking, you have your pace. It is not about the accent, it is about your confidence to say what you want to say. We don't like to talk in English when we are together. It sounds artificial. However we use a lot of English when talking in Spanish:

We use 'Well?' very often. For example, when we want someone to hurry up what they are doing. Also if someone is taking too long to do something easy, we will say to them 'Hey, move your fat ass!'

Yeah, I [Itzela] think we picked it up in a movie. We started using it for an assignment in our English class. We had to do a dialogue, and we thought it would be funny. Also, it is somewhat ironic for us to use it, because we are all *flacas* [skinny].

Yeah, but Paulina and Itzela always think they have fat asses, but they do not!

Another word we like to play with is 'donkey'. We use it with each other when one of us does not understand something the others are saying or doing. We used it to describe folks outside our *clicka* [clique], when they are doing something that we think is too obvious or being really incoherent.

Like when someone in class asks something that they already know!

We have never heard it in an English class. We took it from the Spanish phrase '*qué burro eres!*' We started saying '*qué donkey eres!*' [what a donkey you are!]

Yeah, we kind of invented to use it within our *clicka*.

Oh, there is another word we fool around with 'Loser!' It is not as exclusive as 'donkey' and people even have hand signs for it. You put two fingers up like an 'L', and point to someone. A lot of folks understand that one.

Also, we used to tease each other when someone is doing something dumb or silly, we will call them 'a loser'. But for us, it is only a joke.

Yeah, like when we have an assignment, one of use overdoes it—like putting like drawings of flowers on the paper or stickers to make it look cute—you just don't do that in the university, that's being 'a loser'.

To do more than you need to do, acting like an overachiever, which for us is 'a loser'. It is like using 'donkey', but you can use it more widely. Though, I think 'donkey' is stronger.

Another phrase we like to use is 'You can do it!'. We use it to encourage each other. Like if someone has a difficult event to deal with or is going to a job interview that they might be worried about, we say 'you can do it!' Or we use it joking or in an ironic sense, like when one of us has a very easy assignment in class, we tell them, 'sure you can do it!'

We sort of play with the word 'focus'. We created it from the Spanish word '*visualízalo*'. We tell each other 'to focus' when working on something in class or on an assignment that we do not understand, we tell each other 'to focus', and for us that means to pay attention or realise it. It is a way to jokingly tell someone to work hard to understand something. We mean it to be funny; in fact we use most of these English in a joking or playful way. Like, when we say 'Helloooo?', like 'are you listening?' sort of thing.

I [Paulina] like to play around with the word 'foxy'. So does Itzela. I use it because we are always falling in love with someone. When one of us wants to talk to some guy she is attracted to, we will say to her, '*ya vas de* foxy' [you're going foxy, again] or if you are trying to look good for someone, we will say '*Eres una* foxy' [you are a foxy]. I use it in that kind of context. Or also, I play around with 'horny' if I am involved with a guy, and the others tell me '*Ya estás* horny, *ya estás* horny!' [You are horny now, you are horny now!]. I learned these words from some students who were in the 9th semester when I was in the first semester. I had never used 'bad' words before, but now I am a *pelada* [one who swears a lot].

Recently, a lot of folks are using 'gay', but we use it in a kind of mean spirited way. It is not that we do not accept different sexual orientation, that's cool. I guess we use it a little bit in a discriminating way. In fact we make fun of everyone, and we can sometimes be cruel.

It is somewhat the context here at the *Centro*. You know, we are all women in the clique, and the majority of the students here are women. There are few guys and most of them already have girlfriends. Or some are gay or if they are not gay they are ugly. So we have to look for boyfriends outside the school.

I think the guys here are kind of immature. They are funny and they can make me [Luisa] laugh a lot, but that's it. They are too young, I like older guys. Itzela has had a boyfriend here, but she is the exception. There are too few here and no possibility to choose.

We use 'geek' for someone who overdoes a task in class or in an assignment, like putting stickers on your papers or stay up way too late to make the paper just right. Itzela can be like a 'geek' sometimes. When you do more than is necessary: we say 'how *matadita*, you took it too far!'. I guess 'nerd' is somewhat like 'geek', but for us it is stronger. Actually, we moved from 'nerd' into '*nerdfo*'. Like this guy we always see studying at the self-access centre. He is there with his glasses, books, pens, always reading and studying, way too serious and quiet. We learned this '*nerdfo*' from Edgar and Lalo [members of a male *clika*].

We are not *nerdfos*! No way! Besides just studying, we like to socialise, we enjoy life as well. A *nerdfo* is someone that just wants studying and reading all the time. Or someone that has to work all the time to get a good grade. A *nerdfo* is someone who suffers to get what they want. That's not cool. Getting high grades is good, but you should not have to kill yourself for it. We work on our stuff with the time that is necessary, and not more. Not to be a *nerdfo* means to do your best in the least amount of time possible, so that you get time to take it easy. Who wants to turn their work in a month in advance? It is not cool to start on an assignment the first day it's given, but it is not cool to turn things in late. '*Nerdfo*' is more colloquial than 'nerd'.

Las Malditas very clearly stated, however, that they do not like to interact among themselves in English because they feel that it would be 'too artificial and pretentious'. With a different perspective, *Los Gabos* told us how much they enjoy speaking in English:

> When we speak among ourselves, we code switch a lot. We will start in Spanish and suddenly we will change to English. We do that a lot when we are working on an assignment, any word in English can get us going. But we only use English among ourselves. Many of our classmates think

we talk too fast in English or that we are trying to show off. They think we are trying to mess with them.

Sometimes I [Freda] talk to my siblings in English, and my mother does not understand the language, but she does understand the situation. English can work like a secret code, although that doesn't always work, there can be other people around who are learning it. That's the time to start learning another language!

At school we code switch a lot, mix a lot. Actually, for us it is often using some words in Spanish when talking in English.

What words do we usually use in Spanish? I do not know, a lot. 'Bye' is very common.

'I don't care'. We use it when we think something is not interesting, like *'no me importa'*, 'I do not care what we do'. It sounds light in English; it is good for not making a decision. 'I don't think so' is also lighter than in Spanish. These sound better in English, believe me. 'I guess' is a *muletilla* [cliché], you know, to fill a space when you are thinking.

'Scatterbrain', we use it for everybody else besides ourselves. They don't take it bad. It is a joke. If you do not understand something or act confused, then you are being a 'scatterbrain'. It's meant to be funny, a good joke. It is not an insult. 'Poor devil'. We use it to show pity 'Oh poor devil!' Also, we use 'donkey'. It is perfect for *'burro'*. When somebody does not understand something in class, that can be an example of a 'donkey'. Or when someone is slow, that's also a 'donkey'. It is a joke. It is just between us. It started one day when we did not have anything better to do ... and now it is so common among us.

Another good example of transidiomatic practice is illustrated by *The Video Project* carried out by two of *Los Gabos*. As we have mentioned above, Freda and Braulio are *novios* (a couple). They took part in my Comparative Linguistics course (Angeles). In the classroom, they sit next to each other and hold hands, exchange comments and smiles, but never stop being very attentive and participative.

The objective of this specific course was to explore the comparative aspects of Spanish and English. Each two-student team was in charge of a topic they chose from a list I gave them. One of the last topics was vernacular language, in particular taboo words. Many teams expressed their desire to work with this topic, but it was Freda and Braulio who ended up taking it on. Their presentation was on the last day of the term when all their other courses had already finished. I was surprised that nobody missed that session. For their presentation they chose to make a video, using two young native speakers of English to play the role of traditional teachers. It was staged with these young guys playing the role of the teachers sitting at their desks and with a whiteboard behind showing the students the pronunciation of this rather specialised vocabulary.

The video opens with a rap/rock song playing in the background while the camera focused on a page in a Spanish/English dictionary where the word slang was defined. This was followed by an introduction to what the viewers were about to encounter. The narrator, who is a native English speaker from the United States, explains that this video is to teach the students some English slang words. He tells the viewers that these are just words, though they may perhaps be vulgar to some, they are just words. He does, however, caution the viewers about using these words in the United States.

The scene then switches to a classroom, where another American English speaker is introducing the class for the day. He is seated at a desk and behind him is the white board. He is dressed causally, and begins the class with the words written on the board which he then pronounces for the students. For example:

> Slang words for breasts: Tits, Titties, Boobs, Big titties, etc.
> Slang words for penis: Cock, Dick, Pencil dick, Twigs and berries, Shlong, etc.
> Slang words for butts: Booty, Ass, Grab Ass, Asscrack, Wide load, etc.
> Slang words for vagina: Pussy, Clit, Cunt, Come dumpster, Elephant toe, etc.

Braulio and Freda explained to us, 'we did the video that way to make a combination of something original with something informal and also because we wanted to have fun. It was a topic that had a lot of potential'. To which Braulio remarked, 'People may think that we were only having fun with this video, but it was very important for us. We see its value.' What follows is their comments about the rationale underlying the Video Project. We have decided to leave them in the original interview form to keep track of who is saying what.

Angeles: How would you define the topic of your project?
Braulio: The topic was taboo words, especially sexual slang words that

are taboo. Insults were not considered. For us, insults are more accepted and they are not as strong.

At the beginning we did not know what kind of words we were going to come across. We would not have had problems saying the words in English, though for Freda it would have been difficult to say these words in Spanish.

Freda: I would have felt nervous rather than uncomfortable. Actually it was safer not to say the words in Spanish, because all of us were Spanish speakers. That's why we did not give the translation.

Braulio: Also, we avoided the translation because, in spite of the similarities, we found a lot of variety in English. So for one word in Spanish there are several in English. It is that they were more specific with these sexual terms, while we tend to generalise a lot in terms of sexual terminology. They give the words a figurative connotation. We do that as well but less often ... Let me explain myself, we refer to something very often but with the same word whereas they use different words to refer to the same thing.

Freda: Maybe because we are afraid of being vulgar, that's why we do not use so many synonyms. We choose the word that sounds less strong, that appears less strong.

Angeles: Why was the class so interested in and excited about the presentation? Why were they taking notes of every single word or phrase and showed more motivation than when we studied false cognates or affixes, for example?

Freda: Because taboo words are prohibited and prohibited things are exciting. Most of us use bad words, and we always hear them, but we do not accept it, and we also do not accept that we are interested in this language and how it is used in different places and different situations. However, we are also interested in learning this vernacular in English because we are learning English. It is good because we widen the range of our colloquial English.

Angeles: Are you going to use these words (between you two)?

Braulio: Of course! We have used them when we are talking in Spanish, when we need them, when we have the opportunity, and it is easier to use them in English than in Spanish.

Freda: Yeah, it is more fun!

Braulio: Maybe for us it sounds stronger in Spanish, more offensive. In English, it is only a joke, a light joke. Between us, using these words is like using a secret code. Nobody understands except for us. It has so much potential ... .

Angeles: In the video why did you choose to represent a teaching situation?

Braulio: We thought that it was a great situation to have a teacher teaching something that he would never teach. He would be teaching what is never taught, what is never shown, which is usually left outside the classroom. We also had to represent a traditional teacher to make the situation extreme because the traditional teacher would never say these words. We wanted to make clear that we wanted to teach a lesson, to do a documentary on something that seemed to be serious, that is why we started that way, in a very 'documentary-like way' with the dictionary and then the contrast at the end with the Mexican songs.

Freda: The idea of the Mexican songs was to make a contrast, but, at the same time, to make a connection between how both of these styles of music like to use street vernaculars in their lyrics.

Braulio: I liked the idea of the hip-hop because it is an Afro-American creation that has influenced us a lot. Hip-hop is about conflict in their street culture, and has a very particular way to tell stories that we like. Hip-hop is somewhat like our *corridos* in that it tells stories about conflicts also. That's why hip-hop is very popular here because we had the antecedent of the *corridos* and the *narcocorridos*, which are very similar.

In order to convey the diversity in the transidiomatic practices of students at the *Centro de Idiomas*, we will introduce the third clique, *Las Misteriosas*. Vania, Salia and Marian are three young female students whose clique is somewhat different from the other groups in that they are not *per se* a cohesive clique. The structure of their communication involves Marian interacting with both of them separately and Salia and Vania hardly interacting with each other at all. Marian and Salia are sisters and Vania is Marian's best friend. Another difference from the other cliques is that they do not come from a middle income social context. This aspect makes them shy, quiet and not very communicative, and hence the self-selected names of *Las Misteriosas* (The Mysterious Ones).

Marian and Salia's parents are poor rural farmers, and Vania's background is working class. They are not as active in the social world of most of the students at the *Centro*, and although they are good students, their styles of learning are not always recognised by the teachers at the *Centro*. I (Angeles) met them because they attained a financial government grant for low-income students with above average grades and they asked me to be their tutor, which is a requirement for getting the grant.

Vania is twenty-one years-old and was born in the city of Oaxaca. She is the oldest of three children. Her parents were both quite young and poor when she was born. Her parents were part of an extended family that was their base for survival in the harsh conditions of poverty. When she was little the family lived in a shack, had a basic diet with very few proteins, and it seemed to her that they were always surrounded by problems and conflicts. When she was in elementary school, she was quite introverted, easily frightened by other students and afraid of her teachers, who she saw as abusive. When she entered secondary school she swung to opposite types of behaviour, became rebellious and was almost thrown out of school. In high school she calmed down and attempted to focus on graduating, which for her was difficult.

Like many other students, she sort of drifted in the studying of English at the *Centro* and has not found life in the university as she expected it to be. She has thought several times of dropping out, but with the encouragement from her mother and a close female friend who lives in the States, she has struggled to stay in school. She wants to finish her undergraduate degree and then think about travelling to either the United States or Europe. In terms of her future she states, 'I want to enjoy life as far as I can, be satisfied with my professional life and be better as a person so as to be able to give love to others.'

Vania and Marian are very different in how they like to present themselves. Vania has a light complexion, likes to dress extravagantly, to use makeup and to dye her hair. Marian has a darker skin tone, does not like to use makeup, is a casual dresser and keeps her long hair in a pony tail. They also have different personalities; Marian hardly talks and always appears very serious although once in a while you can get a kind of a timid smile from her, whereas Vania is always smiling and presents herself as a very social person. Marian and Salia are also quite different from each other. Salia is a little bit flamboyant, has some body piercing, likes to use makeup, and wears flashy inexpensive jewellery. In their roles as students, they are also different; while Marian is very dedicated and works hard, Salia tends to put off work and rely on her memory (which sometimes does not work). She compensates for this trait, however, with her facility to talk in class and make herself visible to the teacher (a very important skill in the crowded Mexican classrooms). To overcome her insecurities, Marian practised as a teacher in a small village where some secondary students needed some remedial work to pass their English courses. She also spent her last semester in a university in Chiapas, an experience that has added to her self-esteem.

What Marian and Salia have in common is the poverty of their family's rural background, dealing with the alcoholism of their father and having to take care of their younger siblings. Their father has stayed on the coast while their mother moves back and forth between the coast and their residence in the city. Last year, Salia talked to us about spending her summer with her father and how she had to make *tortillas* at six o'clock every morning and then start preparing lunch immediately after she had finished washing up from breakfast, 'After that summer, I just knew that I didn't want to get married', she stated.

Lately, both of them also share, with their siblings, the responsibility of running the house, since their mother had to move back to their hometown to take care of their father whose illness has worsened. The most difficult part has been taking care of two younger siblings: a girl of eleven, who feels depressed because of her mother's absence and her father's sickness, and a boy of nine who is too active and noisy according to the school teacher and too lazy and disorganised according to his sisters.

There is something else that Marian and Salia share; their disposition to learn English. Both of them are aware that they need to work hard to make progress in this language. Marian's main problem is her shyness, which makes her too quiet for her English teachers' tastes. For Salia, the main problem is her lack of discipline, which manifests itself in her tendency to procrastinate. Since Marian started two years earlier at the programme, she tends to help Salia, encouraging her to keep trying, explaining things to her and giving her advice about how to succeed at school. Both of them are now planning to initiate their little sister into English, because now they know how difficult it is in secondary school and how important it is in life.

Different from *Los Gabos*, who interact very often in English, *Las Misteriosas*, have found that due to their background and personalities, they can construct safe houses with their families at home where they can perform their role as English learners. Vania describes this in the following way:

> I say a lot of things to my mother in English, but she reacts very strongly, 'Get real! We are in Mexico. Our language is Spanish. Besides, I do not understand what you say to me!' But still I talk to her in English. At the

beginning she didn't understand a word. Now she understands more and doesn't get so angry. My brothers get really mad at me. But with my mother I have set myself that goal and now she is accepting it, she can live with it. She used to get angry because she would say that I didn't see the difference between home and school. And, to be honest, sometimes I even change the structures in Spanish. Sometimes I say *rojo carro* (red car) in Spanish instead of *carro rojo* (car red). It is because we are so worried about learning it!

Marian does not involve her mother with her interactions; nevertheless, she still has to explain her behaviour when the mother enters her safe house:

At home sometimes, if I am not too tired, I speak to myself in English. I started like 'This morning when I woke up ... .' One day my mother got into my room and said, 'What are you doing? Who are you talking to?' I explained to her but she didn't seem to understand and keep thinking that I was reading from a book, 'So what? Are you talking to the air, or what?' When she finally understood she said, 'I'll save some money to buy you a tape recorder, then you'll be able to listen to yourself and let's see what you find, maybe you'll find your mistakes and you can correct them.' It made me laugh that my mother said that to me, but actually it is a good idea. She hasn't bought the recorder but I liked that she said that to me.

Reflections

These students' performances of English within the contact zone of the *Centro* (which, as we have seen, extends to other places and times that are not constrained by the school) can be characterised by the use of transidiomatic practices. Jacquemet feels that through these practices, various diasporic and local groups 'recombine their identities by maintaining simultaneous presence in multiplicity of sites and by participating in elective networks spread over transnational territories' (2005: 8).

Transidiomatic practices involve linguistic innovations with heavy borrowing from English though any number of languages could be performed with these communicative recombinations, depending on the 'reterritorialisation needs and wants of the speakers' (ibid., 8). Anyone present in transnational environments, whose talk is mediated by deterritorialised technologies, and who interacts with both present and distant people, will find herself producing transidiomatic practices. In this framework, *deterritorialisation* refers to the diffusion of people and texts around the global world. *Reterritorialisation* represents how people reconfigured themselves and the various texts that they use in this postcolonial globalised world economy (ibid., 9). Jacquemet states that 'language studies must address the progressive globalisation of communicative practices and social formations that result from the increasing mobility of people, languages and texts' (ibid., 4). This involves avoiding neo-liberal fallacies about the dynamics of globalisation and confronting the realities of asymmetrical power relations found within the political economy of talk.

As stated above, and drawing on Jacquemet's ideas, transidiomatic practices for us refers to various forms of communicative practices—such as word play, fluid language compositions, media appropriations, and multiple identity performances—used by language actors in the overall social and cultural context of the globalisation (ibid.).

Furthermore, we think that one of the ways in which these students are exorcising the ghost of the native speaker of English, or disinventing the metadiscursive regime of English standards, is the way they engage in these ludic performances that involve English and Spanish. In both languages, they are seeking ways to have fun by recomposing phrases and ideas, by developing their own concepts about appropriate student behaviours and styles, and by exploring gender and sexual possibilities. For us, they are using their cliques as safe houses within which they can test the boundaries of their learning cultures by playing various language games. The *Centro de Idiomas* as a contact zone between the language regimes of both Spanish and English is a context saturated with various media networks in both languages: music, movies, internet, radios, graffiti, advertisements, television and numerous forms of written textual material. Flowing through all these spaces is an array of spoken languages ranging from the indigenous languages of the native groups of Oaxaca to the diversity of languages brought by the international tourists circulating throughout Oaxaca. This is a contact zone where 'any number of languages could be performed with these communicative recombinations, depending on the 'reterritorialisations needs and wants of the speakers' (ibid., 8). Furthermore, it seems that this is also a context 'mediated by deterritorialised technologies' where the students are interacting with 'both present and distant people' and thus find themselves 'producing transidiomatic practices' (ibid.).

For Freda, this involves what she refers to as code mixing. For her and her clique, this means playing words games between Spanish and English. Using English as a secret code is a form of a game for them though they are aware that it will not be secret for long, because others are also learning the code. They invent and recompose English words to insert them into their vernacular Spanish, because it seems to have a lighter social meaning. Playing with both languages gives them a sense of their own selfhood.

Freda and Braulio's video project on taboo words is an expression of communicative recombinations based upon their 'reterritorialisations needs.' Both felt that they needed to know how to use English in a direct and open sense, not just something from textbooks and classes and, as the reader can see, they are taking high risks with the language they have chosen to learn. It is in situations like this that the students are relocating themselves outside the dichotomy of the native/non-native speakers and moving towards an awareness of themselves in a continuum from being novices or expert language users as they perform their English with a postcolonial accent. As Freda and Braulio become experts in the field of taboo language, they will realise the problematic connotations of the words they are just discovering. Still, the project was fun for them and gave them space to explore their feelings towards taboo words because they felt freer to play within these domains in English. The video included a mixture of Mexican and African-American music, visual puns and a parody of traditional English language instruction subverted by a presentation of taboo words. As we can see, they are aware that they could use language learning as a way to transgress limits within their own social domains. And, as Freda stated, 'Yeah, it is more fun!'

Vania used her English to 'reterritorialise' the linguistic space within her home, where her mother and brothers objected to her English use, but she did not back off. She has even started to play with the word order of her Spanish. Marian has had a similar confrontation with her mother, but finds that her mother relents with the suggestion of acquiring a tape recorder for her English practices. This small event also introduced the realities of social class in the political economy of transidiomatic practices, for Marian's mother's promise of the tape recorder has not been fulfilled for lack of funds.

The comments of Itzela and her clique are strong expressions of 'communicative recombinations', depending on the 'reterritorialisation needs and wants of the speakers'. This involves developing a discourse on what constitutes for them appropriate and inappropriate student behaviour. They apply these norms to themselves and others. Though 'donkey' is a word transported from their Spanish usages and 'loser' one transported in the opposite direction, both words are used to evaluate their own behaviour or those of other students. They are using these words to convey their understanding of the kinds of pressures they feel in their social and academic lives. They are also sorting out the subtleties of what they consider to be the proper norms for interaction and styles of presentation within the classroom.

They pursue these concerns while having fun with the language. A good example of this is the way they have played with the word 'nerd', borrowing it from its English context and hispanicising its meaning in their interactions at the *Centro*. They have composed and imposed a form of student identity with the term *nerdfo*. They judge others for exhibiting the qualities of being a *nerdfo*, but strongly suggesting that they do not fit within that category. In fact, they use the term to define what they do not want to be. Their word play is meant to be more comical than somehow prescriptive for others. In that way they can both play with the language and define what they feel about their own social and personal context.

This playfulness can be heard when using new sexual expressions. 'Foxy' becomes not a term used to evaluate them, but rather to express how they feel about themselves, '*Ya vas de foxy!*'. 'Horny' is used in a similar way, as an expression of their sexual feelings and desires. 'Gay' is more problematic for them and they are not quite sure how far they should push this idea. Their current use of the word is more for describing the sexual politics of heterosexuality at the *Centro*, while at the same time claiming to be open and supportive of sexual diversity among the students at the *Centro*.

Such words as 'donkey', 'nerdfo', 'foxy' and 'horny' suggest a deterritorialised/ reterritorialised dynamic in how they perform their word games. By their uncertainty as to where they actually picked up these words (from each other or other cliques, from movies, or music) they are expressing the deterritorialised quality of vernacular words in both languages. The way they chose to use them in ways that express their feelings (especially 'foxy' and 'horny') illustrates a link between agency and reterritorialisation in these language games.

In terms of various identity locations, such as gender, sexuality, ethnicity and social class, these students are (at least metaphorically) part of 'diasporic social formations in which people have multiple linguistic and cultural allegiances.' For these students, these connections are composed in a whirlpool of multiple intersecting dynamics of media, language education, family, community and their perceptions about their own selfhood. In different ways, they are struggling with whether their use of English will reproduce or counter these processes of social language inequality. It is our argument that these students, by performing English with a postcolonial accent, are trying to find out where they are located in the various 'social hierarchies and power asymmetries' in the political economy of talk and how they can express their needs and desires in this deterritorialised/reterritorialised global world they are entering.

In different ways and with different styles of language use, these young language actors are composing various forms of emerging transidiomatic practices in their performance of English and Spanish. By composing diverse languages games within their learning cultures, they are able to emerge from their safe houses to: use their agency; counter the ideological regimes of both Spanish and English; claim their use rights of creative language performances and; be validated by communicative success. They have located themselves away from the contact zone of the *Centro* to a 'multiplicity of language sites' by participating in selective communication networks 'spread over transnational territories'. (ibid., 8). Now they are ready to be themselves in both languages.

Performing as themselves and as the other

We open this book with Freda and Braulio stating that they want to be themselves in this other language. What do they mean by that? And again, what do the various word games presented above say about these students' desire to 'perform, invent and (re)fashion identities across innumerable domains' (Pennycook, 2006:169)? These concerns allow us to focus on the subjective desires that these students bring to their language encounters within the *Centro de Idiomas*. What follows is a series of statements and illustrations of how these students are performing or giving expression to their agency as they place their subjective hopes and desires into the process of being themselves in both Spanish and English.

This is the way *Los Gabos* express their subjectivity when learning English:

> For me, when you start to learn a new language it is essential to start building phrases and sentences; although I can not express myself completely, I can start structuring my ideas even though it is only bit by bit, but for me it is important to feel I can express myself. To make jokes is very motivating, you know; it means to get rid of that barrier that only allows you to ask the routine questions and to listen to the routine

answers such as, 'What is your name? Where are you from? Do you like Oaxaca? I am Pete, I live in Oregon. Yes, I do'. There is a motivating value in being able to make somebody laugh, to make somebody relax, and to start a friendship (Braulio).

And to make people feel some emotions. This use of the language allows you to create a friendly atmosphere, to be more relaxed, less formal. You start using this language and people realise that you can make jokes, that you can talk! (Freda)

It is very good for your communication and to establish a friendly atmosphere, because the most important thing when communicating is to use ordinary words, the language of everyday! (Braulio)

Our current English teacher is a native speaker, but for me he is more of an authoritarian figure than a guide or a teacher. He is the provider of everything we learn and has the total control of the class. He solves doubts, corrects mistakes, and explains the information that the text includes. The students, in turn, are the recipients who answer the questions, carry out the activities that he tell us to do and we submit to his authority. This situation only allows for a teacher-student interaction where the student only addresses the teacher to solve a doubt, ask to explain something or do the homework. Apart from this there is no communication with him. He evaluates with written exams, filling the blank or writing paragraphs. His teaching is completely based on what the textbooks says. It is impossible to do something different. This means that our feelings are not taken into consideration. It does not matter how you feel, what your problems are or if the student felt bad when the teacher corrected his/her mistake in a rude manner. It seems that there is no place or time for that. The only thing to do is to concentrate in the class and in the explanations and activities and leave aside everything else. (Raimunda)

The subjectivity of Marian and Vania from *Las Misteriosas* is expressed in their very particular way of practising their English in the streets of Oaxaca, a safe house that we can call 'blocking out English':

Usually we talk in English when we have finished our *intercambio*.¹⁷ It is like a game for us. We like to challenge each other. We say 'let's see how many blocks can we keep talking in English'. Sometimes we even get to the *Zócalo* [Ten blocks from where they start] still speaking in English. The first one that switches to Spanish loses. We are making good progress. Each time we do more and more blocks. But sometimes we really get desperate, we feel blocked in our heads, not knowing enough vocabulary.

Even though this is the way we practice, we try to do it in a natural way, like chatting. Vania started this game and really surprised me the first time she spoke to me in English. But little by little I got the idea and started to feel better and better doing it. We sometimes mix our Spanish and English, like the *gringos*, like Spanglish, but after all it is a strategy, isn't it? Once we had the idea to start taking notes of the words that we do not know in English but soon we realised that it was impossible, you know, walking, talking in English and taking notes at the same time! A better idea would be to record it but we haven't done it so far. We have been doing this for a year. As I said it was Vania's idea, she is the crazy one. At the beginning I [Marian] didn't even want to go for an *intercambio*, but she encouraged me saying that 'things will work out' and 'it is not actually that difficult'. So I became less afraid every time. Now I do not get so nervous. If I don't do well, *ni modo* (so what). Anyway, *gringos* also have mistakes and are not ashamed of them, so I shouldn't be ashamed, should I? I told that myself! Sometimes we tell each other that we have to talk more. People in the street just stare at us. Who knows what people in the bus stop think of us? We talk just about everything, our experiences with the *intercambio*, about boys, about people in the street; about this guy who is staring at us. Just the same things we would chat about in Spanish.

Less elaborated but more intimate, Marian with her sister Salia try out a different type of safe house, at home:

At home I sometimes talk in English to Salia, my younger sister, although she does not understand everything, she is making some progress. In fact, at home I say like twenty phrases a day. I have counted them. My

17 An intercambio is an exchange between students at the *Centro* and visiting international students, where they practice both Spanish and English.

family says that they are tired of hearing it all the time. But I can't help it, I swear. It is something already in me. It is not to show off; it is something already part of me.

Both safe houses are constructed because for *Las Misteriosas*, the school is not safe enough to perform their English:

> Here at school we do not talk in English. I [Vania] talk in English when Raimunda [from *Los Gabos*] asks me something in English. She always talks English to everybody, but only on those occasions. We do not feel like doing it because there is no freedom here. Everybody speaks English, knows about mistakes, so one gets too self-conscious about your mistakes and then you make more and they judge you. You really feel it, the criticism, the pressure. Maybe it is just *chaquetas mentales* [a mental block] that we are carrying around with us, but that's why we do not develop our oral skills. But when we speak English to each other, Marian and I, we are aware that we do not criticise each other, we feel free to make mistakes and even laugh about them. And we also try to solve our own doubts together. In the classroom there is a lot of pressure, always with an advanced student willing to criticise you.

Finally, one interesting theme we noted in these narratives about performing English was how many of these students found that English was a space in which they could say things that perhaps they might not want to express in Spanish or not want others to understand. In a sense, English became a safe house where they could be someone else. According to Freda:

> We like to speak English among ourselves because we feel free to say what we want without any limits. We mostly talk about our own experiences and you know, sometimes it is easier to talk about those things in English. You feel like you are not talking, someone else is. It feels like if we said some of these things in Spanish it would sound too harsh, but in English it seems OK.

Marian expresses the same feeling:

> When I get angry, I say things in English. In English they sound less strong. People do not take it as strongly as it sounds in Spanish. I think this is because they do not know the meaning of my English words, but they get the intention because of the tone of my voice. For me, saying harsh thoughts in English sounds more polite or educated, than if I did it in Spanish.

Reflections

Drawing from the work of Ortner, we are using subjectivity to represent those modes of perception, affect, thought, desire and fear that 'animate acting subjects'. These modes are expressed through 'cultural and social formations that shape, organise, and provoke' them (2006: 107). The issue of subjectivity means acknowledging that it is 'a necessary part of understanding how people (try to) act on the world even as they are acted upon' (ibid.). That is, subjectivity is the basis for the expression of agency. Agency endows a series of cultural meanings to the subjective desires, feelings and intentions of social actors (ibid., 110). This approach assumes that social actors that have some awareness of their overall personal and cultural context can, therefore, act upon such conditions (Giddens, 1979). Further, it seeks to find the links between relations of power and authority that frame the subjective feelings and desires of such actors. Thus, agency is a social and cultural construction that is expressed in individual actions which are, in turn, 'embedded in webs of relations, affection and solidarity,' and intermixed with relations of power and solidarity (ibid., 134). Within these webs there are possible patterns of empowerment, the seeking of particular projects of aspiration, and actions of resistance to forms of either physical or ideological subordination (ibid., 152-153).

The comments by the students provide an array of examples of how they are 'animate acting subjects' (Ortner, 2006) as they express their hopes, desires, feelings and fears about how they use both English and Spanish in their everyday lives. For Braulio, it is important that he feels that he can express himself and his desire to connect with others in meaningful ways, or as Freda states 'to make people feel some emotions.' Moreover, Raimunda's strong critique of her native speaking English teacher, who did not allow any of the students' feelings to affect his style of teaching illustrates the link between subjectivity and power relations.

That is, the teacher has the power to block the feelings of the students as part of the instructional context.

Vania and Marian's comments are suggestive of the ways that subjectivity engenders the dynamics of their particular agency. They construct for themselves a game for learning and using their English. They see how many city blocks they can walk together speaking only English. They do this for both practice and pleasure. They feel extremely pleased to be whom they want to be and in the spaces they want to use. They have created a space where they can be themselves in both languages, as they stated, 'who knows what people in the bus stop think of us? We talk just about everything ... the same things we would chat about in Spanish.'

In their comments there are reflections of how they understand their personal and social contexts and how they use that understanding. Vania comments on her family's frustration at her English performance but contends that they have to accept that that is just who she is. These two young ladies are situated in a more working class context than those of the other two cliques. Their fear or timidity about using their English at the *Centro* partly comes from their implicit sense of these class differences. There are also patterns of inequitable power relations among the students. They resolve these fears by taking their safe house beyond the gaze of the other students at the *Centro*.

An intriguing connection between agency and subjectivity is found in Freda and Marian's comments on how they feel they can be someone else when they are using English. Freda feels that certain expressions in English allow her to say things that she would not be comfortable saying in Spanish, whereas Marian feels that English gives her a space where she can more freely express her anger. Ironically, they do not just want to be themselves in this other language, but in some contexts, they want to be the other.

For us, these overall statements reflect the various ways in which these students have performed, reinvented and (re)fashioned their identities 'across innumerable domains' (Pennycook, 2006). These performances are being enacted within their cliques, their classrooms, their families and in the streets. These performances enrich their language learning cultures so that they feel able to invent or refashion themselves throughout diverse social and cultural contexts. Furthermore, how these students seek to be themselves in both of these languages highlights Ortner's distinction between agency as a form of power and agency as a form of intention and desire (2006: 152-153). That is, in this context they use their agency to contest and show resistance to the discursive regimes of standard English and authentic Spanish, while at the same time expressing their intentions and desires to be themselves in that process.

Conclusion

In this chapter we have provided an ethnographic analysis of the word games that these students play within their cliques, and we have illustrated how they have sought to move beyond the existing language ideologies currently being expressed within the multicultural context of the *Centro*. This has involved using their learning culture cliques as safe houses where they attempt to *disinvent* the identity locations of native and non-native speakers of English usages, and in that process, they have become more playful users of their own Spanish vernacular. We have argued that through these actions, these students seek to construct a politics of linguistic affinity based upon language use rather than ownership measured by either authenticity or standardisation. By claiming for themselves the rights of userhood of that language, they are also illustrating how they exorcise the ghost of the native speaker of English. Furthermore, they express this right of userhood by constructing their own forms of transidiomatic practices in both English and Spanish. By this construction they are, in turn, able to perform both as themselves and as the other in both languages. These performances include the expressions of a matrix of their subjective feelings and desires as they use their agency to resist the ideological claims of an authentic Spanish or a Standard English and also to project a vision of a communicative interaction as a more profound script for postcolonial language performance. This script of communicative interaction is composed within the contours of their respective language learning cultures. Within these social spaces, how they perform this new script is an expression of using culture as praxis as they seek out the possibilities of language use beyond the language regimes of both Spanish and English.

This vision of communicative interaction is what we mean by a politics of language affinity. For us, this affinity could be a bridge between the dynamics of multiculturalism and interculturalism within our postcolonial globalised world. Using this bridge could provide the means to move beyond the discursive disciplinary powers of the colonial difference.

Chapter 5

'It is not about the accent, it is about having the confidence to say what you want': Moving between language learning and language use

Introduction

Itzela, in one of our interviews (see chapter four), made the following statement that we are using for the title of this chapter, 'It is not about the accent, it is about having the confidence to say what you want to say.' We feel that her observation represents our journey with these narratives through how these students at the *Centro de Idiomas* have been performing English with a postcolonial accent. Remember that we have been using the idea of accent not only to denote the phonetic quality of these students' speech acts, but also to stress the fact that these language actors are playing in numerous languages, particularly in Spanish and English, and to emphasise how their everyday sociocultural, economic and political actions and practices are taking place in the postcolonial context of Oaxaca. Woven into their accounts there are illustrations of how these students have used their particular forms of agency to seek ways so that their hopes, desires, fears and dreams are part of their language performances. We read Itzela's comment about 'confidence' as an expression of the subjective drive that has framed the students' overall actions and practices in the context of the *Centro*: Claribel and Alberto's confident actions in gaining entrance to the *Centro* in order to pursue their studies were illustrations of the political economy of language education in Oaxaca. Or, how the confidence showed by Nour, Facundo, Jorge, Elena, César and Yolanda as they navigated their ways through the various identity locations of gender, sexuality, ethnicity and social class demonstrated the ways they were pursuing the accumulation of various forms of linguistics and cultural capital. Also, it was the creative confidence of *Los Gabos*, *Las Malditas* and *Las Misteriosas* that allowed them to construct language learning cultures through their formation of their cliques and to find safe houses where they could playfully move back and forth between the contested boarders of the discursive regimes of Spanish and English. These safe houses became their theatre for the performance of their language hopes and desires.

These students, through such confident practices, were exploring different learning projects for exorcising the ghost of the native speaker of English, experimenting with the composition of transidiomatic practices in both languages, and finding out how to be themselves in these performances. This involved confronting the colonial difference in language education at the *Centro*. That difference maintained that English was to be performed within the context of native-speakerism, which in turn engendered questions about authenticity of the students' speech acts in both languages (Woolard, 2005). This confrontation required the students to understand the dynamics of the deterritorialisations of both languages and to be willing to impose their own needs and desires for how they wanted to reterritorialise their language performances based upon successful communicative interactions. We feel that these various practices suggest a movement towards a politics of affinity between language performers within their own language and other postcolonial users of English.[18]

Having said that, let us now introduce the content of this chapter. We will present four stories of how, in this overall context, students are moving away from being language learners to being language users. As a whole, the range of these four stories will allow us to illustrate the various processes that most students face sooner or later in their personal and professional lives as English performers. At the conclusion of their studies, feeling confident that they have scripted their English studies so as to be able to perform as they wish, students often find the time and space to reflect upon the learning that has brought them to where they are. This is the story of the Curriculum Revision Clique. They embarked upon a highly critical metalinguistic journey that allowed them to move from being language learners to language planners. This included a proposal for the construction of a better curriculum for future students enrolled in the B.A. programme at the *Centro*.

Within this growing confidence, language users can begin to envision how to move from being reflective about their learning to being creative or experimental with their performances. These creative activities involve finding ways to be themselves in their language activities that are beyond the hegemony of the classroom or the textbook. The story of the Poetry Group is a good illustration of this movement. Helped by their teacher, who fortunately was also interested in their development, they were able to find ways to be themselves through the process of writing poems.

---

18 The claim that these students are moving towards a politics of affinity between themselves and other postcolonial users of English is based on their own comments and our observations on how their various words games and patterns of social interaction suggest such movements. We are aware that it is more an interpretative move on our part to understand their feelings and concerns than a quantitative proof. The activities of various groups in this chapter offer more collective representations of this movement.

This journey from being a language learner to becoming a language user brings students to a crossroads where they have to move away from the *Centro* and use their performances to enter the outside world of work, politics and social action. The story of Martha captures this transition as she moved from being a student to becoming a teacher. Martha's experiences illustrate many of the attitudes, concerns and difficulties that young adults, who have recently graduated from the programme at the *Centro*, confront as novice teachers. Having gained confidence as an excellent language learner, Martha was able to work on her teaching skills and self esteem in order to become a teacher that her students would believe in.

In the political economy of this globalised postcolonial world that these students are part, the use of English has complex social and political implications. Ervin's story is a daring and challenging account of what such implications can mean in one's everyday life. Ervin is by far one of the more experienced and confident performers presented in this chapter. Along his journey, however, he wanders back and forth between the social and political advantages and obstacles of performing English with a postcolonial accent.

We are using this distinction between language learners and users not to suggest fixed positions of performance, but rather to capture the movement and actions in these students' endeavours. Clearly there are no fixed boundaries between language learning and use, they are co-existing performative events.[19] However, it is in the social and cultural context of language education at the *Centro* where these students are located as learners, and it is the various certification processes of this education that is supposed to award them the right to be located within the domain of being a user of the language. One of the central themes of our narrative has to do with how the students have contested these scripted locations and have been seeking to rewrite that script. The ethnographic accounts in this chapter offer a preview of what this new script will be for language practices and performances. That is to say, it will suggest what might constitute the linguistics praxis of these students' politics of affinity based upon communicative interaction.

Performing as English educators: Whose agency has agency?

In 2002, the faculty at the *Centro* carried out a major evaluation of the curriculum in their undergraduate programme. The evaluation stressed that since the

---

19 Though we do not wish to enter into the hermeneutical dilemma of the dog chasing its own tail, it is clear to us, that language use could in many cases precede language learning. That is why we state that they coexisting activities.

current TESOL programme was more than ten years-old, major updating in the teaching content was needed. It also pointed out that the programme should be structured with more flexibility to cope with the different expectations and interests of students. The language area of the curriculum was one of the first to be evaluated and changed. The English faculty worked together for six months to develop what was thought to be an innovative programme. The outcome was a process-oriented syllabus programme (Nunan, 1988), that was open enough to allow space for teachers to manoeuvre while still making their own planning decisions:

> ... we have chosen not to suggest any particular procedures or techniques that teachers should follow. Instead, we want to provide a brief description of what we understand as some of the aspects of communicative language teaching (CLT). The actual teaching practice, of course, is entirely up to the teacher herself, and is heavily influenced by her own personal style and the particular group she is working with.
>
> (*Facultad de Idiomas*, 2002: 8)

Responding to this pedagogical orientation, and with the concept of 'language as a *set of skills* that ought to be used in real communication' (ibid., 9), the programme does not prescribe the linguistic content or the specific teaching activities that the professor should carry out in order to teach. However, it suggests ways to create the necessary communicative conditions for students to develop their linguistic skills:

> We have chosen instead to give a list of the elements which teachers ought to include in classroom tasks, projects and on tests. What follows, however, is meant to be suggestive, not prescriptive. These will be general components of a foreign language syllabus that, when taken together, form the basis of a strong and comprehensive EFL syllabus.   (ibid.)

Finally, the programme puts special emphasis on students:

> ... teachers are encouraged, whenever possible, to try and engage their students in a process of negotiating the content of the course, a unit of study, or a specific task. Success in language learning depends greatly on the extent to which a teacher can get the students involved in their own

learning; allowing for a negotiation between the teacher and the student is a very effective way of fostering this involvement. (ibid.)

With this pedagogical orientation, the current programme does not prescribe the grammatical content or the specific teaching activities that the teacher should carry out. The stress was on how to create the necessary communicative conditions for students to develop their linguistic skills.

What we (that is, the faculty) thought as innovative was not *per se* shared by the students. In the summer of 2006, the generation of students who had entered under the new programme were close to graduating. In a interesting and challenging exchange of learning concerns, six young women from this generation suggested what they thought to be a more innovative and adequate revision of the English curriculum.

Adriana, Rebeca, Odelma, Dalila, Heidee and Angelica (the Curriculum Revision Clique) started their undergraduate programme four years ago. Adriana and Rebeca are from the city of Oaxaca. The other four are from different parts of the state and moved to the city for their undergraduate studies. Odelma comes from Jalapa del Marquez in the Isthmus area; Dalila comes from Nochixtlan, one of the larger communities of the Mixteca; Heidee and Angelica are from a Mixteca speaking village in this same area.[20] From the beginning of their studies, these young women (except for Rebeca, who has been part of different social groups) formed a rather closed clique. They stood out for their commitment and hard work but also for their quiet and reserved style of behaviour.

To outsiders, it seemed as if they were overwhelmed by the new academic and social context. It turned out that they were not precisely timid; they simply presented their persistence in a low key manner. Little by little, they showed more confidence and assertiveness in their academic work, to the point that all of them decided that, as part of their last year of studies, they would apply for a place in the national mobility programme that allows students to study a semester away from their home institution. All of them were accepted and they spent a semester at UNAM (Universidad Nacional Autónoma de México), the national public university in Mexico City.

There, they quickly learned the difference between the provinces and the metropolitan academic worlds. UNAM is one of the leading educational centres in the world, whereas the Oaxacan state university's academic assets have been

---

20 Heidee and Angelica have co-authored an article, with two of their professors, on 'creating and sharing power through critical dialogue' as a way to become better language educators, learners and researchers (López et al, 2006). This experience certainly helped to enhance their critical awareness.

eclipsed by its political conflicts and limited resources (Martínez Vázquez, 2004b). This difference was very clear to them in terms of English language instruction at the two universities. From this awareness sprang their quest to revise the programme back in Oaxaca. The logic of their argument was anchored on the assumption that since they had spent four years in this programme they knew its weaknesses better than anybody else:

> We are about to graduate and we feel like we do not have the proficiency level we should have at this stage of our language education. We know how to use English grammar but we do not use the language in everyday contexts. To us, it seems that teachers prefer to teach only from their textbook and they focus more on teaching us the structure of the grammar rather than encouraging us to actually use the language. You can see this in the classrooms, where, because there is such contrasting level of language skills among the students, those with lower skills have problems of low-esteem and do not like to participate in class activities. We do not think we are prepared well enough to be good English teachers.

Their sentiments were based upon the experiences they had endured during the four years of their studies. The rationale behind their proposal, therefore, included academic aspects (to improve the programme and to form better prepared teachers) but also psychological issues in order to increase students' self-esteem. All this, they say, would be a way to pay back the institution for their education, which had profoundly affected their lives. Angelica says that:

> Studying at the B.A. programme was the best thing that has happened to me. In my personal experience ... firstly, I have become a multilingual person. Second, I am a pre-service English teacher though I feel capable to teach Spanish as well. Next, during these years I have learned not only the language but also I learned to give a high importance to my first and second languages that are Mixteco and Spanish respectively. I am proud of my language, my culture and, above all, my profession as an English teacher.

The Guide

The Curriculum Revision Clique was aware that if they wanted to propose major changes in the existing programme, they needed more than just their feelings; they had to attain input from other students in their generation, and they needed to find out the views of the faculty and the administrators at the *Centro*. So, for their senior thesis project[21], they carried out their own investigation on how other members of the community felt about the curriculum. From these different bits of information they put together a series of proposals for innovation which was presented to the faculty for their consideration. They were hopeful that their ideas might have an impact on the curriculum reform at the *Centro*.

Their major concerns are stated on a document called *The Guide*, which focuses on the questions of teaching methodology and content. First of all, they proposed an approach to teaching whose central element was to be on students' language needs. They summarised it with the following diagram:

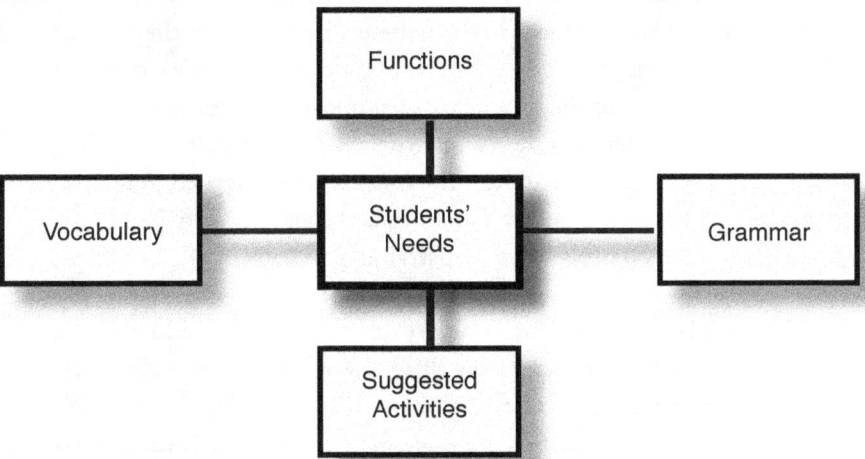

Fig. 2 Teaching model proposed by the Curriculum Revision Clique

In this model, the teacher' decisions about *what* to teach (vocabulary, grammar and functions) and *how* to teach (suggested activities) had to be based on the specific needs of the students the teacher was dealing with. That was their way to conceive of a student-centred approach: everything should evolve around the language needs of the students.

---

21 In Mexico, B.A. students are required to write a dissertation on the area of their studies. In the case of the programme in the *Centro* de Idiomas, this dissertation has a length of sixty pages approximately and it has to be written in English.

In order to ensure that the teacher included all the linguistic aspects they thought the students needed, they worked on long lists of vocabulary items, grammar structures, communicative functions and activities that were spread along the eight English levels of the curriculum.

The reaction of the members of the faculty to this part of the proposal was mixed. While some were very happy to have a guide that will assure a better development, others were concerned about the lack of contextualisation of the content. The latter told the Curriculum Revision Clique that they were expecting to see more elements of what students need in Oaxaca and less about the usual topics of 'going on vacation, keeping on a diet or ordering food in a restaurant'. At this point, these six young women insisted that they needed to know *everything*, arguing that 'our case is completely different (from regular English students) because we are trained to become English teachers and we need to know everything in order to make the best decisions for our students.'

As the negotiations between the students and the faculty over these curriculum issues became more intense, the students felt that they had opened a Pandora's Box. Every time they raised one issue, several more would come up. In particular, they found the experience of proposing the teaching contents for each semester very demanding. Apart from having difficulties deciding how students should be graded and how the four elements of their guide could be combined (grammar, vocabulary, functions and suggested activities), they also found that the overall process was constraining:

> Doing a syllabus turned out to be very difficult and involved a lot of hard work. I learned many things from this project, but the one reality we had to face was the most dramatic: in order to develop a new class syllabus one has to deal with the bureaucracy of the institution. The success of a syllabus depends more on how the administration takes it into account. Most of the times, it is the politics of a school that influences the design of a syllabus, and not the concerns about student learning.

They clearly hope that there could be a different outcome:

> It would be better if the acceptance of a syllabus was not simply a matter of meeting the rules of the institution. Actually an excellent syllabus is when it considers students' needs and not administrative needs. A syllabus should be made to help students in their learning. I would like students

to participate in the design of the syllabus. In that way, teachers will focus the syllabus on students. This kind of involvement by students would demonstrate how seriously they are about the demands of becoming a teacher.

However, they were aware that, in spite of their efforts to make things better, whatever they proposed would not work if teachers did not do their part:

> We are totally sure that having the 'right' textbook is not the solution ... We feel that some teachers only work with the material from the text and they do not try to make the class more interesting. However they could make use of a great tool, their creativity. Everyone can make their own decision as whether they want to be a good teacher or a bad one.

As stated earlier, their concerns are motivated by feeling that they had not been adequately trained for the task of being English teachers. Their concerns were valid. Their levels of English were not as good as the average English level found among students in university programs in Mexico City or in the northern part of the country, where an advanced level of English is an entrance requirement. This demand would be an impossible requirement for the students who enter the English programme at the *Centro*. The majority of the students who wish to enter this programme come out of the public school system, and at best have had only basic instruction in English, which in reality makes them false beginners. The Curriculum Revision Clique understood that it was impossible to raise the entrance requirements:

> When we began with this project our expectations were too high, we assumed that the first year students who entered the *Centro* should have a basic knowledge of English. However, we are aware that many young people in Oaxaca do not have the opportunity to take English courses in addition to the classes they take in secondary and high school. For this reason we dropped the idea of entrance requirements, and proposed instead a training course in order to make students become familiar with the English language.

Thus they renounced their idea of a high English level for the entrance requirements and instead proposed that there should be a two week training course for all students before starting the programme. This course would include linguistic and pedagogical components. The former would deal with issues of basic vocabulary (words and idiomatic expressions) and basic grammar. The latter would focus on the development of learning strategies for the students to gain lexical and grammatical knowledge.

In order for their proposed changes to actually reflect the desires and needs of the students, they also suggested changes in the processes of achievement evaluation. They felt that the evaluations of students' achievements should fulfil two functions: to be able to place students in appropriate classes that actually reflected their skills levels and; to be able to use teaching strategies that would focus on the communicative context those students desired. For them, the achievement evaluation techniques would be framed in terms of having the students develop language performance projects that would be presented every year. According to them, developing these kind of projects

> ... would allow the students to get involved with real contexts of language use. No matter what level or what age, the most important thing is to connect this new information with their real lives in order to make it more useful and meaningful.

In using these everyday language projects as a means of evaluation, they hoped that the approaches of their professors would move away from solely metalanguage issues, and allow for the integration of the four macro linguistic skills. The Curriculum Revision Clique wanted the students to have the freedom to develop their projects according to their relevance to their everyday contexts. The following are some of the examples they provided:

- Talk about things you want to change in your town, in your country or in the world;
- Give a presentation on Oaxacan food, using specialised vocabulary and prepare the food in the classroom from your own recipe, explaining the whole process or even proposing an original way to do it.
- Present a play that you have written, describing the costumes and scenario.
- Explain a problem in Oaxaca (teachers' strikes, indigenous languages in Oaxaca, poor people in Oaxaca, the government, *porros* in the university, etc.), support your ideas with good arguments and propose a solution.

Thus, the Curriculum Revision Clique managed to include the contextualisation element that some of their teachers had asked for. However, they also managed to maintain the students' freedom to decide the content of their English performance. They concluded their argument stating that they believed that their proposal included the academic aspects needed to form better prepared teachers but that it would also cope with psychological issues in order to increase students' self-esteem.

Underlying their innovation, these six highly-committed students were aware that, in spite of what more conventional educators think:

> There is shift going on in language education now, and for the good ... We have gone beyond of traditional ways where students had to perform perfectly and only teachers had the right to judge their work. In the past, students used to play a passive role, sit quietly and receive input. Nowadays we are conscious of the situation and it is our responsibility to improve the teaching/learning process little by little. Let's see how far we can go.

Reflections

This is a very interesting story in terms of the themes that we have been developing in this study. Present here are ironic tales about the accumulation of cultural and linguistic capital; the expression of agency as both a project and a mode of resistance; the struggle of these young ladies so that all the students could be themselves in this other language; and the challenge of the authority of the colonial difference through a movement towards a politics of affinity and the absence of the ghost of the native speaker.

Before these students were the Curriculum Revision Clique, they were seen as a group that was timid and somewhat overwhelmed by the urban complexity of the city of Oaxaca and the cosmopolitan qualities of the university. It turned out, however, that they were aware of the cultural and linguistic capital they were accruing in this context and were quite sophisticated about how to pursue their educational goals and desires. They used their accumulation of cultural capital to obtain scholarships to study at the UNAM in Mexico City. There, they were able to understand the different levels of academic capital between their provisional home university in Oaxaca and the sophisticated world of the national university. But instead of being 'overwhelmed' by these differences, it engendered in them a desire to return to their home context and to struggle to attain for future students a level of academic quality that would be equal to what they had confronted at UNAM. They anchored their authority to seek such curriculum reforms in the fact that since they had suffered through the deficiency of the current programme, they were best located to offer alternatives. Here they were using their collective agency both as part of a quest for a particular project as well as a mode of resistance. It is also where they came upon and confronted the various agencies of the professors and the staff of the *Centro*.

As can be noted by the references to the policy changes adopted by the faculty at the *Centro* in 2002, these were very similar to the changes that were being advocated by the Curriculum Revision Clique. The changes of 2002 were supposed to be student-centred, focused on the communicative competence of the students and open to the participation of the students in the development of programs' goals and objectives. They were not to be grammar-based. In fact, these policy changes were primarily the work of those who were thought to be the progressive members of the faculty. However, by the end of first generation of students that went through this programme, as expressed by this clique, the exact opposite of what they had hoped took place. These students felt all they received was grammar and not communicative skills for the use of English in an everyday context. Nor did they feel that the faculty was student-oriented. Their perception was that the English professors were in fact wed to their course textbook, which for students seemed only to offer boring metalinguistic insights. Some of the more progressive faculty members felt that the students' suggestions would be a return to more traditional forms of instruction and did not reflect current reform movements in educational language. Here is where we encounter whose agency has agency? That is, whose agency is to prevail: the knowing progressive faculty's agency expressed through forms of academic capital based upon what they have accumulated through their involvements in international relations of applied linguistics and TESOL or these young students' agency that was driven from the experiential context of their educational adventures? Another irony here was that what the students' proposal envisioned as a possible brake on their suggested reforms—lack of faculty and administrative support—were the factors that had limited the success of the progressive faculty's proposal for change. That is, even though these policy changes were formally codified, their actual interpretation and application was left to be determined by each faculty member. The Curriculum Revision Clique's view was that no changes had actually taken place. Thus, both the progressive faculty and students had the same hopes and desires about language education, but were being stalled by resistance of the agency of others in the programme who were not, in fact, with the programme.

Thus, whose agency has agency in this tale? Clearly all the various actors are expressing the different ways in which agency can be performed, particularly in terms of differential forms of power and authority. Equally clear is that the faculty and administration have the actual power in this domain, whether it be through authorship of policy changes, in the administrative power of running the programme, or in the informal power of indifference. The power of the students was located in their hopes that their voices could be heard within this context. For us, it was not so important whether what the students were advocating were new methods of language learning or whether they were reinventing traditional styles of language teaching. What was important was that they were stating that the success of their language education was determined in terms of how far they could be themselves in these processes. They wanted a language education and a teaching education that would give them access to using language and teaching in various ways that fit their needs and hopes. For them, their subjectivity as language actors was as important as any particular methods or teaching strategies. In fact, they are searching for a kind of methodology or teaching strategies that could afford spaces for the feelings, hopes and desires of students. Their use of agency as project was not just to achieve a unitary goal, but was about their freedom to be themselves. Also, this freedom was to be affirmed by the successful performance of their communicative language and teaching skills in the context of their everyday lives. As important and insightful the projects of the progressive faculty are for a more valid curriculum, they need to remember that they had advocated that these programs be open to student participation. Ironically, it could be said that the students' challenge to their programme was an indication of its success. We would humbly suggest that the faculty should be looking for ways to blend the students' vision of what their language world should be with their somewhat more pragmatic understanding of the politics of these quests. The faculty needs to remember that these students want *everything*, not jesters or promises, but affirmations of themselves in these processes.

This is where we see the Curriculum Revision Clique challenging the hegemonic authority of the colonial difference through their expression of a politics of language affinity. They were claiming the right to produce knowledge that was valid and useful in their educational context. Further, what they were advocating was not something for themselves, but for future language students at the *Centro*. Since they were all about to graduate, if any of their suggestions came to fruition, it would be for the next generation of students. Their quest is for their language and teaching performances to be validated by successful communicative interaction. They were also suggesting that through a politics of affinity with other English language users and teachers, a social context could be created in which their collective skills and usages could be composed, performed and affirmed. This is reflected in their concerns that students be given spaces that would encourage more rather than less self-esteem and that would facilitate sentiment such as the one expressed by Angelica's statement that her language education provided her with the opportunity to embrace the intercultural spaces between English, Spanish, and her natal language of *Mixteco*, and that such opportunities should be there for other language students in the future.

A further challenge to the colonial difference reflected in these tales was the absence of discourse about the 'ghost of the native speaker'. In all their plans and proposals, the students showed no concern over the role of the native versus the non-native speaker in learning, using or teaching English. For them, these identity locations were not relevant to either their goals or hopes. They had assumed, by their movement through the curriculum at the *Centro* and their adventures at UNAM, that their claims for users' rights over English were non-contestable. Interestingly, this was not a concern of the faculty in their reactions to these proposals. They had all left the confines of this double bind and were performing English with scripts they had composed.

The final irony of this tale is that, since their proposed curriculum revisions were part of their thesis projects and not formal proposals for policy changes, they were left floating in ambiguous spaces of the 'hoped for,' instead of in the spaces where ideas were actually acted upon. No doubt this performance of English with a postcolonial accent will be taken up by other students. In fact, our next story suggests such a direction.[22]

Postcolonial English poetics: Creating and recreating the language

In this section we want to talk about a set of language activities that express the full range of issues we have been exploring in this book. This ethnographic example involves how one of the senior faculty members at the *Centro* used his

---

22 As we were writing the final version of this book, these students told me (Angeles) that before they started with the next step of their careers (two are already working as English teachers and the other four are leaving to England and the States to attain teacher assistantship programs), they wanted to ask the institution to allow a presentation of their project to the English faculty. They are certain that it would be better to address the professors themselves instead of looking for an administrative move to change the curriculum.

English writing class as a forum to allow students to explore how to be critical and creative writers, which resulted in these students putting their creative writings (mainly poems) into a volume which they had printed for the use of others, which in turn allowed another student to use these materials as a means to structure the English class she was teaching. This tale temporarily ends with two current students using the experience of this class for their senior thesis on teaching methodology. Flowing through this tale are the issues of English userhood, the exorcism of the ghost of the native speaker by confronting the authority of the colonial difference, the sharing of cultural capital through being themselves in this other language, and the production of transidiomatic practices to express their linguistic praxis.

This tale begins in the summer of 2004, when, Sam Johnson, one of the senior members of the faculty (though only part time) offered an English writing class. Sam has been a long time advocate of exploring critical and creative methods for his writing classes. Of particular interest to him is how creative writing could be used to help his students both improve their English writing skills as well as find new ways to use the language. The class that he presented at the *Centro* was an elective course on writing in English and he wanted to structure it around ideas on creative writing that he had developed from a work by Gabriele Rico (1983) on natural writing. He thought this would be possible because the class was an elective course, the students were in their fourth year, and they were highly motivated to explore how to improve their writing skills in English. They entered the class assuming that it would be about how to write using a formal or an academic style of English. This was not what Sam had in mind. He wanted them to write about themselves: what they felt, thought or wished for. One of the students summarises how difficult this challenge was for them:

> The first thing he did was to ask us to write anything we thought or felt about ourselves. At the beginning it was very difficult for us, because we were worried about making mistakes and we were not sure what the content should be. Also, we must confess, the topic made us feel uncomfortable. Being asked to write something about oneself is not easy to do. It is not something we were familiar with. On the contrary, for us to write something personal, and to know that it is going to be read by another person that you do not know or trust, is horrible, makes you feel embarrassed, and of course, creates anxiety at the moment of writing. ... Those and many other thoughts knocked

about our brains at the moment of writing. Those thoughts stood in the way of what we really wanted to say and resulted in writings that were monotonous and artificial, and revealed almost nothing about us.

(Cisneros and Valenzuela, 2006: 35)

As would be expected, their first writings were neither promising nor interesting. They were not yet comfortable being themselves in this language. Sam anticipated these results, and with such writing techniques as word clusters, vignettes and mind maps,[23] he encouraged the students not to worry at first about the correctness of their writings, but to experiment with their words and thoughts. These techniques involve a series of exercises in which the students first clustered words together to see what they could do with them and then attempted to place these words into short vignettes either in prose or poetry. As the students began to accept this approach, their fears and worries lessened. According to the students, with the freedom to write about anything they came to feel empowered. That is, they felt the resources for writing were inside of them and by drawing upon these resources, the results were very surprising and the writing was far more authentic, fresh and original than with conventional methods. With this open invitation to write about themselves, their inspirations were awaken, and their creative energy just seemed to flow and grow.

More than two hundred examples of poems and short prose pieces were composed by these students. They had produced written performances expressing a wide range of feelings, thoughts, emotions and fears. By being encouraged to use their language agency in ways that were expressive of their

---

23 Sam, drawing from Rico 1983, defines these terms in the following manner: 'The heart of the method is called clustering. This is an exercise that you do prior to writing. We take a word or phrase, write it on the paper, draw a circle around it, and then whatever word or phrase that comes to mind, we write it down, circle it, and connect it to the first word by a line. At first, it may appear that the words have no relationship to each other. But suddenly the writer feels a shift, and the feeling that he or she needs to write, and comes up with a writing which relates the words to each other and one which is original, fresh and vigorous.

At first we concentrate on short writings called vignettes. These may take the form of a paragraph, a poem, or something else. We do not try to dictate either the form or the outcome. The point is to be able to write in a free manner, and come up with a unified whole. Later on, these principles may be applied to a longer, more structured composition, such as an essay, story, or research paper.

A vignette, unlike a paragraph, is a whole, complete thought or statement on a subject, a fully expressed idea, even a very short story with a fully developed plot. When we write a paragraph, we assume it is part of something finished, which needs something before and after. And we learned that a paragraph has a beginning, middle and an end.

A vignette stands as an aesthetic whole, and it developed naturally from clustering. It can be the length of one paragraph or several, or it can be a free-verse poem or dialogue. The writing of longer pieces is actually a process of composing a series of vignettes, mini-wholes, which later become incorporated into a larger, more comprehensive whole. Writing short vignettes, no more than 10 minutes in length, helps to capture this sense of wholeness'.

subjective states of being, they responded with courageous reflections upon themselves and their personal and social histories. Below we offer several poetic examples of how these students were being themselves.

The poem by Rhomani came from an exercise in which the students were playing 'parallel and balanced rhythms using the phrase 'and I have learned ...' (Johnson et al., 2007, 59). We also see her poem as an exploration of her personal anxieties and self worth.

Anorexia
by Rhomani
And I have learned how to live without it,
Learned how to overcome it,
How to control it,
Even how to reject it when it seems
Like an anxiety inside my body.
We have broken a link, my anorexia and I.

Araceli's poem comes from various cluster activities that dealt with how to use metaphors, that is 'attributing images or qualities to things which they literally could not be' (ibid., 79). Thus, this poem could be read as a metaphor for one's feelings towards alienation.

Sharpened dagger
by Rosa Araceli
Sharpened dagger
Hurting time
Breaking bones
Pure ashes.
Simpler than a gun
More painful than a bomb
Stabbing through the skin
Separating souls.

An earlier poem written by Araceli comes from an exercise in which the students were playing with modelling their writing on the work of other writers. In this activity, they were working with an untitled poem by the American poet Meter Meinke (ibid., 11). Through this modelling, Araceli found a means by which to explore what is involved in intimacy and friendship.

Anonymous Friend
by Rosa Araceli

This is a poem to the blue-eyed guy
Whom I have hurt a million times
Whose faithful and big heart
Has been torn by myself.
You knew to make me feel
To put up with all my whims.
Understanding everything I said
And if you scolded me once
You also gave me another chance.
It was your sincere sight which
Reflected your beautiful child's soul
Bent in defeat, brave man's tears
Because of my failure and my fears
I have scarred you with pain
And I've suffered from your aches
Because when I needed someone to blame
You were there to be my friend
And because
I thought I knew
You were special and fair
Your blue eyes and blond hair
Made me feel and enjoy each day.
Thanks for understanding my despair
And being loyal as you were
Many thanks, dearest friend.
Now, I'm writing this to you
Feeling repentant to what I do
Because I think it was wrong
I ask for your pardon
My beloved friend.
So I write this to forget
For becoming alive again
For being as you were
I write this to your forgiveness
Dearest anonymous blue-eyed friend

As means to use all things learned in this class, they were asked to compose the vignette model around family members. They were to use 'wholeness, images, language rhythms, metaphors, recurrences and creative tension' (ibid., 96).

We were certainly captivated by Elena's poem, for it offers a poetic history of her family and friends in contrast to the ethnographic portrait of her presented in chapter three.

A Wedding Picture

by Elena

'This is a beautiful picture, isn't it?'
'Oh! Yes, it is.'
'What an important day that was. When was this picture taken?'
'Two years ago.'
'Who's that? He looks a little tired.'
'Oh! That's my Grandfather.'
'Can you tell me about him?'
'Sure, heaven is his home. It is good to know that, even thought we miss him. The Family is divided, but please don't think that it is because of his departing. His daughters don't share the same ideas and they couldn't understand that he had to leave us. Everybody loves him and his passing was very painful. Now, everyone continues their normal lives. I hope he blesses his family and smiles because we know he is fine in his recent new home.'
'I'm so sorry about your grandfather's death. Look! Who is he?'
'He is my oldest brother who lives in an amazing and great world—that's what he believes. Alcohol, fun, games, and friends are part of his life. He doesn't know about honesty, earning money and living in a moral way. How enjoyable is his life that he can't see the uncertain and grey future he could live. Can you see this? Can you see the pain? Can you see the barrier he is constructing here? Oh! Dear brother what can we do? If we take different roads, his is bringing pain and disunity to this home. I don't want to see this, I can't stand it and I can't stand his friends; the alcohol and drugs. I can't stand his crazy dark nightlife.'
'Oh! That is so sad. Look—this is your sister. She is pretty. What did you say to her that day?'
'Good luck sister, good luck in your new life, good luck girl. So many things are waiting for you, your new family, your new home, and your new experience with your love. Good luck and thank you. I remember our pranks, your teaching and help. This is a great day, which I will never forget. You look so beautiful in your wedding dress. Good luck sister, good luck friend.'
'Beautiful words. Is that you?'
'Yes, it is. How did I look that day?'
'Well, fine. But you look tired.'
I've been working hard.'
'By the way, did you see your love before he left?'
'I couldn't—I worked that day.'
'Can I tell you something?'
'Yes.'

'You, living in this busy world, do you have time to enjoy life? I can't see your personal life. The clock is ticking and time will never come back. Why are you longing to see him again? You had the opportunity, but you were busy that day. Do you know that the events never take place the same way? Is your family so important to you? So, give them more of your time. What about your Mom—is she immortal? God lent her to you a little while. Time is passing and you are not enjoying it. Go and search for your love—go and enjoy life.'

'Oh! I would like time to stop like in this picture—everything stays the same, nothing changes in it. We looked so happy that day.'

Based upon what they were able to do in this class, ten of the students, with the help of Sam, are working on having these poems published. They have chosen some two hundred poems that will be included in the volume. These poems run from the ones that are fairly ordinary to the ones that are quite exceptional. What is most striking in all of them is the willingness of the writers to be themselves through these poems. They hope that their publication can reach three different types of readers: their classmates, their teachers and the English speaking world. They hope that their classmates will see how it is possible to be creative in their writing in English and that the experience of being themselves can be rewarding and enjoyable. For their teachers, they want them to understand that they need to trust the students in a different way. The teachers have to think beyond their own assumptions and envision what the hopes and aspirations of their students are. They want their teachers to believe in their abilities and above all

> teachers must understand that each student has a different perception of reality and that these perceptions are reflected in their writings. Teachers should respect students' perceptions and not try to change or alter them in some way only because they do not agree with them. (Cisneros and Valenzuela, 2006: 66).

To the English speaking world, they want to say that their English is valid and unique. Through their claim to the userhood of this language, they can 'produce any kind of writing they want' and that their writings can show a diversity of contents and ideas that make references to their 'personal experiences and perspectives'. They want the world to know that they can 'sail on the sea of creativity' in this other language that happens to be English. Or as we would say, while showing the confidence to perform English with a postcolonial accent, they are constructing new spaces for the expression of social beings.

These new spaces are actual safe houses in which they perform according to their imagined communities, accepting the fact that they suffer from eating disorders, that their families are far from perfect, that they can acknowledge their mistakes and that they even are able to confront metaphorical dangerous daggers. Obviously, these linguistic safe houses also function as places where they learn how to live without anxieties, accepting love from others, asking for forgiveness and enjoying memories. For some of them these textual safe houses exist in English and Spanish, either if the latter was there long before they developed an ability to transfer their skills to English or if they started in Spanish after they discovered, through Sam's course, that they could actually write poetry. For others, these houses only stay in English because that may be the only way to warrantee their safety.

Making teaching decisions: The reproduction of English

This tale takes an interesting twist. Sarahi, a fourth year student, has been developing her thesis on the idea of exploring the possibilities of connotative and denotative meanings as a methodological tool for English students. She grew up on the coast of Oaxaca near the city of Pochutla. She came to the city of Oaxaca at the age of fifteen to go to high school and has stayed to continue her studies at the university. She is described by her classmates as a responsible, highly committed student, and 'one of the few who were born to be a teacher'.

She has recently been teaching an English class at the *Centro*. When looking for appropriate material to use in her class, she came across some of the poems that had been written in Sam's class. She found them quite engaging and thought that she might be able to use them to offer her students a different way to learn English. The following is a compound account of how this experiment worked out. The data was taken from our notes and from drafts from her thesis (Cruz, 2006).

Sarahi's English class was very small, only four teenagers, and even though they had some basic level of English, they were not really interested in learning more. She suggested to them they might like to read some poetry, written by students like them, as a way to better understand and use English. She told them that through poems they could learn how to express their feelings in ways that made it easier to say things that were hard to address. Her idea was to present them with one of the students' poems from Sam's class, and then show them how to read through or between the lines as a means of interpretation. She chose a poem written by Tomás. She gave them a brief introduction to the poem, explained how it had been written in an English writing class and then she gave them a copy of the poem to read. Then she asked who would like to read the poem aloud to the class. Sandy volunteered for the task. She read:

> *Nothing that belonged to me*
> *by Tomás*
> I had a pain, but it did not hurt me;
> A big flame inside my body,
> But it did not burn me; sadness, but not sorrow
> I had an anxiety, but not a wish; cold blood, but I was hot;
> A beat, but no heart; many things to say but no energy.
> And words to say them; a big smile, but no lips;
> A poem to write, but no hands, no pencil no paper
> Wherewith to give a shape. I had all these things, and
> Slept and dreamt; but waking up was horrible, because
> I had nothing that belonged to me.

When Sandy finished reading the poem, Sarahi asked the students what their impressions were. They were silent and offered no comments. Nobody wanted to talk. So she decided to try to explain to them the structure of the poem. Their exchanges went as follows:

> *Sarahi*: As you can see, in the poem there are different words that help you to understand the meaning of other words. There are verbs, what tense is it used?
> *Students*: Past
> *Sarahi*: Does anybody have questions about unknown words, or words that you don't understand?
> *Mari*: Yes teacher, I don't know pain, flame, sorrow, beat, *y espéreme* [wait].
> *Rosi*: *Yo tengo otras* [I have others]
> *Sarahi*: OK, before you know the meaning of these words, let's talk about the words that you know. (Cruz, 2006)

Based upon their questions and answers, Sarahi thought it would help to explore the content of the poem. She suggested to the students they try to guess the meaning of the words by looking at the context in which they were presented. This turned out to be quite hard and they had to go line by line through the poem, stopping at each word they did not understand. It went in this fashion:

Sarahi: Who wants to read the first line?
Alberto: I had a pain, but it did not hurt me
Sarahi: Who understands the words in this line?
Alberto: *Tener es en pasado y el* hurt *es como lastimar, no?* [to have is in past tense and hurt is kind of *lastimar*, isn't it?]
Sandy: *Pero está en negativo, entonces es como tenía algo que no lo lastimaba.* [but it is negative, something like he had something that didn't hurt him]
Rosi: *Puede ser* pain *como enfermedad?* [Can pain refer to illness?]
Mari: *¿O un problema también, no* teacher? [or a problem, isn't it teacher?]
Alberto: *Pero si es un enfermedad, como no le va a lastimar, creo que si le duele ...* [but if it is an illness, how is it that it doesn't hurt him?, I think it hurts him].
Sarahi: That is the clue; this line expresses a contradictory feeling.
Sandy: *Entonces* pain *es como algo que lo lastima ... dolor tal vez* [Then, pain is like something that hurts him, an ache maybe]
Sarahi: Exactly
Rosi: *¿Pero cómo que le duele y no le duele?* [But how is it that it hurts but it doesn't hurt?]
Mari: *¿Pero* teacher, *esto no es lo que dice, verdad?* [But, teacher, this is not what it says, isn't it?]
Sarahi: Well, the writer tries to say that ... a pain is something that hurts us, but he says that this pain didn't hurt him.
Mari: *Ah! por eso es contradictorio!* [That's why is contradictory!]
Alberto: *Ah! Como cuando uno no sabe qué tiene o siente* [like when we don't know what exactly has or feels].
Sarahi: Yes, that could be it ... OK. Who wants to read the second line?

When they finished understanding the poem line by line, she decided to work with two words—*sadness* and *sorrow*—to illustrate the use of connotative meaning in poetry. She said she chose these two words because their meanings were popular among teenagers. According to her, they perfectly reflected the feeling when one loses someone. She asked the students to write the words on the whiteboard and write all the ideas that they related with these two words. This is what they said in English about sadness:

> When we first read these lines ... well, I didn't understand all the vocabulary ... and for some words that, but when my students, no, my classmates start to say another ideas of the words I think about, for example, sadness in the word suffering because for me *la tristeza* [sadness] is suffering and I think in bad experiences. I don't like it ... *y ya* [and that's all]. (Alberto)

> *Yo*, I write the word melancholy, well, it is because when we have bad experiences we are sad, *bueno es lo que creo* [well, I believe that]. But the sadness is more than bad memories; we don't like to be sad. It is no good to anybody. (Rosi)

> I am sad when I break with my boyfriend, and I think when you are not with the person that you want. You don't know what to say or think, well ... if your boyfriend or girlfriend don't have love, you can put in a difficult way, *digo* [I mean], you have, ... no, you are sad. (Sandy)

> You feel sadness when you have problems or you don't do what you want or need to do. Because I am sad when my family have problems and I don't help my family or I can do nothing. This sadness is something that I don't like, for example, my friends tell me that it is normal, but I don't know, also I think sadness is like to be alone or need help and nobody help you ... and you don't ... *¿cómo es solucionar?* [how do you say *solucionar*?] ... *Bueno no solucionas problemas*. [OK, you don't solve the problems]. (Mari)

Then Sarahi suggested that they rewrite the sentences of the poem, that is to say, to use the poem to write their own sentences with similar meanings using different words and different grammar, but keeping its message. These are two examples of the task's outcome:

> I think that he has a pain very strong, maybe he is with his family or with his girlfriend and he has feeling very bad with himself and he has many things in his heart but he couldn't get it out of him (Mari).

> This poem expresses sadness, a big feeling. But I think a man is saying this to a woman, like if are love, but you try to say in words and then you can't because you use words that don't explain nothing. But the person who loves you, she can understand (Sandy).

Sarahi concluded her lesson telling them that a poem contains more than words, that it also expresses strong feelings, 'It may be that someone is confused, but in this confusion s/he tries to use logic, and in each word that s/he writes we find clues for understanding what kind of feeling s/he is trying to express' (Cruz, 2006).

What is interesting in Sarahi's experiment was that she was not trying to get her students to write poetry, but rather to use the poem to help the students understand the complexity and diversity of meanings in English. Her confidence to perform with a different teaching script seems to have been reflected in these four somewhat uninterested students. They were making very slow movements towards finding themselves in this other language.

The thesis

There is one more act in this tale (as of now). Two of the students in Sam's class chose to do their senior thesis on their experiences in the class and to offer a model for a creative writing class for the students at the *Centro*. Berenice and Araceli stated that the purpose of their thesis was 'to raise awareness in students and teachers that writing is not one of the most difficult skills to develop when learning a foreign language' (Cisneros and Valenzuela, 2006: 1). They felt from their experiences at the *Centro* that the 'majority of writing courses are based more on the usage of language and on the correction of mistakes rather than on students' ideas' (ibid.). They felt that they had 'the misfortune of living through that in our education formation' where students were required to write on an assigned subject matter, given little or no feedback and were 'never given time or help to generate and organise their ideas' (ibid.). They want their work to 'break down the power relationship that exists between the teacher and student'. They believed that a 'relationship of friendship and confidence between the teacher and the student will make learning an enjoyable and motivating experience' (ibid.).

Their thesis elaborated on many of the ideas that they had learned about in Sam's class. They analysed the way in which the issues of motivation, autonomy and brain mapping would provide the intellectual base that would allow students to enjoy more creative freedom in attempting to write in a different language, which in this case, is English. They reviewed what they had done in the class with Sam and presented what they though a class syllabus for creative writing would entail.

Then they offered their conclusions. First and foremost they wanted to stress that writing in another language could or should be fun and enjoyable. As said above, they stated that 'teachers must understand that each student has a different perception of reality and that these perceptions are reflected in their writings'. They argued that teachers should respect students' perceptions and should not try to change or alter those perceptions 'just because they do not agree with them' (ibid., 66). They invited their teachers to recognise the uniqueness in the writings of the students and to allow for the use of students' own experiences and perspectives in deciding what they wanted to write about. Through their work in Sam's class, they had the experience of dealing with a different way to learn how to write, one that was not based upon doing what they were told but rather based on their own realities. They concluded that 'it is through this type of writing course that students are taught how to stimulate the production and development of ideas and how to organise them to convey clear and powerful messages with a high degree of significance' (ibid., 67).

For our purposes, what is most important here is not so much the profundity of the intellectual base of these ideas on creative writing or how practical such a course would be (though Sam's work leaves little doubt about that) but rather the confidence they had to have felt in order to be able to state what they thought should be done to question power relations in both teaching and access to language use, and to seek a connection with future students through their passionate concern for a better and more enjoyable way to be themselves in these language performances.

Reflections

Though Sam and his students' rational and intellectual focus for these writing activities are somewhat different from the concerns of our analysis, the outcome is quite supportive of what we have been arguing. By contesting geopolitical knowledge production, they have involved themselves in the disinvention of the discursive authority of Standard English and have thus claimed for themselves the right of English userhood. They have refused to recognise the authority of the colonial difference. Furthermore, they have used these rights to express their agency through writing about their own states of being in terms of their feelings, hopes, desires and fears. They boldly proclaim that through these written performances, they can 'sail on the sea of creativity' (ibid.) in this other language that happens to be English. Their declarations avoid the double bind of the dichotomy of the qualities of native versus non-native speakers of English by simply not recognising its presence. They have exorcised the ghost of the native speaker through their creative performances of being themselves in this language. They are no longer located in the social spaces of the 'other'. Through their performances, they are relocating themselves into new personal and social spaces in this other language. This freedom was expressed in various academic roles (writers, critics and editors) and transidiomatic practices (language mixing and remixing and juxtaposing different modes of communication) but above all, it was expressed in the self-awareness of what they were seeking and desiring. They did not see their accumulation of cultural capital as bestowing upon them the ownership of these language activities but as a desire and passion to pass these user rights on to others. They want their poems published so other students, teachers and users of English can see and hear the pride they had in their efforts and compositions, they wanted these performances to be useful in the teaching of English classes and they wanted future students at the *Centro* to have access to the same creative freedom that had been able to attain. These desires and wishes were fulfilled by the agency of another student, Sarahi, who, by using one of their poems, motivated her students to express themselves.

The Poetry Group's agency, like those in the curriculum project, was both an expression of resistance as well as a quest for change. They want to resist the restrictive authority of traditional or standard teaching of English writing and to seek a future that would be open to all students to experiment with. That is, they are expressing their linguistic praxis through a politics of affinity for the creative and enjoyable use of language. This affinity is further expressed in Sarahi's use of the poetic material and Berenice and Araceli's idea about changing the perspective and approach toward the teaching of writing at the *Centro*.

Performing out there: teaching young adults at the university

One way to clearly illustrate that there is not a fixed location between the performances of language learners and users is to explore the activities that are used to English in the classroom. In this context, one can witness how a new script for language use is being composed. Below we present a portrait of Martha, a graduate from the *Centro*, who has been teaching two English classes at the university. These are classes for students in other colleges at the university who need English for their studies. This portrait will focus on how Martha had to find her own confidence in order to have validity as an English teacher to these students. In this tale, we see again confrontations among the colonial difference represented as the hovering of the ghost of the English native speaker, the movement of cultural capital funds in order to support new ways of performing English, and expressions of a politics of affinity through Martha's use of her agency to resist what others wanted her to be.

Martha comes from a family of two generations of teachers. Her parents met when they were studying for their degrees in education. Martha is the youngest of three children and the only girl. Her brothers are ten years older than her. She always enjoyed going to school and being active in school events. When she entered kindergarten, her two favourite games were being a teacher for her dolls and chanting and marching with her school friends during their parents' union demonstrations. She learned from her protesting experiences so well, that once her and her friends threatened the head of the kindergarten to organise a demonstration if she didn't change their classroom teacher. They were against this teacher because of her practice of putting paper balls in their mouths to stop them from talking.

Her time in elementary and secondary school was filled with ballet, piano and English lessons, along with the full range of school requirements and activities. In high school, she made the conscious decision of becoming an atheist, and began thinking about the issues of gender and sexuality. She started questioning her mother's perspective on gender such as, 'You should learn to cook, to be ready when you get married, but your brothers don't need that. They will have someone to cook for them.' It was in those days when she decided to become an English teacher:

> I discovered the magic of learning and teaching a language beyond the limits of 'only being able to have a conversation'. To know other forms of thinking enriches you in the way that you discover the reason underlying these differences, the body language that goes with that new language, and the challenges that you have to face in order to teach not only the sign system but also the meaning that goes with it. I was fascinated when I realised that.

To pursue this goal of being an English teacher, she entered the programme at the *Centro* and was able to graduate as one of their best students. After graduation, she taught English as a part-time instructor in several private elementary schools in Oaxaca and then was able to get a position at the Institute of Education (ICE) at UABJO to teach English to their undergraduate students. She remembers this experience in the following manner:

The ICE is one of the new schools in our university. In 2004 they had their first undergraduates. It has a new building on the main campus, a very impressive white hexagonal two storey building. The first floor holds the administrative offices and the second floor is mainly classrooms. There is also a media room, a computer room and a very nice library.

When they started their B.A., they didn't include English as a compulsory course, but it is now. Currently, the school offers three levels of English classes. I started working on the first level with first year students; I had a class of twenty women and six men. The first day of classes, these students were really angry because they had to take that class, and they didn't like that the class was run from four to five in the afternoon.

Even though they were to be very active students, most of their activities were directed at making trouble for me. I literally had to force them to attend classes and hand in assignments, and I had to be sure that the sitting arrangement did not favour cheating during exams. They were very happy when we had to cancel classes or if during the day their other classes were cancelled so they would not wait for my afternoon class.

The following term they gave me an English class at the second level. My new group was very different from the previous one. There were fifteen women and five men enrolled in the class. At the beginning I was a little nervous because I had heard that these students were very demanding with their professors. One of my former students told me:

'That class is a bunch of nerds, very demanding. You'll miss us!'

The first day of classes I was really afraid of them. When I showed up in the classroom they didn't even recognise me as the English professor. They thought that I was one of their classmates! They did not believe me until I raised my voice to tell them that I was their English professor. I introduced myself in Spanish trying to make the atmosphere friendlier. I asked them what they had learned in the previous semester and the unanimous answered was 'nothing!' I also asked them if they have had some practice with conversation and one responded:

'If repeating is speaking, then we spoke.'

Another student went on:

'Look teacher, what happen was, we think, that we were the first class that our former teacher had ever taught. Thus, we didn't learn that much. But we hope that our experience with you will be better.'

When I heard this I became even more nervous, remembering my former students who told me that I was going to miss them. At that moment I just wanted to leave that place and go back with my former class, thinking that 'these students will freak out if they learn that I had been teaching adults for only one term!' An older male student interrupted my thoughts:

'Professor, what resources do you use to teach? Because, well ... here in the school we have overhead and computer projectors, television sets, actually a whole room for audio and video. So it would be good if you make use of all those resources, don't you think?'

That made me miss my former class even more. They did not care what I used to teach them! But I answered that I was used to work with all those resources. To find a way to end this inquisition, I naively asked them to give me written answers to the following questions: *Why do you want to learn English? What do you want to learn? How do you want to learn?* Their answers ended my naivety; they all stated that they were there because the course was compulsory and that they didn't like English.

The second day of the class, I taught a lesson on simple and progressive verb forms and I didn't face any problems. However, I noticed that one of best female students had a notebook filled with notes on English usage, which she was using to check all the rules that I was explaining. She did that during the whole week. One day, I announced that we were going to have a native speaker to visit the class. So we prepared some questions for him to answer. That day, the students were really shy and afraid to ask the questions and they always checked with me about what he had said. I talked to my guest in English and that was a kind of a test, proving them that I actually could speak in English. From that day on, their attitude changed, in particular that female student that used to check her notes. Everybody showed a real motivation to learn, they participated in class, handed in their assignments, chose to attend classes (I did not have to force them to attend), and if their other classes were cancelled, they waited for my class even though they had to stay for two or three hours. They were even more polite, asking for permission when, on the rare occasion, they had to miss a session.

With her second class, Martha was able to negotiate a level of trust and confidence between herself and the students. In part, this was attained by each of them recognising the agency of the other. Martha did not attempt to convince them of the importance of the class or of the language, only that she could help them get through the class. This meant that she would have to find ways to allow the students to be themselves in this process. This also allowed her to see the diversity of the way students developed their styles of performing. The resistance to English of some, like Eduardo, was grounded in political beliefs, whereas for others, like Mariana, their acceptance or rejection of the value of English was based upon complex personal and social issues. Martha recounts her interactions with Eduardo and Mariana:

> Eduardo is a very nice young man. He is about 19. He is very political and the very first day of the course, when I asked the students about their expectation for the English course we were about to start he wrote in Spanish:
> 'I have strong prejudices against English, but apart from that, this programme and the global situation make learning English necessary. As with any other language, it requires time and dedication to learn it. I don't understand how the institution wants us to learn a language with the overload of information that we already have to absorb.'

Eduardo's negative attitude is obvious. As we can see, he chooses to open his paragraph with 'strong prejudices against English'. Then he states that studying English is an imposition from the institution and from the demands of the current situation. Then he adds that English as a language is not different from any other, implying that it does not have a higher status. He ends up venting his disagreement with the authorities of his school who claim that students can learn English on top of all the other subjects that they have to take.

In spite of (or maybe because of) having said enough about his position towards English, Martha decided to know more about this learner since she realised they both would have to cope with the situation. 'I had to teach and he had to take the course' she told us. So, in one of their conversations Eduardo talked about his learning strategies as a language learner:

> I studied French and a good strategy that I've developed for basic vocabulary is to write the name of objects on cards and paste them next to

the object they refer to. That way I had my bedroom full of French labels. It is a very good strategy to remember words, and it makes a nice learning environment ... I tried to do the same in English, but I couldn't bear it, to have my bedroom full of English words ... it was just unbearable.

In a different way, Mariana, another of Martha's students has established some emotional links between her life at that time and her learning of English. The following account describes an episode of Martha's quest for finding out who her students were.

Mariana was one of my female students. Unlike Eduardo, she wanted to learn English. Mariana showed from the very beginning a strong motivation to learn English. She was very punctual, never missed a class and worked very hard to improve her English. Her commitment was shown in her intelligent questions and well developed assignments. However, three weeks from finishing her course she started missing classes, and when she was there her negative attitude was very overt.

Mariana comes from the Isthmus. She lives with her parents and she is the second of three daughters. Her parents are very traditional and they raised their children to get married 'the right way' which means to stay virgin in order to wear a white dress for their wedding. This shows the community that they are decent women that deserve respect from everybody. However, her older sister became involved with a married man. They now lived together and they never married. Her youngest sister has already run away with her boyfriend. Although he is not married, everybody knows now that she is not a virgin. The hope for her parents is Mariana. So they arranged her marriage with a young man from the community who happens to be in love with her. Her parents are very happy about the arrangement because he is a hardworking man that has found his way in the United States. He plans to take Mariana to the States, where he has a secure job and can offer her a very stable environment for them to raise a family. Mariana's problem is not only that she is not in love with him, but that she envisioned her future life very differently. First of all, she was planning to finish her BA in Education in Oaxaca. Further, she did not see herself as a *chicana* [Mexican-American ethnic identity], trying to find her way in a society she dislikes. That is, she did not want to have an American family and live the American way.

I gave her very strong advice 'Don't get married!' However, as Mariana saw it, there was no solution, because the last thing she wanted to do was to disappoint her parents. At the end of their conversation, Mariana was quite upset and finished our interaction by saying; 'By the way, I won't be in class tomorrow, because I am buying my wedding dress.'

Reflecting on these experiences, Martha seemed to realise, however, that recognising the agency in others does not always mean that there will be agreements on the difference of hope and fears, only that each is aware of others' positions.

Martha's quest to be herself in this language and to find out who her students were was a constant process that repeatedly required her to prove her authority.

Last week I had an interesting experience. I was working on pronunciation, explaining to my students that some letters are silent, for instance the *l* in words like *walk* and *talk* (I wanted them to pronounce them the right way because they were saying wɔlk/ and /tɔlk/ instead of /wɔk/ and /tɔk/). After the explanation we had some practice.

Several days later, a very motivated and hard-working student told me that she had talked to an American friend and he told her that the '*l*' was not silent, and she emphatically added '*and he knows because he is a native speaker*'. At that moment my confidence totally disappeared. And my answer was very stupid. I knew that it was but I had to say something. So I said, 'but he is American and I am teaching you British English. That is the reason of the difference'. It was a lie, so to gain more credibility I gave them a boring mini lecture about regional dialects, and all that stuff that we learn at the BA in TEFL. Only very few students seemed to be interested.

As we see it, Martha was trying to rescue the high respect that she had gained from her students about her teaching. She had managed to turn her class into a group of very cooperative and motivated students who were interested in learning English. As we have seen, she worked on this every day and, after some weeks, they had learned that she was a teacher they can trust. Being a novice teacher with not much experience, she could not afford to lose her educational capital. Thus, her alternative narrative about the varieties of English ('I am teaching you British English') was not only about saving face but also about not losing everything she had done to show them that she, a non-native English teacher, was worth learning from.

In that struggle, it is obvious that she was also coping with her identity, which she seemed to call into question when her students ask her about her English:

> Some days ago, a student asked me what kind of English I was teaching them. Immediately I thought that the answer could be Mexican English. However, I somehow felt that I was not prepared to defend this position, nor I knew how to explain what I meant by Mexican English. It was also about giving a response the students wanted. I do not think that Mexican English was going to be so welcome by students in Oaxaca.

Later on, Martha told us about her way of playing with the differences in English pronunciation styles in order to build her own confidence as an instructor of English. Since she does not have an allegiance to any particular style, she feels that she can play word games with the different pronunciation patterns in British and USA styles between /twenti/ and /twɛni/ or /parti/ and /pardi/. Her reason for not stating a preferred style is that she feels that it would involve performing with a script that she does identify with, that is, she would be trying to be like a native speaker in one English dialect or the other.

This concern for not performing something she was not does involve issues of power, authority and gender. For her, this is expressed in the social fields of proper and improper forms of personal address:

> During the first week of my second level class, I was writing something on the whiteboard when a student asked me:
> '*Oiga miss, ¿qué dice en la última oración?*' [Excuse me, miss, what does the last sentence say]
> The moment I heard the word *miss*, I turned my head and told them not to call me *miss*. They could call me *teacher* or *Martha* but not *miss*. Then they asked me why, since their former teacher had told them to call him 'Mr. Robles', why they couldn't call me 'Miss Reyes'. I answered that only in kindergarten do children call their teachers *misses*; that in the university they wouldn't address the professor that way. I said that because I only had heard that usage in private pre-elementary and elementary schools. During that term, some students used the 'miss' and I really got annoyed.

I had the same reaction when my friends made a joke about my career: *Ya vas a acabar, ¿ no? ahora si ya vas a ser una* miss, [You're about to finish, don't you? Now you're going to be a 'miss'].

Recently I received some information from the International Institute of Education on how to get teaching assistantship in the States. There was a section dealing with the relationship between students and professors and it explicitly explained the way to address a university professor was as 'Dr.', 'Mr.', 'Ms.', 'Mrs.' or ... 'Miss' plus their first name, or just by their first name. When I saw the word 'miss', I realised that my belief about using it only for kindergarten and elementary school was wrong. I also hated the fact that my students in the States would call me 'miss'.

Afterwards I reflected on my annoyance. I recalled my first English classes when I was eight. The first day the teacher told me that the word for '*maestro*' was teacher so I started calling her teacher, and, since then, I have been calling all my English teachers the same way, 'Teacher' for secondary school, 'teacher' for high school, 'teacher' in my private courses in Harmon Hall and even 'teacher' in the university and nobody never corrected me. At the university, we could address them as 'teachers' or use their first names. Even the native-speakers never told us, 'Don't use the word 'teacher', call me 'professor', or 'Miss' or 'Mr.' I only remember one of them that when we called him 'teacher' he answered back saying, 'Student!' I thought it was funny; however he never said that it was inappropriate. I'd never asked him why he did so. I also remember that a classmate that spent a term in a university in the States started using professor instead of 'teacher'. He explained to me that there they used that word. I told him that for me 'professor' meant a very well-prepared experienced and wise scholar, with a long and solid academic career, thus we could not use that indiscriminately at the *Centro*.

Anyway, for me the words 'miss' and 'teacher' have cultural and social connotations. The translation for miss is *señorita* and for teacher is *maestro/a*. In Mexico we use the word 'teacher' to address a person prepared for that profession, which means holding a B.A. degree. A 'teacher' needs the knowledge to teach his/her subject. To call them with that word is to address the fact that they are well prepared to do their job. For instance, among musicians they use the word '*maestro*' to mean a good musician. On the other hand, in Mexico we use the word *señorita* to refer to a woman that is not married, usually a young woman, regardless her academic background. It is also used for young female people whose name we do not know. However, apart from that sense of formality, the word also has gender connotations, for instance, when they say, 'Señorita, porque mi trabajo me ha costado' [Please, call me *miss*, because I have worked for that]; 'Se casa de amarillo porque ya no es señorita' [She is getting married in a yellow dress because she is not a *miss* anymore]; or 'seño para no entrar en controversias' [Use the short *seño* to avoid problems]. That is the how 'señorita' and 'miss' turns into a synonym of virgin and a way to discriminate against women.

Reflections

In this tale we can note how the issue of one's confidence is little more slippery when one is in the classroom not as a protesting student or one who is seeking a means of creative expression, but as one who is supposed to have the authority to teach English. Here the hegemonic authority of the colonial differences is ever present in its appearance as the spectre of the native speaker. Like many non-native speakers of English who find themselves teaching English (Li, 2007), Martha expressed her fears and insecurities about this endeavour. In fact, her validity was affirmed in her class because she was able to converse with the visiting native speaker in front of her students. But her long term acceptance came through having the confidence to be herself in the classroom and to allowing her students the same freedom. She gambled with this authority in her attempt to claim that she was teaching one style of pronunciation instead of another (British/U.S.A.) and then moved to realise that such affiliation was not necessary. She recognised that neither she nor her students can be what they were not; native speakers. But they could be who they wanted to be: users of English for their own needs and desires. This is how she kept the spectre of the native speaker at bay.

Her concern about appropriate modes of personal address was a tale that expressed her cultural capital, her skill at constructing a critical intercultural take on power, authority and gender, and a means to declare her affinity to others through her knowledge of where she is located. Drawing upon her own cultural capital concerning the teaching profession in Mexico, she makes a critical analysis of how 'Miss' might hint at some form of equalitarianism in a North American context, but in her context it applies to realities about class and gender that she has been resisting. For her, it is not about the simple choice of one particular word, but about dealing with the social and political context of that one particular word and where that one particular word would locate her. That location is not where she desires to perform either her English or her personhood. Further, by taking such a critical stand, she suggests to others the importance of knowing who and where one is located in the social fields of power and authority, especially in terms of gender. For us, this is using one's linguistic praxis as means of political affiliation with others in similar domains of practices.

The revenge of the ghost of the native speaker

Ervin graduated from the *Centro* about four years ago. He was noted for his 'gift of gab' and his skill at hyperbolic explanations of his achievements and adventures. As a student he was one of the more political and radical students of his generation and was well known for *Ladrillos Muertos*, wall periodical posters he would put up at the *Centro*. *Ladrillos Muertos* was like an alternative newspaper for the students and addressed a range of domestic and international political issues. Some of his professors considered him to be a critical student though, at times, irresponsible. Others regarded him as one of their best students in terms of his English teaching skills. The following are his comments on his various adventures in the areas of teaching, working in the private sector and other roles he has played while performing his English during the last year's political events in Oaxaca. His tales capture, often quite dramatically, many of the themes we have been addressing in our analysis. He is clearly located within the complex social folds of postcolonial Oaxaca particularly in his dealings with international commerce, police and the drug trade as well as issues of human rights. He finds that his everyday life requires navigating the reality of the colonial difference. It seems that he has successfully exorcised the ghost of the native speaker though its spectre stills haunts his thoughts and actions. And although his attainment of user rights of English is complete, he finds that success has come with personal and political costs. The following is a biographical narrative by Ervin when we asked him to talk about himself:

> Since you wanted to know about me I am going to give you a photo tour. First, I brought you an example of one of the teaching activities that I have used with my students. I think it is a cool thing to do. I called it *My life in a lunch pack*. This is a photo pack of my life. Each photo has its own story. I always start with a photo when I was a little baby. The idea

is to use the tenses and do a lot of speaking. There is a photo with my family, my parents and my only brother. From this photo on my students recognise me. They say that I haven't changed at all. Next photo shows when I was teaching in the *Centro de Idiomas* as part of my social service. I use this to connect with my students. For me, it doesn't matter how we want to see it or how much we talk about education and teaching strategies and all that other bla bla bla, in Oaxaca we are still suffering from the barrier between students and teachers. It doesn't matters if I allow my students to use *tú* [Spanish informal personal pronoun] with me or give them my email address and my cell phone number, I am still the teacher and they are still the students. That block is still there. For me, a way to move beyond this barrier is through this activity, it allows me to be closer to the student and to motivate him or her to study and to learn. Because of this style of teaching, my students fall in love with the class. I discovered that by sharing with them very private or intimate realities about myself, they like the class and me as the teacher better. They also bring their photos and get sentimental and sometimes even cry when they talk about their things, about their family. It is a difficult thing to do. It affects everybody. Besides, the students are not used to the fact that their teacher opens up and tells his life to them. In a way, this shocks them and shocks me.

Actually I started teaching from the second year of the B.A. in an open high school. My university friends invited me to teach English. They said, 'Do you want to be an English teacher here? You will not become rich but you will not starve. This is not a business, you cannot afford luxuries'. Well, my experiences turned out a little different from what they suggested!

In this brief account of his teaching style, we see that he too gives a central role to the quest to be oneself in these language performances. For him this means that he and his students' feelings, hopes, desires and fears are part of the learning context. In this context he has used his linguistic capital to open up language possibilities for his students. At this point in his life, however, he has arrived at a crossroads where he can convert his linguistic capital into economic capital. It also involves his first pact with the devil over the use of his English.

I heard that one of the most important cacao business in Oaxaca was looking for someone with English to help them with their marketing programs. I applied for the job and got it. Here is a photo of me when I started. At the beginning I had to learn about the process of how to process the cacao and my presentations were in Spanish. I had all kinds of groups from tourists to kindergarten kids. From there they realised that I have this ability to talk (my mother says that *'me hierve el buche'* [my mouth boils], and I answer her that 'this is what I make my living from mother, so I have to do it well'). My speeches were incredible, and I started liking it a lot, trying different ways to modulate my voice, to change the intonation. From there they asked me to teach some English courses for sales people and from there to other activities. I even made cacao presentations for the BBC and other TV chains. I was also told to do translations, and other things. They even created the international department in the company, because I was there and they found me useful. I was sort of the international representative of the company, or something like that. They noticed that I also spoke Italian and French, so better for them. They also started sending me to other companies to do all sorts of things related to English. Once I taught English for three months to this TV person who was going to work in Canada. I work intensively with her and she learned. She was very motivated.

Then, they just came and told me, 'We want you to do this and this'. I started feeling that it was too much of an imposition. 'Do this', 'do that'. No negotiation. But they paid good money and I liked that. At that time they started doing international events, and they called me to be a simultaneous translator with the people they wanted to promote their products. Here is photo of me with two soccer players from the States. They were hired to make some ads for the cacao. I had to go to their press conference. At another time this Nigel somebody, a famous TV conductor from England, was here and I had to be his translator. Often I didn't know what my role was supposed to be but I accepted that it had to do with English. Once, they also sent me to the Graphic Art Institute of Oaxaca. There, this very famous artist interviewed me for an English teaching job for the personnel there. When he asked me about my fees, I thought, these *cabrones* [bastards] really have money so I am going to ask for good money. So I told him double of what I regularly charged. He was shocked when he saw the amount. At that moment I realised that I had gone too far. He looked at me and said, 'I didn't know that you English teachers are so fucking uptight about wages!' That same experience happened to me several times with those people. I think that now I know how much I charge to them.

They also called me to help them with restaurants to translate their menus. I had to learn that style of expression; it was rather formal to me. Also, it had to be spotless because it was meant to be published. I have also worked with this woman that wrote a book on Oaxacan cuisine. I liked that. I realised that English was a way to deal with different ways of developing cuisines and because I like cooking I thought that in the future I would be able to combine both of these desires of mine.

Once they asked me to go to this meeting with the cacao people and some internationals who were interested in doing business with them. When we arrived the visitors were talking in English among themselves and they did not notice that I also spoke English. When my bosses realised the situation they asked me to translate what the guys were saying in English, so I translated their conversations. It was very interesting because, I was able to tell my boss that these internationals were trying to fuck us over in terms of what they wanted to pay for the cacao. Eventually they realised that I was translating what they were saying and they asked me to leave the room in order to continue with the negotiations. This is the story of how I was a spy using my English.

In the spaces of this narrative, Ervin is enthralled with the world that English has opened up for him. He feels that he had become an important 'player' in the commercial social classes of Oaxaca. Because of his English skills, he worked on improving the cacao company's international marketing programs, was attaining *palanca* (influence) through the favours he was doing for his bosses, thought he could stand up to the presence of one of Mexico's most noted artists in demanding appropriate reimbursement for offering his English classes, and has even acted as a commercial spy. He felt in full control of his agency. As the following narrative suggests, there were, however, limits to how much control he had.

Look! This photo is the representation of my lack of discipline and responsibility. They took it when they put me in jail for a night. After all these adventures while I was working for the cacao guys, I started to think I was someone important. One night, I was drinking in the *Zócalo* and I got drunk. I began acting obnoxiously; shouting and arguing with everyone. I just thought that I was one of them, one of my bosses, and that I had the power and do whatever I wanted to do. How foolish I was! It makes me laugh now, but at that time I felt I was BIG! But it didn't work. The police were called; they beat me and sent me to spend the night in jail. The next morning they released me, not because I was somebody, but because my bosses didn't want their names to be involved in that event. It was not convenient for them. For them you don't have any value. I learned that you're a thing they can use, like female workers are things that they can touch and use. They fuck with your dignity and your being. Because of English, I came to believe that I was a despotic and powerful person.

One day they sent me to this place to work with someone who had a project on the traditional dancing of Oaxaca. When I arrived I realised they were translating into English various descriptions of the Guelaguetza dances. They were going to use this material in some documentaries and as promotion for their products. You see, even though I only worked for the cacao company, they sent me to all these places and events that had nothing to do with cacao. I was just something they could do with. They could lend me to other companies. They just lend you as if you were a thing, like 'Can I borrow your pen?' My boss would say 'would you like to borrow my translator?', and then they would tell me, 'Go with this person and do what they tell you to do'.

The problem with all this was that they and I did not always see these exchanges in the same way for I felt that by offering my services they were making money, which was not coming to me. One day, when they sent me to translate for an event selling make-up products, which I knew very little about, I got fed up and in the middle of everything I said 'That's it!' and walked away. I was so fed up that I didn't show up to claim my salary. You can see there how irresponsible and rowdy I am. Rebellious, I mean. And I was in debt and I was drinking too much. I am that way. One day I just woke up in the morning and said 'That's it! I don't give a fuck!' That's why I left all that. I worked so much for those bastards, people with power, used to giving orders. That's why I left them. I realised that English can also be used to fuck the people, to exploit the poor. There I learned that when they invite the artisans to an *Expo* of such and such they tell them, 'But remember, I get half of what you sell'. Everything is fraudulent. For them you are a thing that is useful and that's it. But you are disposable. You see, I left them and nothing happened. I was easily replaced. You are nobody for them. They are used to firing male workers and to abusing female ones. I saw that, I saw everything. I saw how they take advantage of their role as bosses. For some time I thought that I was one of them, but fortunately I realised that I don't want to. I used to admire their abilities to create and produce, but soon I found out that the basis of that is dishonesty and lie. The products they sell are medium quality. They buy from the people that work in the fields and they pay too low. Sometimes they asked me for my opinion and when they heard it they would say, 'you're an idiot, but anyway, this is what you have to say' and they gave me the 'official' story. Once I was in charge of one of the branches and they told me, 'Now you are the boss. You can give orders and make them obey you, you can be like us, you can touch them now [referring to female workers]' and he would even show me how to do it.

I left them because that was clashing with my feeling that that's not the way I wanted the world to be. To be honest, I earned a lot of money but I threw it away drinking and partying. I don't care. You see, everything comes with English. My teachers told me that I had a special talent for this but I believe that it was only luck. It happened to me but it could have happened to anybody. I felt so bad even physically that I even had to go to the hospital. I was suffering from partial face paralysis. After that I stayed for months at home.

When I felt better I went back to teaching. I feel better now. I am eating better and not drinking that much. I am even exercising. I like boxing so I went to this gymnasium close to the *Centro de Idiomas*. I became very good friends with the manager. One day he told me that he needed someone to help him because some people from the States were coming to take some photos and to start his webpage. I told him that I could do that because of my English. So now I am in charge of his English web page and I even do boxing presentations in English. You see, English follows me everywhere. I can't get rid of it, fucking English. My life is always around English. Sometimes I think English's affected me emotionally.

Moving between language learning and language use

In this narrative we have very colourful accounts of how Ervin came to feel the limits of his own agency within this overall context. He thought that his *palanca* made him like his bosses, immune from social control, and that he could do whatever he wished. This illusion was sadly altered by spending a night in jail. He offers numerous stories of how he felt used and alienated in his various endeavours within this context. He felt that his English skills had turned him into an object that could be passed around without his consent. He was encountering his own glass ceiling in terms of the worth of his English skills. Furthermore, he found that the cost of being accepted by those with authority meant that he had to abandon his political and social values. Both his physical and mental health was affected. In this context he seemed to have avoided dealing with the authority of colonial difference but not the hegemony of class differences.

He was questioning the wisdom of his pact with the devil when an adventure came along that seemed like something that would allow him to link his English to his political and social points of view. This involved working with the state police in dealing with a drug dealer.

> Recently I had a very dangerous experience related to English. A friend that works as a reporter told me about this job with the state attorney office and the police. He told me they had detained this *gringo* and he didn't speak any Spanish and so they needed a translator. He said, 'Why don't you go and ask for this job? They'll pay you well, really!' I went to check it out. They offer twenty thousands pesos to start with, so I said 'Sure!' I arrived for the job with my camera, my recorder and my notebook, I have learned that a good translator does that, and they told me that we had to travel to this *pueblo* [village], which was not that far from Oaxaca. I was going to go with several policemen that would take care of me. They also told me to prepare some questions in other languages because they didn't know what language their captive spoke. During the drive the police were very nice to me. The journey was four hours long. There in the *pueblo* I learned that they have caught this fucking foreigner who had been growing and selling drugs in the area. He had also been bribing the local authorities and paying local people a lot of money to be able to do his business. But the cops had caught him near his fields in the surrounding hills. They had locked him up in a cottage in the area. At this point they changed the way they were treating me. They told me to leave all my stuff—camera, recorder, notebook—behind, because I would

not need it and it was a two hour walk. We walked for two hours. The captive was kept in this little cottage that was guarded by at least twenty armed cops, you know, these cops in black uniforms with gun belts and bullet proof vests. When we arrived they told me in a very strong tone that I had five minutes with this fucking guy to get everything I could from him: where his fields were and who the other *narcos* in this zone were. They said that he even had his own airplane near by. They told me that from the moment he had been taken the only thing he would say was '*No español, no español!* (No Spanish, No Spanish)!' And they told me I had to find out what this fucker knew. I went inside, and he said the same thing to me, '*No español, no español!*' I tried with English and with Italian and French, I even tried some questions in my broken German. But he didn't seem to understand. Then I thought that, as we have seen in movies, he would open up and negotiate if we were alone, with no cops. So I told them to leave the room. When they left I started with English and he laughed and said in fucking good Spanish, 'Look bastard, I'm gonna give you this suitcase full of money that I have in a house an hour from here. You can divide it with the head of the cops, then I will leave this place and nobody will follow me, understood? You have two fucking minutes to tell him, so make it fucking fast!' So again, someone was giving orders to me! So, like an idiot, I went out and started telling the guy in charge what I had been told. When I finished he said, 'No way! This mother fucker wants to fuck us'! At that very moment we heard a lot of noise and realised that the people from the village were coming to free the drug dealer. When they saw us, they started shooting. You don't know how it feels. You have seen these movies where everybody throws up and passes out. Well it is true! I felt so sick and started vomiting. It feels so horrible that a mother fucker that you don't even know starts shooting at you with a gun. The cops pulled me by the hair and threw me into the truck. They also took the *gringo* and put him in the back of the truck as a shield to protect us. I was hearing all the shootings and the truck going very fast, I fainted for I don't know how long. In movies they say that in those moments you recall all that you have done in your life. Well, I started doing that, thinking about my mother, my father, my brother. Now I know that it is not bullshit, that it really happens, it is stupid, I know. But I was not the only one. The cops were also fucking scared, some crying and some had pissed in their uniform. I had taken this job for all the excitement and for the fucking money and now I was scared to shitless. A whole armed community after you.

That's the ugly thing about English. I never told my parents. Fucking money. They paid me a hundred thousand pesos. They offered me a job there but no way, I didn't accept it. As you can see I have done some dumb things with my English. I have partied very hard with English and made a lot of money, but I have also had some ugly experiences with English.

This social world of criminality and politics is also part of our postcolonial globalised world which Ervin learned about in a very dramatic way. He found that his right to producing his own knowledge was challenged by those who hired him, the police and even the drug dealer. This situation placed him at the crossroads between the hegemonic authority of the colonial difference and everyday reality of social class differences. The following two adventures, though equally dangerous, placed him in a context in which he was clearly using his English to reflect his own beliefs and values. The following is the account of how his English connected him to two different events during the recent social movement in Oaxaca.

Recently I worked with a human rights commission in Oaxaca. You know how those days were with the social struggle in Oaxaca; there were no jobs and there were no tourists in the city. But I have a friend here with a lot of contacts with businessmen and politicians in the city. He called me and asked me if I wanted to do this gig translating for some guys from an international human rights commission. The plan was that we were going to a village that was in conflict with the state government. The village was having its *fiesta patronal* [saint's day party], we would all be pretending to be tourists. That way the state police would not check us going in and take away our cameras and recorders. The observers wanted to interview the *Presidenta Municipal* [village female president] of the community. They wanted this interview because there had been conflicting stories over abuses within the community. As with many other communities in the valley of Oaxaca, conflicts between the faction supporting the PRI and those that were supporting APPO were getting violent. I was to act as the translator between the observers and the *Presidenta* of the community. I told them I would take the job, it sound exciting and important. Apart from being well paid I was going to do something highly risky. When my friend and I arrived we realised that the whole village was covered with signs of *Fuera Ulises* and *Viva la APPO*. So while he was interviewing some people about the *fiesta*, I was trying to get the interview with the *Presidenta*. Actually it was nice to see a woman giving orders to a bunch of male subordinates. We learned from her that it was because the people in this village were supporting the APPO they were being intimidated with guns and beaten. I passed on this information to the guys in the commission and it became part of the official report on human rights abuse in Oaxaca.

Also, during this time, one of the teachers at the *Centro de Idiomas* wanted to interview some of the people working with APPO. So we went to the *Zócalo*, and we met this North American reporter that was carrying his camera and spoke very little Spanish. His name was Brad Will. He was with a friend who worked for *Proceso* [a national Mexican news magazine] who told us, 'This fucking Brad always does interviews but they are never very long because his Spanish is so limited. So, you can help him out!' We laughed and introduced ourselves to him. As we were chatting, a man that had been caught robbing a house was brought by the APPO police to the Zócalo and everybody went over to where he was tied up and started to interview him. You know, at that time that was good news for the reporters, so we took Brad over, and he started talking to him in Spanish but he said something wrong and we immediately corrected him. From then we helped him to carry out his other interviews and we stayed with him for more than three hours. At nine o'clock we left and agreed to meet the following day, but we didn't because of the shooting in *Colonia Reforma*. Two days later, the teacher I had been with, called me and she was very upset, 'Have you heard? This is fucking bad. They killed the *gringo*; the one we helped translating in the *Zócalo*. Brad Will was killed in *Calicanto!*' Later I learned the details. I felt very bad, I had been working with him and now he was dead. I remember that when I was a little kid I used to tell my father that I wanted to be a photographer for the war. Now, many years later, English brings me here, to do this. I had very contradictory feelings, I was very upset that Brad was killed but I felt that it was important that I had been a translator for these radical political events.

In the context of these two tales, Ervin was using his English in a political manner that matched his past actions. He was involved in a dramatic use of his politics of affinity by providing help to those who were struggling for social justice in Oaxaca. Here, he finds a constructive and creative way to use his English for social and political change. He is linked to social forces that are confronting the realities of the colonial difference and social class differences in forms of state violence and repression. Though the accomplishments of these current social struggles were limited, Ervin's involvement affirms for him that he could use his English in ways that would not contradict his own beliefs.

Ervin finished our interview showing us a letter from an elementary school principal inviting him to talk to her students about his career as an English teacher:

> English has given me the opportunity to play so many roles. Out there in the real world, you can do so many things with English. An elementary school invites me every year to tell their students about my profession, about being an English teacher. The programme is called, 'How to live your profession with passion and success'. They want me to motivate the kids, to realise how important English is. I don't know if I have done it with success, but I know that I have done it with passion. I have had a good time; I have had very bad times. I think I like playing with English because I like being a protagonist. It is this context oh English that makes me a protagonist. I love this *rollo del inglés* [role of English]. I am stuck in it but I loved it.'

Here he reasserts the importance of being oneself in language learning and maintaining passion in what one does. This also illustrates that he was able to use his politics of affinity in his drive to teach students how to use and enjoy English.

Reflections

Ervin, in his own style, offers some quite informative insights about performing English with a postcolonial accent. He began his tale with how to use a style of personal involvement with his students in order to reduce the barrier between teacher and student. He feels that this has been very successful and allows for more student commitment to learning. That is, being able to use English as something as real and meaningful offers the means to better learning the language.

In his own personal and political life, however, his English skills have brought him money, notoriety, trouble, and satisfaction.

For him, the ghost of the native speaker of English has come disguised as a devil with whom he has made several pacts. He felt that his English skills gave him the illusion of access to the social worlds of power and privilege within the commercial circles of Oaxaca. But this illusion was rudely disrupted when he attempted to put them into practice. His English skills gave him access to various identity locations, but the limits over who could control his agency led to feelings of being betrayed and used. In other contexts, his agency placed him within the dramatic world of police and drug dealers[24] and the complex and equally dangerous worlds of politics and human rights issues. His very concrete and daily use of English in these adventures offers insights into the problematic quality of the politics of language affinity. Whereas in the other stories in this study the students strove for such a politics, Ervin was and is still living it as a part of his daily life. Like the infamous pacts made with the devil at the crossroads of life, he finds himself in a love/hate relation with English and with the social and political worlds that were opened to him through English. We do not often hear of such dilemmas in the lives of language learners and clearly Ervin's style of explanation adds a theatrical quality to these tales. With all the various ideological claims that are made for the advantages of additional language acquisition, it is refreshing to hear about the everyday complexities of such achievements. Equally insightful is his final affirmation that for all the troubles that he feels English has brought him; he loves the reality of it. It is, after all, his language to use.

Conclusion

These four stories ethnographically illustrate the various processes these students encounter in their personal and professional lives as their performances took them from being language learners to language users. We think these stories on curriculum revision, poetry experimentation, on-site teaching decision-making, and navigating the daily realities of the colonial difference, are illuminating with respect to the confidence to say what one wants to say, and to say it with one's

---

24 In this tale Ervin finds out that what he thought might have been an act of social responsibility, enmeshed him in the very dangerous crossroads of both colonial and social class differences. This entailed the over determined social folds of politics, police, drug dealers and community relations. It is way beyond the scope of this work to address the politics of the economy and drugs in Mexico (Castells, 2000b). Suffice to say, these forces have profound influences in the composition and performance of everyday lives in Mexico

particular postcolonial accent. They have rewritten the script in terms of how to use and present their language performances in various linguistics contexts.

In these stories, we see the absence, or exorcism, of the ghost of the native speaker in different ways. In the cases of the Curriculum Revision Clique and the Poetry Group, the ghost is simply absent. In the various projects, guides, and models offered by the Curriculum Revision Clique, there was no discussion if the English that was taught should be modelled in terms of meeting some kind of standards: their concern was that what was to be taught should meet the needs of the students in terms of their communication desires. Though there was the absence of the ghost of the native speaker in their story, there were no absences of issues of power and authority. Their attempt to envision new ways of teaching English quickly placed them in the contested zone of who had or did not have the authority to make changes in the curriculum. They found that their communication desires were thwarted directly or indirectly by faculty and administrators at the *Centro*. The Poetry Group never felt nor desired that their writing was a demonstration of their command over assumed standards of English, but that it was to illustrate that they were quite able to navigate their ways in the seas of creative expression in this language. In both cases, the ghost was exorcised by refusing to allow this spectre's entrance into the theatre of their performances. As we stated earlier, this theatre was for them a safe house where they were free to imagine who they were and who they wanted to be. In the case of Martha, the ghost hovered around her classroom and threatened her creditability. She found at first that her students were either hostile or indifferent towards her. They directed their dislike for the schools' requirement of an English class at her and questioned her command over the language. Her linguistic slight of hand in claiming that she was using British English instead of that of the USA only compounded the problem. By seeking ways in which she and her students could be themselves in these language activities, she provided the means to exorcise this ghost. Ervin never worried about whether his language performances were or were not meeting the standards of English; he was more worried and confused about the pact that he made with this devil concerning this thing called English. This pact had placed him in numerous conflicts not over his command of English, but rather over whether he, or those who sought his skills, would have the authority to define how his English was to be used. His exorcism involved his acceptance of his passion for using this language in the way he wanted to. All four of these tales show us that, in their refusal to allow the ghost of native-speakerism to monitor their performances, they were also removing themselves from the hegemonic authority of the colonial difference.

These young language actors were resisting the authority of the language regime of English to set the standards of their performance and, as noted above, writing scripts that fit their needs and aspirations. For us, it is interesting that in the contexts of these actions, they did not face any challenges to their authenticity as Spanish speakers nor their identities as Mexican. Thus, in the confidence of their performances, they were moving away from the safety of their learning cultures towards the more problematic location of being language users in the multicultural and multilingual context of Oaxaca and beyond. The Curriculum Revision Clique confidently placed themselves within the discursive spaces of debates over how languages were to be taught. The Poetry Group found the confidence to publish their creative writing works for various audiences and to add their voice to issues of language education. Martha built her confidence as a language teacher by trusting the concerns and interests of her students and by maintaining her own social commitments. Ervin's confidence withstood the exotic and problematic quality of his various adventures in the use of English.

Furthermore, one can also note, within these activities, the presence of an emerging politics of affinity. As previously mentioned in the reflection sections of this chapter, the actions of these young language actors were not just directed towards their own immediate goals, but were concerned with opening new spaces for the learning and use of language for future students. They want to pass on to others the possibilities they had attained or envisioned; their quests were not directed towards the ownership of their successes, but directed towards making their quests available and useful for other learners in the future. They were not interested in turning their learning cultural experiences into a set of 'how to' recipes. Their interests were directed towards suggesting other kinds of possibilities. Even the quixotic tales of Ervin end with a plea that future students maintain a passion for learning. It is to these dynamics that we will address in the concluding chapter of this study.

Part III
Chapter Six

Towards a politics of language affinity

Introduction

We have come to the end of this journey to understand how these young students at the *Centro de Idiomas* have been performing English with a postcolonial accent. We presented a diversity of their stories and their activities: Claribel and Alberto's tales about how they gained access to the *Centro*; the activities of Nour, Facundo, Jorge, Elena, César and Yolanda as they composed their young adultness from their various identity locations and how, in that process, they sought various means to accumulate forms of linguistic and cultural capital; the adventures of *Los Gabos, Las Malditas* and *Las Misteriosas* cliques as they used their learning cultures as safe houses where they could playfully move back and forth between the contested language regimes located within the social spaces of the *Centro*; the creative encounters of the Curriculum Revision Clique and the Poetry Group to change how English was to be taught at the *Centro* and; the personal journeys of Martha and Ervin through the worlds of Spanish and English beyond the context of the *Centro*. Their tales, encounters and achievements during these journeys, though particular to their personal histories and backgrounds, were not any more exceptional than many other stories of students at the *Centro*, they just happened to be the ones we were able to present.[25]

Through all these various tales of language activities and practices, we found three recurring themes; a) the students wanting to find ways to be themselves, that is, having their desires, hopes and values included in the process of adding English to their already existing linguistic contexts; b) wanting their language performances, especially in terms of English, to be validated by their communicative success and not by assumptions of standards or authenticity, and c) regarding the addition of English to their language repertoire as a means to link themselves to other English language learners within their immediate context and to other English language users throughout the postcolonial world.

---

25 There are other possible themes in these performances that we plan to explore in future research. We would be interested to know how these performances encourage changing the structure, semantic potential and discursive conventions of English and Spanish. That is, being themselves in these performances they could be setting in to motion new forms of language accommodations (Canagarajah, 2007: Personal communication).

They felt that their English skills would be a means for all these language users to communicate to each other about the realities and richness of their particular cultures.

We have framed their performances within our conceptual and theoretical journey in order to understand these activities and practices. This framework entailed merging the descriptive prowess of applied linguistics with the interpretative flexibility of cultural anthropology. With this framework, we addressed a series of critical questions on language, identity, agency and culture that allowed us to illustrate how these students, in their everyday lives, were navigating the hegemonic terrains of the multicultural and multilingual social fields in postcolonial Mexico and Oaxaca.

However, we have presented this journey in a top down fashion, that is, we began the overall tale by placing it in the context of the existing dynamics of the postcolonial globalised world economy in which we live. We stated that this was a social reality framed in terms of coexisting forces of multiculturalism: difference, inequality and disconnection (García Canclini, 2004), and interculturalism: the quest for forms of equivalent differences and substantive connections (Dietz, 2003). We felt that within these existing forms of cultural diversity (gender, sexuality, ethnicity, social class and nationality), there were various practices being composed that encouraged several forms of negotiation which sought to go beyond existing forms of power and authority towards a politics of affinity (Haraway, 1991; Mouffe, 2005). Furthermore, these multicultural and intercultural activities exist within a postcolonial context in which the hegemonic forces of the colonial difference determine who would have the power and authority to direct such negotiation towards more justice in the world (Mignolo, 2005). For numerous political and economic reasons, English has been proclaimed as the language that would dominate the forms of social interaction in this postcolonial globalised world economy (Brutt-Griffler, 2002; Canagarajah, 1999; Hamel, 2003; Holborow, 1999; Macedo, et al., 2003; McKay, 2002; Pennycook, 1998; Phillipson, 1992; Seidlhofer, 2001; Widdowson, 2003).

From the discursive perspectives of applied linguistics and cultural anthropology, we wanted to know how these young students at the *Centro de Idiomas* were located in the aforementioned social forces (Clemente and Higgins, 2006). We started from the idea of *learning cultures*, a social and cultural form of analysis for both discourses, which led us to review the hegemonic patterns of native-speakerism (Holliday, 2005) as the form of symbolic power within the domain of language learning, which in turn moved us on to the question of the disinvention of language regimes (Makoni and Pennycook, 2006). From this we concluded that we could locate the realities of these young students by proposing that they were performing English with a postcolonial accent (Block, 2003; Bourdieu, 1991; Clemente, 2003; Clemente and Higgins, 2006; Holliday, 2005; Jacquemet, 2005; Makoni and Pennycook, 2006).

To develop this conclusion, we will reverse the direction, and work from the bottom up. That is, we want to show how the feelings, desires, hopes, fears, and values expressed by the students who strive to be themselves in these language activities articulate to the above issues and concepts. This will compel us to use our agency as investigators and interpreters to find a reasonable way to provide an interpretative analysis, that is, to connect the journey of these students to our journey.

The social, cultural and linguistic realities of the peoples of Oaxaca have for a long time been formed in the overall political and economic dynamics of this postcolonial society (Hernández Díaz, 2007; Martínez Vázquez, 2007). Claribel and Alberto's short narratives illustrated how both their entrance into the university world and their access to the programme provided by the *Centro* are embedded in these dynamics. The collection of portraits of Nour, Facundo, Jorge, Elena, César and Yolanda showed how, through their struggles to compose their young adultness, they were also constructing the stages from which they would be able to present their performances of English with a postcolonial accent. How each of them dealt with their issues of gender, sexuality, social class, ethnicity, and nationality implicated a search for who they wanted to be. As young, imaginative and intelligent students, they are open and reflective about what they are doing, including what attaining of English as an additional language means to them and the effect it has in their personal and social lives. Since they are struggling to find the means to express and understand the variety of feelings and emotions they are dealing with in composing their adultness, it is no surprise that they would bring these same concerns to their language activities. This locates them within the concerns of language standards and forms of the authenticity of one's cultural self (Butler, 1999; Pennycook, 2006; Woolard, 2005). This, in turn, places the performances of their identities and language activities into the complex and confusing social folds of the postcolonial globalised world economy and the contradictions of the social realities of multiculturalism and interculturalism framed by the hegemonic forces of the colonial difference (Dietz, 2003; García Canclini, 2004; Mignolo, 2005). They did not find this context either daunting or constraining or one that would prevent the expression of their hopes and desires. Each, in their particular styles, found ways to attain their education and language goals (the accumulation of linguistic and cultural capital) and enter upon the stage of the *Centro* to begin performing English with a postcolonial accent.

In the activities and practices of the three cliques we presented—*Los Gabos, Las Malditas* and *Las Misteriosas*—we see the emergence of this desire to be themselves in both English and Spanish. In playing between the language regimes of both languages, and being sensitive to the other language system (including the multi-media) in the multicultural context of Oaxaca, they began their disinvention of English standards by advocating for their English user rights. Their achievements were based on both their creativity in these two languages to perform various transidiomatic practices, and their capacity to be themselves in these language activities (Jacquemet, 2005; Kandiah, 1998; Ortner, 2006; Pennycook, 2006). They used their learning cultures as safe houses in which they could rehearse their performances with a postcolonial accent (Canagarajah, 2004; Clemente, 2003; Cantoral, 2005). Throughout all these activities there was a conscious desire to step outside the double bind of the opposition between native and non-native speakers of English and to proclaim that the validity of their performances should be based upon their communicative success (Holliday, 2005). This was an expression of using their agency both as a mode of resistance and as a way to seek a project of linguistic affinity with other language users who are also attempting to add English to their linguistic repertoire. Through these actions, they directly challenged the hegemonic authority of the colonial difference by stating that they were willing and capable of producing knowledge about language use that is valid and important. This implied recognising that both languages regimes, Spanish and English in the postcolonial context of Oaxaca, were in the process of being deterritorialised. The performances of these students also suggest how they could reterritorialise (Jacquemet, 2005) these languages regimes to meet their needs and desires for the use of communicative interaction to validate their language skills (Clemente and Higgins, 2007a). For these cliques, this meant using whatever specific elements they had learned from outside their safe houses (English classrooms, movies, internet, etc.) as a means to reterritorialise their linguistic context so they were free to play in between the language regimes of English and Spanish. In this context they felt that they could practice their ludic activities without fear of being judged or penalised. It was in the doing of their communicative interaction performances where they were able to construct spaces to be themselves.

The actions of the Curriculum Revision Clique and the Poetry Group to change how English was to be taught at the *Centro*, as well as the personal histories of how Martha and Ervin wandered through the world of Spanish and English beyond the context of the *Centro*, brought these journeys to a new beginning. That is, now they are more users than learners of English and it is they who are proclaiming the authenticity of their own Mexican and Spanish-speaking identities (Woolard, 2005). All four of these stories illustrate why we have stated that a focus on performance allows us to provide more ethnographic texture to the interplay between culture, language, agency and identity (Pennycook, 2004). How the Curriculum Revision Clique and the Poetry Group situated themselves to challenge the teaching of English at the *Centro*; how Martha's critical and reflective look at the way she constantly had to compose who she was in order to teach English and; how Ervin's tales of the pact with the devil he made with English are all dramatic expressions of how these actors, in their everyday lives, are weaving together their use of culture, language, agency and identity in order to be themselves. Furthermore, in each of these quotidian dramas, they are acting out their rejection of the colonial difference, particularly, in terms of native-speakerism, as a disciplinary power in how they pursue their desires to be themselves. In the doing of their performances of English with a postcolonial accent, instead of just being non-native speaking students, they are disinventing the authority of the language regime of Standard English and claiming the authenticity of what is to be an English language user (Makoni and Pennycook, 2006; Woolard, 2005). They are attempting to mediate the social practices of difference, inequality and disconnection found within the dynamics of multiculturalism by using language performances to deal with cultural diversity (gender, sexuality, ethnicity, social class and ableness) so as to be able to construct social actions that seek to go beyond existing forms of power and authority. That is, they want to use the process of interculturalism to compose a politics of affinity (Haraway, 1991; Mouffe, 2005).

To explain what we mean by politics of affinity or more specifically, a politics of language affinity, we have had to leave the journey of these students and return to our conceptual and theoretical journey. Though we feel that we have connected these two journeys, the conceptual language is ours. The students that have been presented here are all quite bright and intellectually inquisitive and would, in some cases, see their behaviours and activities in these terms, but we have been the ones framing these practices within the discourses of disinventing language regimes, postcolonialism, multiculturalism and interculturalism. After all, that's what we do.

Drawing upon what we understand to be the feelings, hopes and desires of these students, we want to suggest that a politics of affinity requires a critical look at the importance of the claim of language use over that of language ownership (Byrnes, 2005). The argument we will develop offers a conceptual framework for interpreting the everyday language performances of these students and how these performances could act as counter hegemonic forces to various language regimes that they are confronting. The argument neither claims to be an empirical demonstration of those social realities or a predictive instrument for evaluating levels of language learning. That is for others to explore. We are offering a way to provide a critical ethnographic read of these social practices and activities. The validity of our readings stands on how reasonable it is in representing these everyday language activities and its confirmation would be determined by comparative analysis of other performances of English with postcolonial accents.

Politics of affinity

Within the various discourses of the postcolonial world, the issues and consequences of identity politics has been a volatile and contested social drama (Bhabha, 1994; Trinh, 1989; Nicholson and Seidman, 1995; Spivak, 1999). This has been an arena in which both political debates and social movements have pondered how political actions could be based upon one's various identity locations, such as gender, sexuality, social class, nationality, and religious beliefs (Bauman, 2003). Certainly, current political conflicts have been dominated by a mixture of religious and national identity struggles (Grillo, 2005; Hagelund, 2007). Running counter to these concerns have been attempts to articulate a politics of what Dietz (2003) would see as interculturalism and Haraway (1991) has referred to as politics of affinity. That would be a set of principles and actions based not upon the shared identity of the social actors but rather upon shared hopes and desires for a different world. That is, the fight against sexism, homophobia and racism would not *per se* be based on one's identity as woman, gay or as person of colour, but rather on shared or affiliated positions of social justices (Higgins and Coen, 2000). Historically, social movements have drawn from both the strategies of identities and affiliations and have split over these same issues as well (Bonfil Batalla, 1988; Fanon, 1963; Laclau and

Mouffe, 1985; Melucci, 1989). A politics of affinity would locate the issues of identities within the dynamics of interculturalism by seeking alliances based upon shared concerns and hopes. Such a stance would require a means of successful communicative interaction (Clemente and Higgins, 2007b). This is where we see the connection of students' performances of English with a postcolonial accent with the politics of affinity.

As these students were exploring who they were and who they wanted to be, their actions were also suggestive of how a context for a politics of affinity could be constructed. This is implied in the various dramas of Nour, Facundo, Jorge, Elena, César and Yolanda as they move through their different identity locations while composing their adultness. This can be seen in comments by Raimunda and Freda about how they felt that the addition of English to their language skills did not weaken their identities, that is, their connection to being Mexican or Oaxacan. On the contrary, this addition represented a strength by giving them the means to explain to someone from Japan or Kenya who they were and at the same time be able to learn who these other people were. All the illustrations presented in this book (Jorge's wish to use English as a political weapon, Elena's desire to use her English as a bridge to other worlds, *Los Gabos* and *Las Malditas* way to use transidiomatic practices to extend their desires to connect with others, the ways *Las Misteriosas* were able to be other persons in English, and all of the individual and collective actions of the actors in chapter five) have something in common: they speak of a quest to cross through various social locations in order to seek various forms of communicative interaction. In this quest the students are composing what Konne and Norton (2003) refer to as *imagined communities*. Drawing from Anderson's original idea, they see *imagined communities* as 'groups of people, not immediately tangible and accessible, with whom we connect through the power of the imagination' (Kanno and Norton, 2003: 241). They content that by 'imagining ourselves bonded with our fellow compatriots across space and time, we can feel a sense of community with people we have not yet met, but perhaps hope to meet one day' (ibid.).[26]

Within their communities, either real or imagined, these students have moved away from *being* non-native speakers of English towards a location where they are *doing* successful forms of intercultural communication. We are not saying

26 One of the future domains of research that we will explore involves what would be the ethnographic means to represent how, when students constructed their safe houses, they seem to be locating themselves in the overlapping social fields of learning cultures, communities of practices, and imagined communities. We plan to explore the varieties of safe houses that student use at the *Centro* and how these activities could be framed within these complementary models of social action.

that each and every one of these young social actors are intentionally trying to cure the ills of the world. What we are saying is that by their collective actions, they are suggesting a way towards communicating about both the joys and ills of the postcolonial globalised world we live in.

We are suggesting that the basis for this quest to be themselves and to communicate with others derives from these students' claim on the use of these languages and not the ownership of them (Byrnes, 2005). However one attempts to use or reuse the idea of ownership, this is a concept linked to the conceptual and behavioural values of capitalism (Marx, 1967). It assumes that singular actors can or do have control over their singular situations or contexts (Bauman, 1973). In the case of languages, this encourages an ideological system, where those who are the language authorities or gatekeepers (symbolically the owners) are able to state who and how a language is to be performed and maintained. That is, the gatekeepers of a particular language, in this case English, are able to establish the exchange value of the language and who the participants in such exchanges will be (Bourdieu, 1991). Marx's discourse on the difference between use values and exchange values offers some 'useful' ideas for our argument. For him, items that have use values express utilitarian quantities and are exchangeable for other items of equivalent worth. Such exchanges enhance the value to all the participants in the actions; no one *per se* gains more than others. Where exchange values dominate the forms of interchanges, the process does not require transfers of an equivalent value, but rather transfers with an increase in value for some and a decrease in value for the others. The social interaction that is dominated by exchange values has no history other than that of the transaction, whereas social interactions composed through the logic of use values are based on the collective and connected histories of those involved (Marx, 1967).

These comments by Marx are suggestive of Bakhtin's insight that all utterances are connected to utterances from the past as well as to those in the future (1986). Utterances are forms of social interaction that are anchored in past actions that will engender future actions. In the composition of utterances, speakers draw from their past performances as the means by which to compose new ones (Bauman, 2006). This is also similar to how Bauman explains the dynamics of culture as praxis (1973). For Bauman, culture is not about past traditions but involves how cultural actors see and act upon possibilities, that is, how they compose a future. Verbal, social and cultural interactions are not based upon the ownership of the means of interaction, but on how the histories of such interactions have been used. No one can be the owner of a particular utterance, or, more precisely, one can only be the owner of utterances in a social context that gives the illusion of such possibilities (Bell and Gardiner, 1998). Through what Marx has referred to as the fetishism of commodities, the inverse is both, symbolically and materially, the reality (Marx, 1967). Thus, within the postcolonial globalised world economy both the means of production and communication are privately owned and the numerous social spaces in this context are ideologically framed with the belief of individual ownership, and this includes our acts of spoken language (Holborow, 1999).

In humble but profound ways, these young language actors in Oaxaca are challenging these contexts and the corresponding assumptions by performing with their postcolonial accent. By wanting to be themselves in these performances and through claiming the userhood of languages, they are connecting themselves to histories of language interaction. They are participating in forms of an emerging politics of affinity that seeks to articulate the hopes of intercultural interaction in order to mediate hegemonic tendencies of alienation contained in the existing forms of multiculturalism. They are stepping outside of the double bind of the colonial difference. This consists of their activities that contribute to the disinvention of language regimes, particularly those of Standard English and the authenticity of Spanish. Such disinventions would not be for the development of new forms of language ownerships but rather for the search for the use of equivalent performances, seeking modes of successful communication.

In such a context, we would all share Derrida's feeling that 'I speak only one language but is not my own' (1998: 1). We would paraphrase this idea to say that for all the languages we speak, none of them are ours for they come out of our profound social histories, are performed in culturally rich channels of interactive communication and lead towards a future in which all our accents will be valued. This would require the existence of a social world in which the value of translation would be self evident, and perhaps these young students from Oaxaca could help us learn how to translate such dynamics.

What is implied by this ethnography?

Now, no doubt you are asking yourself what these abstract and utopian concerns have to do with language learning and teaching. Well, we will leave these perhaps imaginative spaces in order to offer a few thoughts on what we think the practical possibilities of our analysis are.

Like many other works in the areas of education and ethnography, our work is a textured and thick look at many of the everyday learning activities of these students in the multicultural and multilingual context of postcolonial Oaxaca. We strongly feel that in order to compose suggestions on classroom education, such ideas need to be based upon clear and reasonable presentations of what happens in these particular learning and teaching situations. That is the most practical result of an ethnographic account.

However, since many of the readers of this work will be from the area of language learning and teaching, especially in the area of additional language acquisition, we assume that their questions would be more direct, since they would want to know what all this means for them in the classroom: What method does this suggest? What kind of learning materials would be needed? What kind of classroom management would be required? What does this say about behavioural or cognitive approaches to language learning?

Though we have our own views on these particular issues (Clemente, 2003), we do not have any direct answers or suggestions in this context. But more valuable than that, we would humbly suggest that language teachers should look at what these students' major concerns are: to be themselves in language learning processes; to have their communicative successes be the means to validate their performances and; to seek ways to communicate with other additional language learners in the postcolonial world.

For us, these concerns of the students are similar to many themes within the discourse of critical pedagogy. Their concern to be themselves in their language performances through communicative success parallels Norton and Toohey's claim that the advocates of critical pedagogies are seeking to radically change language education through understanding how the diversity of students' subjectivities affects learning (2004). These students' quest for a politics of affinity with other additional language learners throughout the postcolonial world, echoes both Pennycook's concern to deconstruct the politics of othering that are present in language education and to invent a politics of difference (2001) and Canagarajah's wish to compose a language learning context that has 'a more egalitarian context of transnational relations and multilingual communication' (2006a: 38). Further, the overall quality of their performances with a postcolonial accent expresses the sentiment of Luke and Graham to search for a critical cosmopolitanism that would act as counter-hegemonic forces to corporate capitalist use of 'technocratic English' (2007:12).

We want to make it clear that we are not suggesting that the teaching style at the *Centro* is *per se* an example of critical pedagogy or that the teaching styles of professors at the *Centro* engendered the students' use of a postcolonial accent. Actually it was the other way around. Throughout all their performances these students were asking for a critical pedagogy that could fit with their feelings and attitudes. For us, it is the way in which the students used their agency to reformulate their language education that encouraged their postcolonial accent. We would suggest that these students were ahead of the faculty, and it is the faculty that needs to catch up with them by developing a critical pedagogy that allows the students to be themselves in these language performances and not to be contained within the hegemonic authority of native-speakerism.[27]

By listening to the concerns of these students, we truly believe that the reader could address any of the above issues. S/he would focus on contextualising what the students and teachers are trying to do, where and when they are doing the learning, and how they are doing it. Letting the students be themselves while learning the language would require open and critical exchanges between all the actors in the process. Teachers and learners would have to know how to express their concerns each to one another beyond the traditional authoritarian structures in the classroom. Teachers and learners would have to participate in a joint exorcism of the hovering of the ghost of the native speaker, be on their guard for attempts to impose claims of authenticity of language performances, compose critical and imaginative ways to subvert the colonial difference and find connections between the social spaces of multiculturalism and interculturalism. They would have to find collective ways to disinvent or subvert the hegemonic demands of conflicting language regimes in their learning context. In terms of accessing the achievements of new language activities it would be worthwhile to follow Canagarajah's suggestions that we 'develop instruments with imagination and creativity to access proficiency in the complex communicative needs of English as a lingua franca' (2006b: 240) and further such tests should be 'interactive, collaborative and performative' (ibid.).

But, are we not just repeating our early abstract claims? We do not think so. We feel that these suggestions could be within the frameworks of a new stage on which to teach and learn. It would be the collective agency of teachers and learners that would compose the scripts for such performances.

27 Based upon our research, we wish to investigate if the subjective desires of these students could be used to generate teaching styles that could be critical and transformative. This would involved understanding what are the connecting or non-connecting relations between the imagine communities of the students to those of the faculty. For an example of the direction this research will take see the special issue of *Mextesol Journal on Critical Pedagogies in the Mexican ELT Classroom* (Clemente, 2006).

Some readers may think that we are simply suggesting the use of the communicative approach to language teaching since the students stress so strongly communicative success.[28] The answer to that is that our argument is not about the issues of what methods, teaching materials or modes of classroom organisation should be used. Instead, language teachers could ask themselves what actions could be taken in order to meet the concerns that these students, and their students, have expressed. It would not be a situation of who would own the means of learning and teaching, but rather how all actors could be using their various forms of agency to create a context in which we all have only one language that is expressed with a diversity of postcolonial accents. Are these still utopian assumptions? Yes, but only because they have not been used yet! (Freire, 1970).

---

28 To analyse why CLT has failed to address these issues falls out of the purpose of this book. We hope that the reader will feel motivated to reflect upon how the rationale behind some language approaches and methods have favoured hegemonic discourses as can be witnessed in the invention of language regimes, native-speakerism, othering, and have left aside aspects such as the construction of identities, the exercise of agency or the performance of cultural realities (Gee, 1996; Holliday, 2005; Kumaravadivelu, 2003, 2006, 2007; Pennycook, 2001; Sullivan, 2000).

Appendix

On methodology

> What I shall have to say here is neither difficult nor contentious; the only merit I should like claim for it is that of being true, at least in parts.
>
> (Austin, 1962,1)

The methodology that we have used in this ethnography is best expressed in our understanding of Kumaravadivelu's argument on beyond methods (2006). In several works (2003 and 2006) he has developed a discourse that he refers to as post-methodology, in which he suggests that the context of both the researcher and the researched should set, and encourage, appropriate strategies of investigation. That context would include the social, cultural and political realities of those involved in the research. Further, he stresses that there are no sets of techniques or stratagems to follow, but that one has to make various critical and reflective choices as to how to attain the appropriate information and data that can best represent the social dynamics one has been investigating (Kumaravadivelu, 2007). In that spirit, we offer a summary of the critical and reflective methodological choices we made to develop this ethnography.

Let us start with our concept of ethnography. Ethnography is a critical means for recording and interpreting the social practices of cultural actors in their everyday lives (Bourdieu, 1977; Geertz, 1973), and how those activities are reproduced within the overall socio-cultural context of these actors. Ethnography gives particular importance to the locations of such social identities as gender, ethnicity, sexuality and social class (Baron and Kotthoff, 2001; Eckert and McConnell-Ginet, 2003). Ethnographic representations are the means for illustrating the universalistic features of cultural processes (Bauman, 1973), the complexity of social diversity (Higgins and Coen, 2000), and the particularities of the micro-practices that human actors use in the creation of their symbolic actions, such as learning languages (Canagarajah, 1999; Holliday, 2005; Clemente, 2003).

Currently, there are a variety of ethnographic styles dealing with education, the classroom and language. There is the in-depth use of ethnography to explicate and develop educational policy, such as Woods' pioneering works that began in

England (1993) and has continued through the works of Beach and Dovemark (2007), Jeffrey (2006) and Troman, et al. (2006); there is the micro-ethnographic exploration of language, identity and ethnicity in the works of Rampton (1997), Maybin (2006) and others; there is the use of the classroom as a naturalistic context for the analysis of conversion and utterances (González García, 2007); there is the use of ethnography for the radical analysis of education and schools, such as the works by Canagarajah (1999) Foley (2007) and McLaren (1997); and there is, finally, the work on training learners to carry out their own ethnographies (Roberts, et al., 2001). As a postcolonial or postmethodological gesture, our methods are informed by these various styles; but, at the same time, they are not like them.

In order to explain this, we need to give the background to our ethnography and then explain the various methods we used.

How we started

We have been working over the last four years on ethnographically representing the cultural and language activities of students and teachers at the *Centro de Idiomas*. We began with a seminar on culture, language and ethnography. The seminar was held at the *Centro de Idiomas* and both students and faculty were invited to participate. We explained that we were about to begin an ethnography on the *Centro* and we wanted to use this seminar to explore the issues that such a project would entail. We were also seeking their participation and collaboration in this project. The first plan for the ethnography emerged from this seminar; ten students volunteered to work with us on various topics. One team selected a group of students from different years to track throughout two academic terms in order to see how they were doing in their classes and what they felt about them. Another team organised and carried out a demographic survey of the students at the *Centro* and a third team focused on the social interaction of the students there. Two students had separate projects: one dealt with the reasons students had for entering the *Centro* and the other looked at what student teaching was like. At the end of the first year of the project, the students organised their findings into a panel presentation that was given at a local anthropology conference. Furthermore, these students used the material from their projects to develop their undergraduate theses.

This first collaborative phase of the project established the base for our ethnography. From there, we collected various life histories of students and professors, carried out numerous interviews with the students on a wide range of issues dealing with language learning and use and the various investments that students have made in pursuing their goals. We had lengthy conversations with students (in Spanish) on how they have formed their own learning cultures and how these learning cultures provided them with safe houses for their pursuit of English. We also had observational data on student social life and their styles of participation in their classrooms. All this data collection was done in collaboration with the students. From these various data bases, we composed how these students were performing English with a postcolonial accent.

Here it is worth re-emphasising what we stated in the prologue. These ethnographic data bases have been presented in various narrative styles throughout the text. We share Bial's contention that the strongest method for knowledge formation is through the narrativisation of the actions and behaviours of the social actors being represented (2004). We have not done an ethnography of speech, communication or language *per se*. We have done an ethnography of the social and cultural context of the performances of these language practices of these students. Our data was gathered in the form of interviews, observation notes, speech transcripts, protocols, etc., and was woven together in a narrative form with the purpose to illustrate and interpret the context within which these actions take place. This mode of presentation also allows us to show how these students perceive and interpret that context and their location within it. To explain what particular methods were used, we will review them chapter by chapter.

In chapter one, we embarked upon our own critical readings and interpretations of the discourses of applied linguistics and cultural anthropology in order to locate our project within these discursive spaces.

In chapter two, there were three primary methodological activities. For the opening portraits, we selected two students' stories that were representative of the two main ways to get into the *Centro*. To work on the main body of the chapter, we developed an instrument to carry out the census of the *Centro* for which we were assisted by the INEGI (National Institute of Statistics, Geography and Informatics). The instrument was piloted, modified and given to all the students at the *Centro*. Eighty per cent of the questionnaires were answered and analysed. The information was used to contextualise the general information we provided on the educational system in Mexico. The third set of activities consisted in helping the students enrolled in a course called 'Research Methods in Education', to organise several debates on different topics. The topics were selected and analysed by the students according to their own perceptions of the relevant issues at the *Centro*. The topics were on the issues of identity, social class, gender, sexuality, nationality and the quality of education and social ambiance at the *Centro*. The thirty students that were involved in this project invited the *Centro* community (students and faculty) to participate in ten different debates. The debates were recorded, transcribed and analysed by the student organisers.

Chapter three involved numerous lengthy interviews with several students from first to fifth year in the programme. From them, we chose six students who would represent the diversity of actors that make up the community of the *Centro de Idiomas*. A very important element used to compose their portraits were the different documents that these students produced, either as part of their academic lives (assignments, class work, theses, etc.) or requested by us (diaries, reflections, etc.). The compositions of these portraits involved translating and transcribing the interviews, complementing them with the written documents, editing them into narratives and then asking the students their opinions of their portraits.

Chapter four was a mixture of methodological approaches, observations of classroom and of social interaction (as students and student-teachers), detailed interviews with the different social groups on the structure of their cliques, the styles of their language usages, and their views on their education processes, their professors and the institution. As in the previous chapter, we made use of all the written documents that we thought could add texture to our ethnography.

Chapter five was also a mixture of approaches, though here there was a greater use of materials produced by the students themselves. The narratives on the Curriculum Revision Clique and the Poetry Group were a combination of the actual materials they produced (the guide, the poems and the theses) as well as the interviews with them on the importance of what they were doing. In the case of the Curriculum Revision Clique, we also included the recording of three work meetings that they had with the faculty, and in the case of the Poetry Group, we corresponded by email with Sam Johnson, the professor in charge of the writing course. The material on Martha and Ervin were combinations of their own narratives (some of them offered and produced spontaneously), interviews with them on what they had said or written, and our reflections on how to interpret them. This last step was a constant methodological activity on our part during the whole project.

Finally, chapter six was composed by bringing all these various narratives, observations and interpretations into some kind of coherent conclusion.

To sum up, we think that our methodology was context-driven, most of it in the form of secondary data, listening to the voices of the actors of the community, letting them interpret their own texts and actions. Our way of doing ethnography was motivated by our quest to seek alternative expressions and interpretations, to describe constructions of identities, forms of resistance (articulated and non-articulated) and socio-cultural realities (Kumaravadivelu, 2006) that necessarily go beyond the boundaries of the school settings. In other words, we contend that ours was a postcolonial methodology that recognised, as Kumaravadivelu states, 'the cultural complexity as well as the competing worlds of discourses that exist in the classroom' (1993), as well as outside of it. We refer to this as ethnographic praxis (Higgins and Coen, 2000).

For us, ethnographic praxis involves explaining what our politics of representation and responsibility are. Our methodology is framed by our collaborative work with the students in this project and by the fact that Angeles is a faculty member of the *Centro de Idiomas*. That required that we developed a particular kind of trust with these students to work beyond the power differential between themselves as students and ourselves as different types of representatives of the power structure of the university world. In turn, this involved all of us doing the best we could to move away from the traditional roles of student/teacher and researched/researcher towards being able to perform as collaborators and friends who were able to work together. This meant that we were all open to feedback, suggestions and criticism. Further, this allowed for the interviews to become arenas for the exchange of ideas and the challenge of assumptions. With the conclusion of the writing of the text, the students were all able to read and offer suggestions and corrections. It was interesting that many wished to use their own names in the text, whereas others preferred pen names that they thought match their styles.

At the same time, we are aware that our efforts were only partial and limited. The realities of the power differences between students/teachers/university structures are still intact despite our efforts. That is, we could only alter or restructure these relations within the social spaces of our particular interaction, as to what effect that will have on the overall structure remains to be seen. Furthermore, although we worked collaboratively with the students, the conceptual language that we used to represent their wishes, desires and hopes was ours. We framed their desire to be themselves in this other language, their wish to have their skills validated through communicative success and their quest to connect with other users of English within the postcolonial world as performing English with a postcolonial accent. Also, it is our interpretation that these actions and performances can be read as an emerging expression of a politics of affinity. In our exchanges and dialogues the students have found these arguments to be compelling and reasonable representations of their views and activities. It remains for future researchers to find out how they update these understandings in their future performances of English.

The above is our position in terms of politics of representation and responsibility. One has to talk about how one came to represent these young language actors within the existing power structures of knowledge production. Not to do so would be to aid and abet the production of the colonial difference. Our politics of responsibility involves offering as clearly and as distinctly as is possible the hopes and desires of these students and to find arenas where these voices can be heard. It is their voices that are more important than any particular suggestions or agendas that we might like to offer for educational change. We are advocating that the search for such changes should begin with their concerns.

Finally, in order to keep in our pursuit of doing ethnography *with* (as opposed to *on* or *for*) (Cameron et al., 1992) the actors of the community of the *Centro de Idiomas*, we built a website (www.performingenglish.uabjo.mx) that has updates on what these students are currently doing with their language performances and that would allow the readers to maintain direct contact with the students further exemplifying their transidiomatic practices. Our suggestion for the development of a website is an element in which readers who have interest in such issues can establish their own contacts and connections with these language actors. The idea of this website is not that we feel that our relationship with these young language actors is fraught with tensions, but rather that these tensions might emerge within our readership wondering about our politics of representation and responsibility.

References

Anderson, B. (1991) *Imagined communities*, London: Verso Books.
Ashcroft, B., Griffiths G., and Tiffin, H. (1998) *Post-colonial studies*, London: Routledge.
Austin, J. L. (1962) *How to do things with words*, Oxford: Oxford University Press.
Bakhtin, M. (1986) *Speech genres and other late essays*, Austin: University of Texas Press.
Barabas, A. M. and Bartolomé, M. A. (1999) *Configuraciones étnicas en Oaxaca: Perspectivas etnográficas para las Autonomías*, México, D. F.: Instituto Nacional de Antropología e Historia and Instituto Nacional Indigenista.
Baron, B. and Kotthoff H. (2001) *Gender in interaction*, Amsterdam: John Benjamins.
Bauman, R. (2006) Commentary: Indirect indexicality, identity, and performance: Dialogic observations, *Journal of Linguistic Anthropology*, 15 (1): 145-150.
Bauman, Z. (1973) *Culture as praxis*, London: Routledge and Kegan Paul.
Bauman, Z. (2003) *Liquid modernity*, London: Routledge and Kegan Paul.
Beach, D. and Dovemark, M. (2007) *Education and the commodity problem: Ethnographic investigations of creativity and performativity in Swedish schools,* London: the Tufnell Press.
Bell, M. and Gardiner, M. (1998) *Bakhtin and the human sciences*, London: Sage Publications.
Bhabha, H. (1994) *The Location of Culture*, London: Routledge.
Bial, H. (2004) Introduction, in Bail, H. (ed.) *The Performance Studies Reader*, New York: Routledge.
Blackman, S. (2004) *Chilling out: The cultural politics of substance consumption, Youth and drug policy*, Maidenhead: Open University Press.
Block, D. (2003) *The social turn in second language acquisition*, Edinburgh: Edinburgh University Press.
Bonfil Batalla, G. (1988) Los conceptos de diferencia y subordinación en el estudio de las culturas populares, in Aguirre, G. (ed.) *Teoría e investigación en la antropología social Mexicana*, México, D.F.: INAH.
Bourdieu, P. (1977) *Outlines for a theory of practice*, Cambridge: Cambridge University Press.
Bourdieu, P. (1991) *Language and symbolic power*, Cambridge: Polity Press.
Breen, M. (2001) Postscript: new directions for research on learner contributions, in Breen, M. (ed.) *Learner contributions to language learning,* London: Longman.
Brutt-Griffler, J. (2002) *World English: A Study of its development*, Clevedon: Multilingual Matters.
Butler, J. (1999) Performativity's Social Magic, in Shusterman, R., (ed.) *Bourdieu: A Critical Reader*, London: Blackwell Publishers.
Butler, J. (2004) Performative acts and gender constitution: an essay in phenomenology and feminist theory, in Bial, H. (ed.) *The performance studies reader*, Routledge: London.
Byrnes, H. (2005) Renting language in the ownership society, Inaugural lecture presented at George M. Roth Distinguished Professor of German, 24 October, Georgetown University, Washington, D.C.

Cameron, D. (1997) Performing gender identity: Young men's talk and the construction of heterosexual masculinity, in Johnson, S. and Mienhoff, U. (eds.) *Language and masculinity*, Oxford: Blackwell.
Cameron, D., Frazer, E., Harvey, P., Rampton, B. and Richardson, K. (1992) *Researching languages: Issues of power and method*, London, Routledge.
Canagarajah, S. (1999) *Resisting linguistic imperialism in English teaching*, Oxford: Oxford University Press.
Canagarajah, S. (2004) Subversive identities, pedagogical safe houses, and critical learning, in Norton, B. and Toohey, K. (eds.) *Critical pedagogies and language learning*. Cambridge: Cambridge University Press.
Canagarajah, S. (2006a) Negotiating the local in English as a lingua franca. *Annual Review of Applied Linguistics*, 26: 197-218.
Canagarajah, S. (2006b) Changing communicative needs, revised assessment objectives: Testing English as an international language. *Language Assessment Quarterly*, 3 (3): 229-242.
Candlin, C. (2001) *Sociolinguistics and social theory*, London: Pearson.
Candlin, C. (1990) What happens when applied linguistics goes critical?, in Halliday, M. A. K., Gibbons, J. and Nicholas, H. (eds.) *Learning, keeping and using language*, Amsterdam: John Benjamins.
Cantoral, S. (2005) *Identidad, cultura y educación*, Mexico, D.F.: UPN.
Castells, M. (2000a) *The information age: Economy, society, and culture—the power of identity*. Vol. 2., Oxford: Blackwell Publishers.
Castells, M. (2000b) *The Information age: Economy, society, and culture—end of millennium*. Vol. 3. Oxford: Blackwell Publishers.
Cisneros, B. and Valenzuela, R. (2006) *Overcoming fears and increasing Autonomy in writing*. Tesis (B.A.), Mexico: Facultad de Idiomas, Universidad Autónoma Benito Juárez de Oaxaca.
Clemente, A. (1998) *SLA Research on self-direction: Theoretical and practical issues*, Thesis (PhD), London: Institute Of Education, University of London.
Clemente, A. (2003) Learning cultures and counselling: Teacher/learner interaction within a self-directed scheme, in, Palfreyman D., and Smith R. (eds.) *Learner autonomy across cultures*, London: Palgraves.
Clemente, A. (ed.) (2006) *Mextesol: Special issue on critical pedagogies*, 30 (2), Mexico: Mextesol.
Clemente, A. and Higgins, M. (2003) The production of learning cultures: The interface between applied linguistics and anthropology, *Proceedings from Congreso de Lingüística Aplicada*, 3-5 May 2003, Mexico D.F.: CELE-UNAM.
Clemente, A. and Higgins, M. (2004) Whose English is it anyway? Ethnography of Facultad de Idiomas Oaxaca, México, Paper presented at the *37th Annual BAAL Meeting*, 9-11 September. London.
Clemente, A. and Higgins, M. (2005) The Subversion of the native in language learning: From the exotic to the standard, Paper presented at the *38th Annual BAAL Meeting*, 15-17 September. Bristol, England.
Clemente, A. and. Higgins, M. (2006) Que 'donkey' eres! Disinventing standard English! An ethnographic case from Oaxaca, Mexico, Paper presented at the *Ethnography and Education Conference*, 10-11 September, 2006, Oxford.

References

Clemente, A. and. Higgins, M. (2007a) Performing English with a postcolonial accent: An Ethnographic example from Oaxaca, Mexico. Paper presented at the *Conference of International Society for Language Studies*, 11-13 April, Hawaii.

Clemente, A. and Higgins, M. (2007b) English as a linguistic and intellectual weapon against native-speakerism, Paper presented at the Conference *Tuning in: Learners of language, language of learners,* 24-26, May, Sabancı University in Istanbul, Turkey.

Clemente, A. and Kissinger, D. (1994) *El proyecto de autoacceso en Oaxaca,* Oaxaca: UABJO.

Cook, V. (1996) Competence and multi-competence, in Brown, G, Malmkjaer, K., and Williams, J. (eds.) *Performance and Competence in second language acquisition,* Cambridge: Cambridge University Press.

Cruz, S. (2006) The teaching of connotative and dennotative meaning in an Englsih class in the *Centro de Idiomas,* unpublished manuscript, Mexico, Oaxaca: UABJO.

Derrida, J. (1998) *Monolingualism of the other or prosthesis of origin,* Stanford, CA: Stanford University Press.

Dietz, G. (2003) *Multiculturalismo, interculturalidad y educación,* Granada: Universidad de Granada.

DeHay, T. (2007) A postcolonial perspective (work in progress), *Swirl: A Journal of Post-Discourses* [online], 5 (12), www.sou.edu/English/IDTC/Issues/postclo/Resources/Terry/deHay.htm [Accessed 20 March 2007]

Eckert, P, and McConnell-Ginet S. (2003) *Gender and language,* Cambridge: Cambridge University Press.

Facultad de Idiomas (2002) *English language curriculum,* Oaxaca: Facultad de Idiomas. Universidad Autónoma Benito Juárez de Oaxaca.

Fanon, F. (1963) *The wretched of the earth,* New York: Grove Press.

Foley, D. (2007) Collaborative ethnography: Blending activist and reflective practices, Plenary presented at the *Second International Qualitative Research Conference,* 30 May-1 June, Guanajuato, Mexico.

Freire, P. (1970) *Pedagogía del oprimido,* Mexico, D. F.: Siglo Veintiuno Editores.

Gal, S. (1989) Language and political economy, in *Annual Review of Anthropology,* Vol. 18: 345-367.

Galeano, E. (1985) *Memory of fire: Genesis,* New York: Norton Books.

García Canclini, N. (2004) *Diferentes, desiguales y desconectados: Mapas de la interculturalidad,* Barcelona: Gedisa Editorial.

Gee, J. P. (1996) *Social linguistics and literacies,* New York: Routledge Falmer.

Geertz, C. (1973) *The interpretation of culture,* New York: Basic Books.

Giddens, A. (1979) *Central problems in social theory,* Berkeley: University of California Press.

Goffman, E. (1959) *The presentation of self in everyday life,* New York: Anchor Books.

González García, J. (2007) La construcción conjunta del conocimiento a partir de narraciones: Una propuesta metodología, Paper presented at the *Second Internacional Qualitative Research Conference,* 30 May-1 June, Guanajuato, México.

González Casanova, P. (1986) *El poder al pueblo,* México, D. F.: Océano.

Grillo, R. D. (2005) *Backlash against diversity? Identity and cultural politics in European cities.* Oxford: Centre on Migration, Policy and Society Working Paper No.14.

Gutmann, M. (2002) *The romance of democracy,* Berkeley: University of California Press.

Hagelund, A. (2007) 'But they are Norwegians!' Talking about culture at school, *Ethnography and Education*, Vol. 2 (1): 127-143.

Halliday, M. (1978) *Language as social semiotic*, London: Arnold.

Hamel, R. E. (2003) *Language empires, linguistic imperialism, and the future of global languages*, Unpublished paper, México D. F.: Universidad Autónoma Metropolitana, Department of Anthropology.

Haraway, D. (1991) *Simians, cyborgs, and women*, New York: Routledge.

Hedges, W. (2006) *Performance theory*, [online] www.sou.edu/English/IDTC/People/theory/austin.htm [Accessed 25 March 2007]

Hernández Díaz, J. (ed.) (2000) *Inclusión y diversidad: Discusiones recientes sobre la educación indígena en México*, Oaxaca, Mexico: Fondo Editorial IEEPO.

Hernández Díaz, J. (ed.) (2007) *Ciudadanías diferenciadas en un estado multicultural: los usos y costumbres en Oaxaca*. Mexico, D. F.: Siglo Veintiuno Editores/UABJO.

Higgins, M. (1997) *Somos tocayos*, Oaxaca, Mexico: Instituto Oaxaqueño de las Culturas.

Higgins, M, and Coen, T. (2000) *Streets, bedrooms and patios: The ordinariness of diversity in urban Oaxaca*, Austin: University of Texas Press.

Holborow, M. (1999) *The politics of English*, London: Sage Publications.

Holland, J., Ramazanoglu, C., Sharpe, S. and Thomson, R. (2004) *The male in the head: young people, heterosexuality and power*, London: the Tufnell Press.

Holliday, A. (2005) *The struggle to teach English as an international language*, Oxford: Oxford University Press.

Hymes, D. (1971) *On communicative competence*, Philadelphia: University of Pennsylvania Press.

Jacquemet, M. (2005) Transidiomatic practices: Language and power in the age of Globalization, *Language and Communication*, 25 (1): 257-277.

Jeffrey, B. (ed.) (2006) *Creative learning practices: European experiences*, London: the Tufnell Press.

Johnson, S., Cisneros, B., Valenzuela, A., Castellanos, A., Ignacio, M., Alonso P., López, R., Martínez, W., Jerónimo, E., González, A., and Toral, T. (2007) *The book: selections from students compositions*, Oaxaca: Facultad de Idiomas. Universidad Autónoma Benito Juárez de Oaxaca.

Kachru, B.B. (1986) *The alchemy of English*, Oxford: Pergamon Press.

Kandiah, T. (1998) Epiphanies of the deathless native user's manifold avatars: postcolonial perspective on the native speaker, in, Singh, R (ed.) *The native speaker: Multilingual perspectives*, New Delhi: Sage Publications.

Kanno,Y. and Norton, B. (2003) Imagined communities and educational possibilities: Introduction, *in Journal of Language, Identity, and Education*, 2(4): 241-249

Kissinger, D. (2006) Learning English can be a drag: The Language School in Oaxaca as a pedagogical safe house, Paper presented at the *AAAL Meeting*, 17-20 September. Montreal.

Kramsch, C. (1993) *Context and Culture in Language Teaching*, Oxford: Oxford University Press.

Kramsch, C. (ed.). (2002) *Language acquisition and language socialization: Ecological perspectives*, London: Continuum International Publishing.

Kumaravadivelu, B. (1993) The name of the problem and the problem of naming: methodological aspects of problem-based pedagogy, in Crookes, G., and Gass, S. M., (eds.) *Problems in a pedagogical context: integrating theory and practice*, Clevedon: Multilingual Matters.

Kumaravadivelu, B. (2003) *Beyond methods: Macrostrategies for language teaching*, New Haven and London: Yale University Press.
Kumaravadivelu, B. (2006) *Understanding language teaching: From method to postmethod*, New Jersey: Lawrence Erlbaum.
Kumaravadivelu, B. (2007) Interrogating cultural complexities in the classroom, Plenary presented at the *Second International Qualitative Research Conference*, Guanajuato, Guanajuato, Mexico. 30 May 30-1.
Laclau, E. and. Mouffe, C. (1985) *Hegemony and socialist strategy*, London: Verso.
Lantolf, J. and Thorne, S. (2006) *Sociocultural theory and the sociogenesis of second language development*, New York: Oxford University Press.
Lave, J., and Wenger, E. (1991) *Situated learning: Legitimate peripheral participation*, Cambridge: Cambridge University Press.
López, M., Stakhnevich, J., Leon, H., and Morales, A. (2006) Teacher educators and pre-service English teachers creating and sharing power through critical dialogue in a multilingual setting, in Clemente, A. (ed.) *Mextesol special issues: Critical pedagogies*, 30(2): 83-108.
Li, X. (2007) Identity puzzles: Am I a course instructor or a nonnative speaker?, in Mantero, M. (ed.), *Identity and second language learning*. Charlotte, N.C: IAP.
Luke, A., Luke, C., and Graham, P. (2007) Globalization, Corporatism, and Critical Language Education, *International Multilingual Research Journal*, 1 (1): 1-13.
Macedo, D., Dendrinos B., and Gounari P. (2003) *The hegemony of English*, Boulder, Co.: Paradigm Publishers.
Makoni, S. and Pennycook, A. (eds.) (2006) *Disinventing and reconstituting languages*. Clevedon: Multilingual Matters.
Martínez Vásquez, V. R. (2004a) *La educación en Oaxaca*, Oaxaca: IISUABJO.
Martínez Vásquez, V. R. (2004b) Modelos de universidad: El caso de la UABJO, *Cuadernos del Sur*, 10 (20): 87-108.
Martínez Vásquez, V.R (2007) *Autoritarismo, movimiento popular y crisis política: Oaxaca 2006*, Oaxaca: IISUABJO.
Marx, K. (1967) *Capital*: Vols. 1 and. 2., New York: International Publishers.
Marx, K and Engels, F. (1974) *La ideología alemana*. Mexico, D.F.: Cultura Popular.
Maybin, J. (2006) *Children's voices: Talk, knowledge and identity*, Basingstoke: Palgrave Macmillan.
McKay, S. L. (2002) *Teaching English as an international language*, Oxford: Oxford University Press.
McKenzie, J. (2004) The liminal-norm, in Bial (ed.) *The performance studies reader*, London: Routledge.
McLaren, P. (1997) *Revolutionary multiculturalism*, Boulder: Westview Press.
Melucci, A. (1989) *Nomads of the present*. Philadelphia: Temple University Press.
Mignolo, W. (2002) The geopolitics of knowledge and the colonial difference, *The South Atlantic Quarterly*, 101(1): 56-95.
Mignolo, W. (2005) Prophets facing sidewise: The geopolitics of knowledge and the colonial difference, *Social Epistemology*, 19 (1): 111-127.
Mouffe, C. (2005) *The return of the political*, New York: Verso Press.
Murphy, A., Stepick, A ,. Morris, E., Winter, M. (2002) *La cabeza de jano: La desigualdad social en Oaxaca*, Oaxaca, México: Fondo Editorial de la Unidad de Proyectos Estratégicos, IEEPO.

Nahmad, S. (2000) Derechos lingüísticos de los indígenas de México, in Hernández Díaz J. (ed.), *Inclusión y diversidad: Discusiones recientes sobre la educación indígena en México*, Oaxaca, Mexico: IEEPO.
Nicholson, L. and Seidman S. (eds.) (1995) *Social Postmodernism: Beyond identity politics*, Cambridge: Cambridge University Press.
Norton, B. (2000) *Identity and language learning: Gender, ethnicity, and educational change*, Harlow, England: Longman/Pearson Education.
Norton, B. (2001) Non-participation, imagined communities, and the language classroom. in Breen, M. (ed.), *Learner contributions to language learning: New directions in research* Harlow, England: Pearson Education.
Norton, B. and Toohey K. (eds.) (2004) *Critical pedagogies and language learning*, Cambridge: Cambridge University Press.
Nunan, D. (1988) *Syllabus design*, Oxford: Oxford University Press.
Ortner, S. (2006) *Anthropology and social theory*, Durham: Duke University Press.
Pavlenko, A. (2002) Poststructuralist approaches to the study of social factors in second language learning and use, in, Cook V. (ed.), *Portraits of the L2 user*, London: Multilingual Matters.
Pennycook, A. (1998) *English and the discourses of colonialism*, London: Routledge.
Pennycook, A. (2001) *Critical applied linguistics: A critical introduction*, London: Erlbaum Publishers.
Pennycook, A. (2004) Performativity and language studies, *Critical Inquiry in Language Studies: An International Journal* 1 (1): 1-19.
Pennycook, A. (2006) The myth of English as an International language, in Makoni S., and Pennycook, A. (eds.) *Disinvesting and reconstituting languages*, Clevedon: Multilingual Matters.
Pennycook, A. (2007) *Global Englishes and transcultural flows*, London: Routledge.
Phillipson, R. (1992) *Linguistics imperialism*, Oxford: Oxford University Press.
Pratt, M. L. (1991) Arts in the contact zone, *Profession*, 91: 33-40.
Ramanathan, V. (2005) *The English-vernacular divide*, Clevedon: Multilingual Matters.
Rampton, B. (1997) Second language learning in late modernity, *The Modern Language Journal*, 81 (3): 329-333.
Roberts, C., Byram, M., Barro, A., Jordan, S., and Street, B. (2001) *Language learners as ethnographers*, Clevedon: Multilingual Matters.
Rico, G. (1983) *Writing the natural way*, Los Angeles: J. P. Tarcher.
Sayer, P., Clemente, A. and Higgins, M. (2004) Learning/teaching English in Oaxaca, Mexico: Teachers, language and identity, paper presented at the *AAAL Meeting*, 1-4 May, Portland, Oregon. USA.
Sayer, P., Clemente, A., Kissinger, D. and Higgins, M. (2005) The diversity of ordinary English language learners in Oaxaca, paper presented at the *AILA 2005*, 24-29 July, Madison, Wisconsin.
Schechner, R. (2003) *Performance theory: Revised edition*, London: Routledge.
Seidlhofer, B. (2001) Closing a conceptual gap: The case for a description of English as a lingua franca, *International Journal of Applied Linguistics*, 11 (2): 133-158.
Said, E. (1993) *Culture and imperialism*, New York: Vintage.
Spivak, G. (1999) *A critique of postcolonial reason*, Cambridge, MA.: Harvard University Press.
Stephen, L. (2005) *Zapotec women: Gender, Class and Ethnicity in Globalised Oaxaca*, Durham, NC: Duke University Press.

Sullivan, P. (2000) Playfulness as mediation in communicative language teaching in a Vietnamese classroom, in, Lantolf (ed.) *Sociocultural theory and second language learning,* Oxford: Oxford University Press.
Trinh, T. M. (1989) *Woman, native, other,* Bloomington: Indiana University Press.
Troman, G., Jeffrey, B., and Beach, D. (eds.) (2006) *Researching education policy: Ethnographic experiences,* London: the Tufnell Press.
Turner, V. (1974) *Dramas, fields, and metaphors,* Ithaca: Cornell University Press.
Vygotsky, L. (1986) *Mind in society,* Cambridge, MA.: Harvard University Press.
Wertsch, J. (1991) *Voices of the mind,* London: Harvester-Wheatsheaf.
Widdowson, H. G. (2003) *Defining issues in English language teaching,* Oxford: Oxford University Press.
Weiss, E., Guerra, I., Hernández, J., Grijalva, O., Avalos, J. (2006) What is the meaning of School? High School and Youth in Mexico. Paper presented at the *Oxford Ethnography and Education Conference,* 10-11 September, Oxford, England.
Woods, P. (1993) *Critical events in teaching and learning,* London: Falmer Press.
Woolard, K. (2005) Language and identity choice in Catalonia: The interplay of contrasting ideologies of linguistic authority, Paper presented at the *International Conference on Regulations of Societal Multilingualism in Linguistic Polices* 1-3 June 2005, Berlin.
Woolard, K. and Schieffelin, B. (1994) Language ideology, *Annual Review of Anthropology,* 23: 55-82.
Young, R. J. (2003) *Postcolonialism: A very short introduction,* Oxford: Oxford University Press.

www.ingramcontent.com/pod-product-compliance
Lightning Source LLC
Chambersburg PA
CBHW050556170426
43201CB00011B/1719